W9-CMG-097

HITLER'S
WAR ON
*RUSSIA

OSPREY
PUBLISHING

Key to military symbols

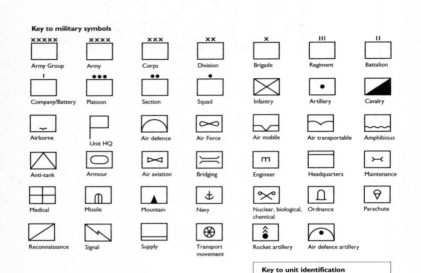

Army Group	Army	Corps	Division	Brigade	Regiment	Battalion
Company/Battery	Platoon	Section	Squad	Infantry	Artillery	Cavalry
Airborne	Unit HQ	Air defence	Air Force	Air mobile	Air transportable	Amphibious
Anti-tank	Armour	Air aviation	Bridging	Engineer	Headquarters	Maintenance
Medical	Missile	Mountain	Navy	Nuclear, biological, chemical	Ordnance	Parachute
Reconnaissance	Signal	Supply	Transport movement	Rocket artillery	Air defence artillery	

Key to unit identification

Unit identifier — Parent unit — Commander
(+) with added elements
(–) less elements

HITLER'S
WAR ON
RUSSIA

CHARLES D. WINCHESTER

First published in Great Britain in 2007 by Osprey Publishing,
Midland House, West Way, Botley, Oxford OX2 0PH, United Kingdom.
443 Park Avenue South, New York, NY 10016, USA.
Email: info@ospreypublishing.com

Text and illustrations previously published as *Ostfront*, 1998.

© 2007 Osprey Publishing Ltd

All rights reserved. Apart from any fair dealing for the purpose of private study,
research, criticism or review, as permitted under the Copyright, Designs and
Patents Act, 1988, no part of this publication may be reproduced, stored in a
retrieval system, or transmitted in any form or by any means, electronic, electrical,
chemical, mechanical, optical, photocopying, recording or otherwise, without the
prior written permission of the copyright owner. Enquiries should be addressed
to the Publisher.

Every attempt has been made by the Publisher to secure the appropriate
permissions for materials reproduced in this book. If there has been any oversight
we will be happy to rectify the situation and a written submission should be made
to the Publisher.

A CIP catalogue record for this book is available from the British Library

ISBN: 978 1 84603 195 3

The author has asserted his right under the Copyright, Designs and Patents Act,
1988, to be identified as the author of this book.

Typeset in ITC Stone Serif, Gills Sans, AT Quay Sans, Bembo and Minion Condensed
Index by Margaret Vaudrey
Originated by PDQ Media, Bungay, UK
Printed and bound in China through Bookbuilders

07 08 09 10 11   10 9 8 7 6 5 4 3 2 1

For a catalogue of all books published by Osprey please contact:

NORTH AMERICA
Osprey Direct c/o Random House Distribution Center
400 Hahn Road, Westminster, MD 21157, USA
E-mail: info@ospreydirect.com

ALL OTHER REGIONS
Osprey Direct UK, P.O. Box 140, Wellingborough, Northants, NN8 2FA, UK
E-mail: info@ospreydirect.co.uk

www.ospreypublishing.com

Front cover: German troops out on the snow near Toropec, January 1942.
(Bundesarchiv)

Photos in pull-out section are from the R. Tomasi collection

Dedication: For Jo. *Ruth 1:16*

This is a revised and substantially expanded version of the text used in Osprey's illustrated history of the Russo-German conflict, *Ostfront*, published in 1998. It is a military history, which is not to say that it is solely concerned with generals and tanks, but that it incorporates almost every other historical discipline. Political history is obviously crucial to this story; but so is economic, social, religious and technological history, and not just of Germany and Russia but of all the belligerent nations in the Second World War.

The political transformation of eastern Europe and the former Soviet Union during the 1990s renders redundant both the phraseology and the spelling of earlier histories of this war. For instance, wartime German accounts refer to their enemies as 'Russian'. Of course, their opponents came from all the constituent republics of the USSR. The Union of Soviet Socialist Republics had a population of about 190 million in 1940: it included 170 discrete races, which spoke 140 different languages. However, 14 of these peoples made up 94 per cent of the total: 90 million Great Russians, 40 million Ukranians, and ten million White Russians. Many are now independent nations, but in the days of the USSR it was politically correct to call everyone 'Soviet'. On the other hand, even President Gorbachev could slip up in public and say 'Russian' when he meant 'Soviet'. This book uses the two expressions interchangeably. I have been equally haphazard with the expressions 'Red Army' and 'Soviet Army'. The USSR's army was officially re-titled the Soviet Army in 1944, but its opponents called them Reds until the end of the war, and subsequent publications tend to use both phrases indiscriminately.

Place names in this story are a minefield of linguistic and political traps. Stalin shifted the Polish frontier westwards after the war, so many German place names are now Polish. After storming the coastal fortress of Königsberg in 1945, the Soviets seized the area for themselves and renamed it Kaliningrad; it remains a political and geographic anomaly, still awaiting resolution today. German place names throughout the Baltic Republics have changed. Leningrad has reverted to being St Petersburg. The industrial centre of Kharkov is more correctly Char'kov when transliterated from Russian, and modern maps spell it in its Ukranian rendition, Harkiv. I have stuck to Kharkov, since this is the form used in most books published in the last 50 years, and I apply the same policy to other towns and cities.

Statistics are unavoidable in this narrative, but by nature unreliable. This conflict was won as much on the factory floors as on the battlefields, but few published sets of figures for German and Russian wartime manufacturing totals agree. There are similar problems assessing numbers of vehicles or aircraft actually serviceable at any given time. Many numbers that have been quoted in book after book turn out to have no reliable basis in original wartime documents. P. J. O'Rourke's first law of social sciences says that 'The more precise the figure, the more general the lie'. Unfortunately, numbers do matter. German intelligence persistently underestimated Red Army strength by about 20 per cent – a million men from 1943. Hitler never believed the summaries of Russian production he received, perhaps because they suggested he should start packing for South America right away. The salient point that will emerge is that Russian tank factories built more T-34s than the sum total of Panzer IIs, Panzer IIIs, Panzer IVs, Panthers, Tigers and other exotica that German industry assembled, and America built more M4 Shermans than the Russians built T-34s. For impressively long periods, even the British were building tanks and aircraft faster than the Germans. With almost the whole of the European coal and steel industry under its control, the German war economy failed miserably to provide the weapons its army required.

★
CONTENTS

★
INTRODUCTION

'Poland will be depopulated and settled with Germans ...
As for the rest ... the fate of Russia will be exactly the same.'
ADOLF HITLER

For many German families the Second World War is synonymous with the Russian front. It was where the overwhelming majority of German servicemen fought, and where more than three-quarters of their 3.9 million dead lie buried.[1] In 1945 the Russian front came to Germany. It engulfed East Prussia and Saxony, and surged all the way to the Elbe, while two million Soviet soldiers stormed Berlin, the would-be capital of Hitler's 'Thousand Year Reich'.

The Second World War is known in Russia as 'The Great Patriotic War'. If the war only became truly 'patriotic' after the invaders were exposed as genocidal enslavers and not the liberators many people had hoped them to be, there was no doubting its great scale. Hitler's invasion pitted the largest national armies ever assembled against each other. The front stretched from the Arctic Circle to the shores of the Black Sea. Operations took place over unprecedented distances. German forces advanced more than 1,000 miles into the Soviet Union; at its greatest extent, their operational front stretched to nearly 2,000 miles. Individual campaigns took place over greater areas than previous wars. The gap smashed in the German lines by the Soviet winter offensive in December 1942 was wider than the entire Western Front in the First World War.

It is salutary to compare the scale of operations on the Russian front with those in western Europe. In August 1944, 38 Allied divisions fighting on a 75-mile front in France encircled 20 German divisions; after 27 days' combat, they destroyed the German forces in Normandy and took 90,000 prisoners. At the same time the Soviet forces mounted three offensives. Along the borders of Romania 92 Soviet divisions and

6 tank/mechanized corps attacked 47 German and Romanian divisions on a frontage of 450 miles; they encircled 18 German divisions and took 100,000 prisoners in a week. Meanwhile, 86 Soviet divisions and 10 tank/mechanized corps attacked across southern Poland and destroyed nearly 40 German divisions in the process. The third Soviet offensive, which had been under way since 22 June, involved 172 divisions and 12 tank/mechanized corps in an advance of 400 miles along a 600-mile front; it overwhelmed 67 German divisions, of which 17 were never to reappear on the German order of battle.

By late 1944 there were 91 Allied divisions in France, Belgium and the Netherlands, facing 65 German divisions across a 250-mile front. In the east, 560 Soviet divisions were fighting 235 German divisions across a 2,000-mile front, driving them rapidly westwards. So there is a strong argument that the Soviet Union had already won the war by 1944, whether the western Allies finally opened a second front or not.[2]

The human cost of the war is so beyond the experience of western Europeans or Americans that it is hard to imagine. To compare the scale of casualties, about 2.5 per cent of the British population was killed or injured during the Second World War; American casualties were 0.6 per cent. In the USSR, the death toll is currently estimated at ten million military and 17 million civilian deaths, representing nearly 20 per cent of the pre-war population. Every three months, the Russians lost more men than America lost in the whole war. Another statistic gives pause for thought. Twice as many soldiers were killed on the Eastern Front in 1941–45 than in all the theatres of war of 1914–18 put together. By mid-1943 the German High Command calculated it was losing 3,000 men per day, every day, most of them in Russia.

Neither side limited its killing to military personnel. The War in the East was a biblical war of conquest conducted with 20th-century technology. As it was Hitler's war, there was never any prospect of it ending in a conventional peace treaty. The German dictator intended far more than just moving a border here and annexing a province there. He was not going to accept reparation payments or negotiate a treaty in the wake of military victory. Hitler planned nothing less than a war of extermination, eliminating the Communist regime, the Jews, and indeed most of the population of eastern Europe. He and his followers regarded the Slavic peoples as sub-humans, to be enslaved or exterminated by the superior, Aryan race: the Germans. The conquered territories would become German colonies, with new German cities linked to the Reich by *Autobahn* and railroad. The Russian steppe was to be dotted with German soldier-colonists establishing what the Nazis regarded as brave outposts of civilization in a barbarous land. This was total war, in its purest and most horrific form. One side or the other would be annihilated.

The full extent of Hitler's grotesque war aims was known only to the upper echelons of the Nazi hierarchy. After the war, many German generals would persuade both the Nuremberg prosecutors and western military historians that they had not known of these aims. In 1945 British and American officers found it difficult to accept that fellow officers and gentlemen – who had fought a largely 'clean' war in the west – could have been implicated in the horrors being reported in the east. Unfortunately, more recent investigation has exposed the disagreeable truth that the German Army was indeed deeply implicated. Heinrich Himmler, chief executor of the 'Final Solution', described the Holocaust as 'a page of Glory in our history which has never been written and never is to be written'. However, the days are long past when the SS could serve as the alibi of a nation. It is now a matter of record that a disturbingly high number of German Army and police units participated in the slaughter of Jews, gypsies, Communist government officials, their families and other civilians. The Hamburg Institute for Social Research organized a controversial exhibition in 1995 that revealed the extent of army involvement. Pro-German forces raised in the Baltic States, the Ukraine, Croatia, Slovakia, Romania and Hungary took part with varying degrees of enthusiasm too.

The Wehrmacht High Command was invited to the Berghof by Hitler on the eve of the attack on Poland in 1939. The loss of so much territory to Poland under the terms of the Versailles Treaty had never been accepted by the Germans, and they would probably have gone to war to recover it even if Hitler had never come to power. But Hitler invested the campaign with far more than territorial objectives. His address to the generals anticipated both the nature of German rule in the east and the nature of his war against the USSR:

> in the East I have put my death's head formations in place with the command relentlessly and without compassion to send into death many women and children of Polish origin and language ... Poland will be depopulated and settled with Germans ... As for the rest ... the fate of Russia will be exactly the same.[3]

One officer recorded in his diary how Hermann Göring literally danced with glee at Hitler's words.

The German Army treated Soviet prisoners-of-war with extraordinary and unprecedented cruelty. A Russian soldier captured by the Germans had less chance of surviving captivity than British or American servicemen captured by the Japanese, who had a 40 per cent mortality rate in the jungle prison camps. Five million Soviet servicemen were taken prisoner in the Second World War, and three million of them died: a mortality rate of 60 per cent. By contrast, the death rate of British and American soldiers captured by the Germans in the Second World War was 3.6 per cent.

At his trial at Nuremberg, SS-Obergruppenführer von dem Bach-Zelewski said: 'If, for decades, a doctrine is preached that the Slav race is an inferior race, and that the Jews are not even human at all, then such an explosion is inevitable.' About three million Germans were captured by the Russians during the war, and a third of them died. However, this is an average that conceals the extent of Russian revenge in the early part of the war. More than half the total of German prisoners were captured in 1945, and most of them survived, even if imprisoned for ten years, as most of them were. However, only a relative handful of the men captured in 1942–43 saw Germany again: of the approximately 100,000 members of the 6th Army that surrendered at Stalingrad, only one in 20 survived to be repatriated in 1955.

If the role of Adolf Hitler is central to the nature and the course of the War in the East, that of his enemy and eventual nemesis, Iosif Vissarionovich Dzhugashvili – or Stalin, as the world knew him – was hardly less important. There was considerable truth to the idea that 'only Stalin got us into this mess, and only Stalin can get us out', although it was not a sentiment to voice in Russia if you valued your life. Stalin bears personal responsibility for the weakness of the Soviet armed forces in 1941, and the readiness of the Russian and Ukranian peasantry to welcome a foreign invader who promised to drive out the Communists and abolish the collective farms. It was on his orders that countless soldiers were sacrificed in premature, over-ambitious offensives beyond the operational abilities of the army that Stalin had beheaded in 1937. Yet as the war progressed, Stalin learned to listen to his best generals, to rely on them rather than the Party apparatchiks whose political reliability was no substitute for military competence. Enigmatic and inhuman, the workaholic Stalin visited neither the front lines nor the factories; indeed, he seldom left the Kremlin.[4] From his Spartan office there, he exerted a steadily more decisive grip on the war. The former revolutionary appointed himself Marshal of the Soviet Union, and strode about in glittering uniforms surrounded by bemedalled officers in big hats. The legend of Stalin the military chief took root and, reason notwithstanding, endures to this day in Russia. Only Stalin could have forced through the industrialization of the USSR in the 1930s with such brutal lack of concern over the human cost. If they had been aware of his methods, one suspects the Nazi leadership would have thoroughly approved. As it was, Hitler and his henchmen had no idea the Soviet Union had already won the arms race by 1939. The greatest achievement of Stalin's regime was to win it a second time, to remove so much of Soviet heavy industry to safety in 1941 and still manage to increase output beyond that of German industry, which had most of western Europe under its control.

'Truth', the proverb says 'is the daughter of Time', and only with the passage of years has a balanced account of Hitler's War in the East become feasible. Post-war Soviet accounts were created to feed the vanity of Stalin. As soon as the tide of battle had turned, the ageing tyrant, who had never served in any army, strove to create a myth of military genius just as Hitler had done. Successive 'histories' sought to demonstrate Stalin's military genius. After his death, Khruschev demanded similar treatment, necessitating a complete revision of Soviet history, and another radical overhaul was required after his overthrow. After the 'decades of stagnation', President Mikhail Gorbachev swept away the surviving gerontocracy and instituted reforms intended to improve the system. Unfortunately for him and his regime, they led to the disintegration of the Soviet empire that Stalin had established in eastern Europe. The Soviet Union only outlasted its former satellites by less than two years before it splintered along ancient national boundaries. The Baltic States escaped to join the west; the Ukraine is still trying to follow suit, although Belarus remains stuck in a time-warp. As the political geography of eastern Europe has been transformed, so the history of the Great Patriotic War has been liberated from the dead hands of Communist functionaries.

For the 50-year period that the Soviet history of the war was massaged to suit the ruling clique, western readers relied heavily on German accounts of the War in the East. Some are classics of war literature, and others are extremely valuable for the light they cast on German grand strategy and on the operational realities of armoured warfare across enormous battlefields. Yet, as will be seen, even a commander of indisputable brilliance like Von Manstein was capable of twisting the facts. His literary sleight of hand in *Lost Victories* was as hard to detect as his shift of Panzer divisions to the south of Kharkov in 1943, and no less effective. The common impression given by German accounts is that the Soviets enjoyed insurmountable numerical and material superiority, yet had it not been for Hitler's lunatic decisions, German professionalism could have defeated the 'Asiatic hordes'. There is a degree of truth here, but it is far from the whole story. Some of the generals who advanced this thesis had also entertained the hope, fostered by Goebbels, that the western Allies might strike a deal with Hitler and join forces with the Wehrmacht against the Communists.

This book does not attempt to cover every battle of the war in detail. Certain battles, for instance Stalingrad and Kursk, receive more extended treatment, while other major actions are relegated to a paragraph or two. However, it is important to note that in terms of combat losses, no single battle or campaign dominated the history of the Russian front. German losses mounted at a remarkably consistent rate from June 1941 until 1945; on a graph of losses against time, the greatest battles appear as small deviations in a generally smooth upward curve. The German Army in the east (the 'Ostheer') was depleted by month-on-month attrition that consistently exceeded the flow of replacements.[5] It is in this context that the many brilliant feats of arms by generals such as Von Manstein, Guderian or Model should be seen. They won some spectacular victories against numerically superior forces, and some of their operations are still studied in military academies, and for good reason, but they did not arrest the overall progress of the war.

Nevertheless, the battles of Stalingrad and Kursk were recognized at the time as battles of special significance. The former was a defeat of unparalleled magnitude for the German Army. Germany had accelerated its call-up to provide the manpower for the 1942 offensive in Russia. The complete and utter failure of Hitler's strategy left the Ostheer no prospect of realizing the German dictator's boundless objectives in the east. Hitler quietly agreed to pull back his forces opposite Moscow into more defensible positions. Even he now accepted that the swastika would never fly above the Kremlin. Kursk was another disaster for the Germans. Although their casualties in the battle, especially tank losses, are wildly exaggerated in almost every English language account, its political impact is beyond dispute. For the first time in the Second World War a major strategic offensive mounted by the Wehrmacht in summer had been brought to a halt. As successive Russian offensives drove back the front line in the late summer of 1943, Germany's allies opened negotiations with Moscow. Only inside the concrete bunkers of the 'Wolf's Lair' could you fail to know which way the wind was blowing.[6]

CHAPTER ONE

★

HITLER AND THE WEHRMACHT 1941

'There's only one duty: to Germanize this country by the immigration of Germans and look upon the natives as Redskins.'

ADOLF HITLER

After the war many German generals recorded their dismay and bewilderment that Germany had plunged into Russia in 1941 without defeating or making peace with Britain. For a generation of soldiers who had been junior officers in the First World War, this was the height of foolishness. It was widely believed that Germany's defeat in 1918 was the result of fighting on two fronts at once. However, it is difficult to find much evidence that the generals opposed a two-front war in 1941. In fact, the German Army's senior leadership agreed that it would take a five-month campaign to destroy the Soviet Army, occupy the major cities of the western USSR and march into Moscow. Nor were they alone in this assessment: in London, the joint intelligence committee predicted that Moscow would fall within six months. In Washington, President Roosevelt received even earlier estimates of German victory. In 1941 the only military figures who believed the Russians could win a war with Germany were Stalin's senior commanders.

Hitler's invasion of the Soviet Union was not an opportunistic swipe at the last major opponent left on the board, prompted by his forces' inability to cross the English Channel. Since the First World War he had dreamed of destroying Russia, seizing the western republics of the USSR as 'living space' (*Lebensraum*) for a new German empire. It was sketched out interminably in his book,

Mein Kampf. German generals who said, after 1945, that they had been surprised when Hitler ordered them to the east were being disingenuous. Perhaps they were maintaining the army's avowedly apolitical stance, adopted in the 1920s to mask its blind indifference to the fate of the Weimar democracy.

In *Mein Kampf* Hitler stated several pre-conditions necessary for Germany to begin its drive to the east. He wanted an agreement with the British, an alliance with the Italians and the destruction of France's military power. If the Führer added new justifications in 1940, claiming that the USSR represented an immediate military threat to Germany, he was really excusing himself from attempting the invasion of Britain. The only surprise in Hitler's policy towards the USSR had been his temporary alliance with Stalin, the Nazi–Soviet Pact, that consigned Poland to oblivion in 1939. Even before the Luftwaffe failed to subdue the RAF above southern England in the Battle of Britain, Hitler ordered Field Marshal von Brauchitsch to prepare new plans for an invasion of the USSR, but they remained no more than feasibility studies while the German generals peered across the Dover straits, contemplating Operation *Sea Lion*, the proposed amphibious assault across the English Channel. Hitler's navy chief, Admiral Raeder, expressed his deep unease at the prospect. The grievous losses suffered by the Kriegsmarine off Norway ruled out any serious attempt to frustrate what he knew would be a vigorous reaction by the Royal Navy. And the flat-bottomed Rhine barges, the only available means of shipping the German Army to Kent, would be vulnerable to any sort of seaway, let alone enemy attack. The Luftwaffe continued to mount sortie after sortie against British airfields, unaware that British industry was already building more aircraft and more tanks per month than the German factories. Hitler prevaricated, conscious of the enormity of his decision. An unsuccessful invasion of England would spell the end of his regime, and him.

While Hitler pondered his options, Mussolini ordered an invasion of his own. On 28 October 1940, the Italian army in Albania invaded Greece, *Il Duce* already planning a grand Roman victory parade through Athens. It was not to be. The Greeks counter-attacked and drove the invaders back across the border.

In November Hitler was still unable to bring himself to issue the detailed orders requested by his generals. The OKH (*Oberkommando des Heeres* – Army High Command) had been told to prepare plans for an invasion of Russia, but no objectives or timetable had been laid down. This reflected Hitler's failure to persuade two potential allies to join his crusade against Bolshevism. He had tried to secure active military cooperation from Vichy France, but this had come to nothing. General Franco – whose forces had received so much aid from Germany and Italy in the civil war – stubbornly refused to allow Axis forces into Spain to attack Gibraltar and thus win the campaign in the Mediterranean. The most he would offer was a division of volunteers for service in Russia.

In December 1940 the Italian Army of Libya was demolished by a far smaller British and Commonwealth force. Italian soldiers surrendered in droves and Italy's African empire looked poised to vanish. The Greeks continued to drive back the Italians in Albania. The future of the Fascist regime in Italy looked bleak. Hitler realized that he would have to intervene to rescue his ally from the consequences of his folly. On 13 December he issued orders for the invasion of Greece, to take place early in the spring of 1941.

Five days later he issued Directive 21, ordering Operation *Barbarossa*, the invasion of Russia, to be launched on 15 May 1941. The objective was to destroy the Red Army in western Russia, armoured forces advancing rapidly to block any attempt to retreat into the hinterland. German forces were to push as far east as a line from Archangel to the River Volga, bringing the remaining Russian industries in the Urals within range of the Luftwaffe. Hitler assumed that defeat on such a scale would lead to the overthrow or collapse of the Communist regime. Whom or what he thought he might negotiate with at that point was never really addressed, since the extermination of millions of Soviet civilians was explicitly included in German plans. Although his senior commanders would win great victories by sticking to the precepts of the military theorist Carl von Clausewitz, they tended to overlook his conclusions on total war. 'Russia', Clausewitz wrote, 'is not a country that can be formally conquered.' He thought it too large to be occupied by the armies of the early 19th century, and certainly not by the 500,000 men Bonaparte had employed in 1812. Clausewitz argued that only internal disunity could bring Russia down. Yet by pursuing Hitler's racist vision, the German Army did not stoke dissent in the USSR; it left the people no choice but to fight or die.

The German diversion to Greece turned into an offensive throughout the Balkans after a *coup d'état* in Belgrade orchestrated by British agents. Prince Paul, the regent of Yugoslavia, had made his peace with Hitler, signing a pact with Germany and allowing German troops passage for their forthcoming assault. But the Yugoslav army, led by General Simović, seized power on the night of 26–27 March in the name of the young King Peter. Simović probably intended to steer a more neutral path, rather than throw in his lot with the British and Greeks, as they hoped, but Hitler did not even wait to speak to him. The German forces were ordered to attack with 'merciless harshness'. Nazis did not do nuance. A more diplomatically astute policy might have divided the artificial Yugoslav state along the lines that re-emerged in the 1990s. As it was, some Croat units effectively changed sides once the invasion was under way.

The invasion of Greece and Yugoslavia began on 6 April. Systematic bombing of Belgrade was reported to have killed 17,000 people, an estimate that has been repeated ever since, but it appears extraordinarily high given the numbers and types of aircraft and their bomb loads. The Yugoslav forces had neither the men, the motivation nor the equipment to survive a conventional battle with the Germans and Yugoslavia surrendered on 17 April. Meanwhile, German troops raced into Greece, making deadly use of their air superiority, and crushed everything in their path. Greece surrendered on 20 April, and the British Commonwealth forces that had landed there began yet another withdrawal to the sea, hammered by German air attacks. At the same time, a detachment of German mechanized troops deployed to Italy's aid in North Africa launched its counter-attack. Under the inspiring leadership of Erwin Rommel, the Germans drove the British back into Egypt.

The Balkan adventure had been another spectacular triumph for German arms, but it imposed a significant delay on the invasion of Russia. At the end of May Operation *Barbarossa* was postponed until 22 June.

———

The staggering success of Blitzkrieg in Poland in September 1939 and then France and the Low Countries in 1940 took everyone by surprise. No army in Europe had managed to resist the combination of Panzer divisions and dive-bombers – the Germans had apparently perfected the recipe for victory. What the defeated Allies did not know is that the speed and apparent ease of the German success was as much a surprise to most German officers as to their enemies. The breakthrough in 1940, the armoured offensive through the Ardennes and the subsequent storming of the Meuse, had been opposed by the General Staff. General von Manstein had been demoted from his position as Field Marshal von Rundstedt's chief of staff for advocating this strategy with such impertinence, and was posted to an infantry corps in the rear. Hitler's generals had recommended a scaled-down Schlieffen plan, the famous right-flanking manoeuvre that had nearly brought Germany victory in 1914. This is precisely what the British and French High Commands expected them to do, and led the French to deploy their best units to the Belgian frontier, with orders to fight the decisive battle as far inside that country as possible.

Unfortunately, Hitler overruled his cautious generals. The Panzer divisions raced through the Ardennes and blew a hole in the Allied front that could not be sealed. It did rather help that the French army neglected to retain any significant forces in reserve, a clunking error of judgement that should not be overlooked when seeking to explain the worst defeat in its history.

The great victory in France had two important consequences, neither of which would be apparent until German forces were deep inside the Soviet Union in 1941. Firstly, the German High Command believed that their tactics represented nothing less than a military revolution: a clear break with the experience of the First World War when the defence had held every advantage. 'Blitzkrieg' (the term was invented by the Allies to describe what had been done to them) reversed the situation. Fast-moving tank formations with air support could bypass centres of resistance, drive deep behind the front line and overwhelm the defence. The parallel with the stormtroop tactics of 1915–18 was not accidental. Unfortunately for Germany, the similarities between the 1918 *Kaiserschlacht* offensive and Operation *Barbarossa* would not end there. Hitler shared the generals' conviction that the technology and tactical methods that brought victory in France had universal application. Yet he drew a second conclusion: that his intuitive leadership, grounded in his front-line experiences in the First World War, gave him a unique insight into military affairs. It was he who had insisted on the victorious strategy of 1940, not the General Staff. When the campaign in Russia began to falter in 1941, Hitler would have the confidence to overrule his commanders again, eventually appointing himself as the commander-in-chief.

The overwhelming bulk of the German Army consisted of foot soldiers. In June 1941 the German Army fielded 175 infantry divisions, 21 Panzer divisions and 15 motorized infantry divisions. Two-thirds of the infantry divisions that took part in the invasion of Russia relied on horse-drawn wagons to carry their supplies. Most field artillery batteries were horse-drawn too, so the infantry marched at the same pace as their fathers did in 1914. Each German infantry regiment included teams of soldiers tasked with looking after the horses. Their deadly modern machine-guns and mortars were taken into position and supplied by horse-drawn wagons. The Germans were not able to use the railways, because it took months to convert the Russian wide-gauge track to European gauge, and the Soviets evacuated or destroyed most of their rolling stock. So the strategic mobility of most German units was no greater than that of Napoleon Bonaparte's *Grande Armée* of 1812.

German infantry divisions consisted of three infantry regiments, each of three battalions, and an artillery regiment with 36 105mm guns and 12 150mm guns. The anti-tank *Abteilung* consisted of three companies, each of 12 37mm guns. The infantry battalions had three infantry companies of about 180 men, a machine-gun company – three pairs of 7.92mm general-purpose machine-guns – and a mortar company with three pairs of 81mm mortars.

The Panzer divisions had been reorganized since the French campaign, their tank strength reduced to free up enough vehicles to double the number of divisions. By June 1941, each Panzer division included two or three battalions of tanks (with an average total strength of about 150 vehicles); four (sometimes six) battalions of truck-mounted infantry (designated *Panzergrenadier* in 1942); one reconnaissance battalion on motorcycles; an artillery regiment with 36 105mm guns; three self-propelled anti-tank companies with a dozen or so 37mm or 50mm guns mounted on obsolete tank chassis; plus armoured reconnaissance squadrons, engineer and anti-aircraft companies.

German tank regiments were supposed to include two companies of Panzerkampfwagen (PzKpfw or Panzer) IIIs, armed with 37mm or 50mm guns, and one company of Panzer IVs with a short-barrelled 75mm gun intended for direct-fire support of the infantry. However, in 1941 the Panzer divisions fielded a total of 3,648 tanks (as opposed to the 2,445 of 1940) but only 1,000 were Panzer IIIs and there were only about 450 Panzer IVs. Although the diminutive Panzer I had disappeared from front-line service, many tank battalions were still equipped with Panzer IIs armed with a 20mm gun; others relied on the Czech-built Panzer 35 and Panzer 38(t).

The motorized infantry divisions were smaller than the standard divisions, with six instead of nine infantry battalions, but all mounted in trucks. Their artillery pieces were towed by lorries or half-tracked prime movers. Their reconnaissance units included motorcycles and armoured cars. In 1942 a battalion of self-propelled guns or tanks was added, and half-track armoured personnel carriers appeared in greater numbers, but in the initial campaign they were essentially infantry units, albeit with greater mobility.

The Luftwaffe had made an enormous contribution to the German victory in France. During the critical breakthrough at Sedan, the German armoured commanders had gambled that air power could substitute for the heavy artillery they would not have time to push through the Ardennes forest. While Messerschmitt Bf-109s dominated the Allied fighters, German twin-engine bombers and Junkers Ju-87 'Stukas' delivered accurate bombing attacks that knocked out most French artillery and pulverized strongpoints defending the Meuse. The massive French heavy tanks, armoured leviathans immune to infantry anti-tank guns, were destroyed by air attacks while on trains carrying them to the front.

The close coordination between ground and air forces was to be repeated in the attack on Russia. Yet German production policy was so haphazard that the losses over France and in the Battle of Britain had not been made good. Hitler launched the attack on the USSR with about 200 fewer aircraft than he had been able to deploy for the attack in the west in 1940. The Luftwaffe had a total of 1,945 aircraft available for Operation *Barbarossa*. Luftflotte 3 had some 660 aircraft in France and Belgium; 190 aircraft were retained for defence of German airspace; Luftflotte 5 was in Norway, and the 10th Air Corps in the Mediterranean. The total in the east included 150 transports and about 80 liaison aircraft. Some 1,400 combat aircraft took part in the initial attack on 22 June: 510 twin-engine bombers (Dornier Do-17, Junkers Ju-88, Heinkel He-111); 290 Junkers Ju-87 dive-bombers; 440 Messerschmitt Bf-109 single-engine fighters; 40 Messerschmitt Bf-110 twin-engine fighters; 120 reconnaissance aircraft (Junkers Ju-86, Focke-Wulf Fw 189, etc.).

Germany's allies provided nearly 1,000 additional machines, but of varying quality. Finland had 230 fighters, 41 bombers and 36 dedicated ground-attack aircraft; Romania provided 423 aircraft and Italy supplied about 100 aircraft to support its forces attached to Army Group South in July 1941. The Hungarian contingent was backed by two air regiments; together with the Croatian Air Legion, this added another 60 aircraft.

Three aspects of the German Air Force deserve comment here. There were no four-engined heavy bombers of the sort entering service in the USA and UK; promising designs like the Dornier Do-19 and Junkers Ju-19 had been cancelled in 1937. The Heinkel He-177, the only heavy bomber under development, was hamstrung by a demand for dive-bombing capability and would never be successful. Long-range attacks on Soviet industrial centres – or the rail network – would not be possible. Secondly, the provision of fewer than 200 transport aircraft to service military forces from the Baltic Sea to the Crimea was clearly inadequate. Thirdly, German aircraft production and pilot-training programmes barely sufficed to keep the Luftwaffe at its then size: if the air force suffered heavy losses in fighters, bombers or transports, it would not be able to replace them with any speed. The Luftwaffe, like the army, was not ready for a prolonged conflict.

Almost a third of German infantry divisions remained in western and southern Europe, leaving 120 for the invasion of Russia. This is an extraordinary number of men to leave out of the equation in a war to the death. A total of 38 divisions enjoyed peacetime garrison duties from Germany to the Low Countries and France. Eight divisions had an even easier time in Norway, which would retain an enormous occupation force until the end of the war. Seven divisions had a less cushy time in the Balkans, where the local resistance could be vicious in the extreme. German forces were supported by 14 Finnish, 14 Romanian, four Italian and two Slovak divisions. Spain provided enough volunteers to create the 'Azul' (Blue) Division, which was incorporated into the German Army as the 250th Division in July 1941. Hungary provided its 'Rapid Corps' of three brigades, including 160 light tanks. The allied contingents were a useful source of extra manpower, but multiplied Germany's existing logistic problems. They all had different equipment, requiring different sets of spares, and German units were already filled out with a staggering variety of captured vehicles. Motor transport units drove a mixture of lorries drawn from all across German-occupied Europe. Most of the allied forces did not cross the Soviet frontier until July, and many were used for rear-area security when they did. German strategy also had to ensure that the mutually hostile Hungarian and Romanian contingents were kept apart. They had spent much of the 1930s preparing to fight each other, similar to the Slovaks and Hungarians, who had actually fought a border war.

The postponement of *Barbarossa* caused by the Balkan campaign was once advanced as the primary explanation for the failure of the ensuing campaign in 1941. In fact the spring thaw came late that year, reducing most roads to a sea of liquid mud throughout May. Many river valleys were still flooded at the beginning of June. So an earlier assault was unlikely to have made much faster progress; and in any case, Hitler's strategic indecision once the invasion was under way cost far more time. As we will see, his armies got to within 200 miles of Moscow, then sat down for six weeks until they resumed the advance. However, the Balkan campaign involved a lot of mileage for German motor transport and tanks. Von Kleist's 1st Panzer Group, the cutting edge of Army Group South, would begin *Barbarossa* with nearly a third of its tanks at workshops in Germany. The airborne invasion of Crete had been a pyrrhic victory for the Luftwaffe, with the effective destruction of its élite 7th Airborne Division. The assault on Crete had been extremely costly in aircraft as well as paratroopers: 146 Junkers Ju-52s were destroyed and another 150 damaged in May 1941. This spelt the end – at least in the short term – of German airborne operations. The possible contribution of Germany's superbly trained paratroopers to *Barbarossa* is one of the more intriguing 'what ifs' of the campaign. One mission discussed before the battle for Crete was for airborne forces to help the Panzer divisions hold the outer ring of a 'pocket' until the infantry could arrive; something that the hard-pressed mechanized forces might have found valuable in the summer of 1941.[1] In the event, the reconstituted airborne division was employed as conventional infantry on the Leningrad front from late 1941 to early 1943. It was a shocking waste of superbly aggressive soldiers.

German hopes rested on a relatively small section of the total forces deployed. The success or failure of Hitler's planned knock-out blow in Russia would depend on 19 Panzer divisions. (Two, the 15th and 21st, were with Rommel in North Africa.) Their task would be to repeat their success of 1940, breaking through the enemy front line to trap the Soviet forces between the hammer and anvil. Thanks to the reorganization there were now twice as many Panzer divisions as in 1940, but they would be operating across a vastly greater area. Paris is little more than 200 miles from the German frontier. On 21 May 1940 the front line extended from the Channel coast to the Meuse – a distance of 250 miles. Yet in Russia the front line would expand from 800 miles to about 1,500 miles as the Germans reached Moscow. The supply lines would stretch back for 1,000 miles.

The German forces had many strengths: combat experience in Poland and France allied to excellent training methods had created a highly professional army, brimming with confidence. The Luftwaffe had one of the world's best fighter aircraft, and its aircrew were superbly trained. Morale was extremely high, and from the front-line soldiers to the General Staff there were few men who doubted Hitler's judgement when he said that one good kick would bring down the whole rotten edifice of Russian Communism.

The weaknesses of the German forces were less evident. There were no new bomber aircraft being developed to replace the existing fleet; the tanks were neither well armed nor well protected by comparison with the latest Soviet types; mechanized units were equipped with dozens of different types of vehicles, which shared few common parts and had to be returned to Germany for maintenance. Hitler effectively had two armies: a small mechanized core of some 35 armoured or motorized divisions, and a large unmechanized mass of old-style infantry divisions dependent on horse transport.

The Germans planned to win victory in the east in one intensive Blitzkrieg campaign. Since the Russians would be beaten before their famously cold winter set in — enough senior officers had served on the Eastern Front in the First World War to remember just how cold it could be — OKH decreed that the army would not require winter clothing. Some quantities of cold weather gear were supposed to be ordered, but only for the 60 or so divisions earmarked for occupation duties. Only one top commander demurred - Field Marshal Milch quietly ignored a direct order from Hitler and set about organizing winter uniforms for all 800,000 Luftwaffe personnel he suspected would still be needed in Russia as the snows started to fall. Army units would not be so lucky.

CHAPTER TWO

★

THE RED ARMY

'How can you have a revolution without firing squads?'

V. I. LENIN

Until Stalin had most of its members murdered, it had been assumed before the war that the Main Military Council would exercise supreme command of the Red Army; however, Stalin established a new 'High Command Headquarters' (*Stavka Glavno Komandovaniya*, abbreviated hereafter to *Stavka*) on 23 June 1941. It was supposed to be chaired by his comrade, Commissar of Defence Semyon Timoshenko. The members were Stalin; Marshal (and Politburo member) Klim Voroshilov; foreign minister Molotov; the Chief of the General Staff, General Georgi Zhukov; the Deputy Commissar of Defence, Semyon Budenny; and the Commissar of the Navy, Nikolai Kuznetzov. Zhukov was not in Moscow, having been sent to the front with all three deputy chiefs of the General Staff to find out what was going on. In July, Boris Shaposhnikov became Chief of the General Staff and it was announced that Stalin would be chairing the *Stavka*. By then, as we will see, Stalin's confidence had completely returned and he announced himself as supreme commander of the Soviet forces on 8 August.

Stavka did not meet as a committee, and its members were seldom in the same place at the same time. On 10 July 1941 Stalin established an intermediate command level between *Stavka* and the army groups: high commands for the north-western, western, and south-western sectors of the USSR. They were led by men picked more for their loyalty than their brains: Voroshilov, Timoshenko and Budenny. These additional, intermediate commands were a failure, since Stalin reserved all critical decisions for himself, and they were abolished in 1942.

The Soviet Union had 171 infantry divisions in the western USSR to meet the German invasion, with new armies assembling further east along the Dnepr and Dvina rivers. There were 20 mechanized corps, 'tank heavy' formations, each with two tank divisions (with a total authorized strength of 750–1,000 tanks), a single truck-borne infantry regiment and supporting troops. However, the corps organization had only just been introduced; many corps had their component divisions widely separated, and few had ever functioned together. Not many of the tank divisions were at full strength. Their vehicles were mostly light tanks, poorly protected and thinly armoured. Lacking radios, they communicated with signal flags, which had all manner of obvious drawbacks. Low standards of maintenance meant that many of them broke down the moment they had to deploy in June 1941.

The standard Soviet infantry division was similar to the German: nine battalions in three regiments, with an artillery regiment of 36 guns (theoretically 24 76mm guns and 12 122mm howitzers) plus supporting troops. However, most divisions were significantly under strength in the summer of 1941. On average, they had 8,000 men against an authorized strength of 14,483.

Unlike the Luftwaffe, the Soviet Air Force was not an independent branch of the military, but part of the army. Stalin took a keen – unwelcome – interest in it, with the inevitable result that reports were kept very positive, and statistics of everything from output to aircrew training faked. One undisguisable consequence was an appalling accident rate. The Red Army had more than 10,000 aircraft in 1941, but many were obsolete and serviceability was poor (about 50 per cent). Since few aircraft had radios, and there was no radar system to coordinate them, tactics were primitive by the standards of 1940. Barrier patrols, of the sort flown in the First World War, absorbed large numbers of aircraft but failed to intercept German raids. Even if the Russian fighters did find the enemy, their pilots were trained to fly the sort of tight formations that the RAF had favoured in 1939 – a system rapidly discredited in action against the loose formations of German fighters. Pilots who have to spend a lot of time checking where they are in the formation are not looking out for the enemy, and the proverbial 'Hun in the Sun' did not give second chances.

In terms of total mobilized strength, the Soviet and German forces were on a par, with about three million men each, although the Soviet Union had another million personnel between Moscow, the Caucasus, Siberia and the frontier with Japanese-occupied Manchuria. Yet in Germany it was assumed the numbers would not matter. General Halder's intelligence summary to Hitler concluded that the Red Army was leaderless.

From 1936 to 1939, Stalin had ordered the execution of almost all his senior military officers, and of an astonishing proportion of junior commanders too: three out of five Marshals of the Soviet Union, all 11 deputy defence commissars, the commander of every Military District, 14 out of 16 army commanders, 60 out of 67 corps commanders, 136 out of 199 division commanders and half of all regimental commanders. In numerical terms, 40,000 of the Red Army's 80,000 commissioned officers were arrested, and of those 15,000 were shot. While the pace of the slaughter had slowed after 1939, the terror had yet to run its full course. The disastrous campaign against Finland in the winter of 1939–40 led to new arrests for treason at a number of bases. Failure at the front was dealt with in summary Bolshevik style, 'the discipline of the revolver'. The commander of the 44th Infantry Division extricated a few survivors from a Finnish encirclement, only to be shot on the orders of Stalin's henchman Lev Mekhlis.

Nearly 200 years previously, Voltaire had observed that the occasional execution of an admiral was necessary to encourage the others, but the wholesale massacre of the Soviet officer corps drastically reduced the effectiveness of its armed forces. At the time of the German invasion, only a quarter of Red Army officers had been in their jobs for more than 12 months. The purge was so comprehensive that most senior positions were filled by men out of their professional depth. Only 7.6 per cent of the surviving officers had a higher military education; most had a secondary education and nothing more.[1] The purge exterminated a generation of officers who had developed armoured forces integrated with air power and even paratroops, and who had gained combat experience since the Russian

Civil War. As Khruschev observed after Stalin's death, 'The cadre of leaders who gained military experience in Spain and the Far East was almost completely liquidated ... The policy led also to undermined military discipline, because for several years officers of all ranks and even soldiers in the Party and Komsomol cells were taught to "unmask" their superiors as hidden enemies.'[2] Fear verging on paranoia left most officers afraid to do anything other than obey literally their written orders. Anyone exercising 'initiative' was likely to feel the cold muzzle of a pistol on the back of the neck.

The Soviet Union's pre-war population was approximately 190 million people, more than double the population of Germany – 80 million. It was a very different Russia from the country Germany had defeated in 1917. On the Eastern Front in the First World War, Russian armies were much less well equipped than their German opponents. Poor procurement decisions – huge fortresses packed with siege artillery, but not enough field guns – rather than lack of heavy industry handicapped them from the start.[3] In their early battles in 1941 the Germans found the Red Army to be hopelessly disorganized, and the Russians abandoned vast quantities of equipment. But there always appeared to be more to replace what was lost. Worse, some Soviet weapons and tanks were demonstrably better than their German equivalents.

Russian industry had been transformed under the Communist regime: coal and steel production vastly exceeded pre-1914 levels. Oil production figures should have given Hitler pause for thought too. The USSR's oil fields supplied 33 million tons of crude oil in 1941, compared to Germany's 5.7 million (of which 3.9 million was synthetic oil extracted from coal). Romanian oil, which Germany managed to secure, added another 5 million tons a year to the Axis side of the balance sheet, but in a war of machines, this was a staggering imbalance.

Russia's massive new factories, like the tank plant at Kharkov, were not just building more tanks than Germany; by 1941 they were building bigger tanks, and better. Stalin's purges of the Red Army are well known, but they tend to overshadow the massive expansion of the Soviet armed forces during the 1930s. Whatever his long-term intentions, Stalin was amassing the capability to overrun central Europe. The Red Army had 1.6 million men under arms in 1938, and five million by 1941. Tank production increased from around 1,600 vehicles per annum in 1937 to 3,000 by 1939, and 1,700 in the first half of 1941. Russian factories built 5,400 artillery pieces in 1937, 12,300 in 1938 and 17,100 in 1939. Aircraft production rose from 4,400 in 1937 to 10,600 in 1940.

German tank production was only 2,200 per annum as late as 1940. Numerical disadvantage was one thing; the later Russian BT tanks and the T-26 carried 37mm and later 45mm guns, and the T-34 and KV-1 entering production in 1940 were superior to any German tank either in service or on the drawing board. Stalin's crash industrialization programme began with the 1928 Five-Year Plan. These giant strides in heavy industry had been achieved at terrible human cost. Working conditions were as bad as anything Marx had encountered in 19th-century industrial slums, and Stalin's dark mills were on a truly satanic scale. Unrealistic production quotas were set, and then increased. Failure was not an option, so the systematic faking of production statistics began, a practice that became a permanent feature of Soviet-style industry. A more rational, humane strategy might have brought greater results, but the cold-blooded ideologue in the Kremlin knew no other method than terror – he even had his young industrial supremo, Russia's equivalent to Albert Speer, killed after the war. The political, military and psychological consequences of Stalinism would profoundly affect the War in the East.

Like a number of his fellow Bolshevik revolutionaries, Iosif Vissarionovich Dzhugashvili adopted a pseudonym. His choice of 'Stalin' ('Man of Steel') is not just easier to spell; it suggests just what an image problem the young Georgian had. Jailed several times by the Tsarist authorities, Stalin was a professional revolutionary who never actually held down a job in his life. After Lenin's death in 1923, many senior figures in the Communist Party imagined themselves to be part of a collective leadership, but Stalin manoeuvred them all aside. By the time of the German invasion, Stalin had been the undisputed dictator of the Soviet Union for nearly 20 years. Indeed, such was the Machiavellian subtlety of his rise to power that it is difficult to identify when his 'rule' actually began. Many of his comrades certainly found out too late.

Stalin tried to command the Soviet armed forces – more than ten million men and women – just as Lenin had controlled the Red forces in the Civil War. Time and again during the Second World War, Stalin would circumvent the chain of command by sending '*Stavka* representatives' to the various 'fronts', as the Red Army referred to its army groups. Lenin used to dispatch trusted leather-coated Bolshevik fanatics to oversee Red Army formations, because he never really trusted generals, many of them former officers of the Tsarist army. Stalin trusted very few of the leaders who survived his purges, so he tended to send those commanders he did have faith in to trouble-spots or sectors where a major offensive was planned. Sometimes this helped; certainly the presence of the commander of the Red Army's artillery, Nikolai Voronov, at a front headquarters, ensured a formidable barrage would be laid down to support an attack. But it often led to confusion, divided counsels and a muddled chain of command, which gave rise to débâcles like the Kertsch peninsula in May 1942 (see Chapter Four). Fighting generals like Rokossovsky and Konev hated having *Stavka* top brass breathing down their necks while they were trying to win a battle.

While Soviet industrial output soared under Stalin's regime, agricultural productivity slumped. Since the overwhelming bulk of the Soviet population lived in small villages, and most of the Red Army was recruited from the countryside – as well as most senior commanders who survived the purges[4] – the young soldiers who faced the German invader were still living with the consequences of collectivization. Peasant farms were reorganized into collective farms with merciless enthusiasm by Party officials. *Kulaks* (the marginally better-off peasants) were to be 'liquidated' as 'class enemies'. The reign of terror across the countryside touched every village, and although grain was still shipped into the cities, there was widespread starvation, particularly in the Ukraine. Several million people died in the years of famine; millions of others were alive in 1941 only because they had survived by eating grass, shoe leather or even human flesh.

Most of the Bolshevik leadership came from urban backgrounds and had an almost superstitious fear of Russia's peasant population. The peasant soldiers of 1914 had practically worshipped the Tsar, and the Communist regime meant little to rural communities struggling to farm in Russia's unforgiving climate. Yet their determination to control the countryside, to abolish private farms and direct agricultural production from Moscow, probably caused what they were seeking to prevent. The largely apolitical peasantry conceived a deep loathing for the regime. Resistance was passive: the productivity of collective farms would remain so bad for 50 years that even by the 1980s, the 5 per cent or so of privately cultivated land (allowed after Stalin's death) supplied more than a quarter of the USSR's food stocks. When the German forces invaded, they were welcomed as liberators across the Ukraine, and attempts by Moscow to create partisan movements across western Russia were sabotaged by the villagers who betrayed the guerrillas to the Germans. Their hopes were soon dashed, of course, as the German invaders regarded them as *Untermensch*, racial inferiors to be exterminated or exploited as slave labour. As for abolishing collective farms, more than one Nazi observed that if collective farms had not been introduced, the Germans would have had to invent them. They were tailor-made feudal estates for the new German rulers.

The Bolshevik Old Guard, the original revolutionaries catapulted to power in 1917, knew a great deal about Stalin. The Party cadres were not unanimously behind him either: nearly a quarter of them voted against him in what they foolishly thought was a secret ballot in 1934. Stalin had the old Bolsheviks arrested and shot, and commenced a thorough purge of the Communist Party too. Of the 1,966 delegates to the 17th Party Congress, 1,108 had been arrested by the 18th Congress in 1939, by which time three-quarters of the central committee elected in 1934 had also been shot. It is a grim truth that Stalin killed many more Communists than Hitler.

Although a number of Soviet officers were arrested on trumped-up charges in the early 1930s, two institutions had so far largely escaped Stalin's terror – the armed forces and the instruments of terror themselves, the NKVD (the Russian acronym for 'People's Commissariat of Internal Affairs'; previous titles for the Communist secret police included Cheka and OGPU, later titles include MVD and KGB). Half-a-dozen generals were seized when the show trials of former leading Communists Zinoviev and Kamenev began in 1936. The army's most senior advocate of mechanization, Marshal Mikhail Tukachevsky, was demoted after increasingly public clashes with Stalin's civil war cronies Marshals Voroshilov and Budenny. In early 1937 Stalin moved against the NKVD; Commissar-General Yagoda was arrested along with some 3,000 of his officers. Yagoda himself was tried and executed with Party theorist Bukharin the following year. Tukachevsky was arrested in May 1937 and shot on 12 June; the firing squad was commanded by his friend Marshal Blyukher, who was unaware that his own death warrant was already lying on Stalin's desk, signed.

The activities of Nazi mass murderers will be described in later chapters, but it is important to recognize, as was difficult for the western Allies at the time and for many people even after the war, that it was the Communist regime that actually pioneered mass executions by poison gas. So called 'enemies of the people' were killed in specially converted trucks, rigged to pipe carbon monoxide from the exhaust gases into the sealed rear compartment where the prisoners were shackled. At one killing centre outside Moscow, a stud farm near the village of Butovo, more than 20,000 people were murdered in 1937–38. In the grounds of a dacha owned by the NKVD near the Kommunarka State Farm, Moscow, Stalin's former colleagues Bukharin and Rykov, and latterly Yagoda and the NKVD chiefs themselves, were put to death. The commander of the local death squad, Vasili Blokhin, killed thousands of victims by shooting them in the back of the head with a pistol; he wore a leather apron and long gloves to keep the spatter off his uniform.[5]

In the days of the Tsars, national administration was remote, almost irrelevant, compared to local concerns. Under Stalin, the hand of government could not be avoided. Industry had made its 'great leap forward', the entire rural economy re-shaped and the 'class struggle' kept to the fore – Stalin claimed it would intensify as the last surviving elements of capitalism fought to prevent the final victory of socialism. The ideological veneer was accepted by Party activists, but society had been brutalized and life cheapened. Recent studies suggest western estimates of 11 million deaths in the 1930s should be revised to 16, or even 19, million. By the time the armed forces were purged in 1937 there were some seven million people held in remote labour camps, the *gulag*.[6] Another seven or eight million people were herded off to these camps between 1937 and the German invasion in 1941. The unfortunate prisoners were condemned to work as slaves in the mining and forestry industries across the bleak wilderness of Siberia. In the Vorkuta coal mines the temperature is below freezing for more than half the year. Prisoners worked outside at the Kolmya River gold mines in temperatures of -50°C. In such conditions, fewer than 10 per cent of the people arrested in the mid-1930s were still alive in 1941. Some camps were simply execution centres for political opponents, with no pretence of any 'work': in the Baikal-Amur camps the NKVD resorted to mass shootings, rather than wait for starvation or disease to eliminate the 'enemies of the people'. No lists of these camps were ever published, and the *gulag* system was never mentioned in the media, but everyone was aware of the threat – the possibility of being taken up on the way to work, or of the NKVD knocking on the door in the small hours of the morning.

The system was also exported. Any potential focus for opposition to future Communist rule was eliminated in Soviet-occupied Poland in 1939 and the Baltic States in 1940. To be a teacher, political activist, trade union leader or military officer was enough to guarantee arrest. In a single night in June 1941, one week before the German invasion, the NKVD deported 132,000 people from Latvia, Lithuania and Estonia to the Russian interior. NKVD records from 1940 detail the removal of 15,031 Polish officers from prisoner-of-war camps where they had been held since September 1939. The same records make it clear these men never arrived in other camps. They disappeared. Not until 1989 did the Soviet government admit their fate, although one of the killing fields, at Katyn outside Smolensk, was unearthed by German troops in 1943. Mass graves there contained 4,000 bodies, all shot in the back of the head.

The Red Army at war 1939–40

The Nazi–Soviet Pact enabled Stalin to occupy the Baltic Republics of Latvia, Lithuania and Estonia, as well as eastern Poland. Finland, which achieved independence in 1917 and extracted territorial concessions from the Bolsheviks during the Russian Civil War, was next. Stalin demanded that the border be moved 25 miles further away from Leningrad. His intention was to create a defensive zone as far to the west as possible, in readiness for the likely confrontation with Germany. When the Finns refused, Stalin ordered the troops of the Leningrad Military District to teach them a lesson.

Although the Leningrad Military District commanded the assault, divisions were dispatched to the front from several other areas, often at short notice. Late November is not the best time to begin military operations in Finland, but in the atmosphere described above, nobody was going to object. Marshal Voroshilov assured Stalin that Red Army tanks would be driving through Helsinki within a week. But Tukachevsky, who had developed the Russian tank units, was dead, along with most of his colleagues. All Voroshilov had done was to introduce compulsory dance lessons for Red Army officers.

The Finns had fortified the Karelian isthmus, and the crude tactical methods adopted by the Red Army failed utterly. To the north of Lake Ladoga, Russian divisions struggled along the few roads, only to be cut off by Finnish ski troops. The 44th Rifle Division, rushed up from the Kiev Military District, was surrounded, broken into remnants unable to support each other – and annihilated. Newsreels showed roads choked with tanks and equipment, frozen corpses of Russian soldiers stacked around them like chopped timber, the whole ghastly scene partly hidden by snow falls. The Red Army suffered more than 200,000 casualties. Only sheer weight of numbers enabled the Soviets to prevail. The Finns mobilized just about every able-bodied man to create an army about 600,000 strong, but it was weak in artillery and supported by just 250 aircraft. The Soviets employed nearly a million men, and by mid-January 1940 enough heavy guns and ammunition had been brought forward to commence a 16-day bombardment of the defences. The Red Army bludgeoned its way to Viipuri, despite heavy snowstorms in late February. An armistice was agreed on 13 March and the disputed territory incorporated into the USSR.

The Winter War appeared to confirm the German High Command's perception of the Red Army: an old-fashioned ponderous mass, just like the army Germany had defeated in the First World War. Its equipment did not appear terribly impressive. The tanks the Red Army deployed to Finland were either light tanks that proved highly vulnerable to anti-tank guns, or super-heavy, multi-turreted monsters that got bogged down on remote forest tracks. Its officers had presided over a shambles that would have discredited the Tsarist army of 1914 – or even 1905. Occurring just as Hitler was preparing his offensive in the west, the Red Army's performance in Finland suggested that it would be no match for the Wehrmacht.

Although Voroshilov was replaced as Defence Commissar by Marshal Timoshenko, and political commissars in military units lost their role as 'co-commanders', the Winter War led neither to meaningful reforms nor to the end of the purges. The commission to review the battle tactics in Finland was chaired by a military Luddite, the ageing cavalry chief Marshal Budenny (described to Von Rundstedt in 1941 by a captured Russian officer as 'a man with a very large moustache but a very small brain'). Although the terror had slowed down, officers were still vanishing in the night to face charges of treason up to and beyond 22 June 1941.

Marshal Tukachevsky's remaining disciples managed to reverse an earlier decision to break up the mechanized corps and distribute tanks piecemeal among the infantry. Eight mechanized corps were authorized in the summer of 1940 and another 21 ordered in February 1941, but they would not be combat-ready by the time of the invasion. However, even the new Chief of the General Staff, Georgi Zhukov, could not prevent Stalin ordering the disarming of the fortifications along the Russian border. Having obtained new buffer territories from Finland through the Baltic States, Poland and northern Romania, Stalin insisted that defences be built along his new frontier, and the old positions – the 'Stalin Line' – were stripped to provide material and weapons for them. The Red Army ended up with two sets of incomplete fortifications. The decision to deploy 'forward' had similar repercussions for the Soviet air arm. Air regiments were brought westward to primitive fields with no facilities, or to civilian airstrips. The German invasion caught a large proportion of front-line aircraft on the ground, jammed wing-tip to wing-tip, waiting for their new bases to be completed.

Zhukov owed his elevation to the one success of Stalin's Red Army, administering a comprehensive defeat to the Japanese in Manchuria. In the summer of 1938, border incidents between the Japanese and Soviets culminated in a small battle at Lake Khasan, 70 miles from Vladivostock. The following spring, the Japanese Kwangtung army seized the village of Nomonhan, on the remote border between Manchuria and Outer Mongolia, the River Khalkin-Gol. Zhukov masterminded a counter-attack, deploying some 60,000 troops and 500 tanks in a battle of encirclement which anticipated the larger-scale battles of 1941–45. Soviet losses were about 23,000; Japanese casualties were more than 61,000. Japan made peace, and although major Soviet forces would remain to watch the border until Japan attacked Pearl Harbor, the Japanese Army had lost its appetite for war with the USSR.

Promoted to command the Kiev Military District, Zhukov worked energetically to repair the damage done by the purges. He emphasized that the Red Army would have to fight with what it had now, not what was due to come along in a year or two. In a wargame of a possible German invasion, he commanded the attackers and ran rings around his opponent, General Pavlov. Appointed Chief of Staff in February 1941, he was so convinced of the inevitability of a Russo-German war that he urged Stalin to attack immediately.

Today, Zhukov is Russia's most famous commander of the Second World War, and one of the architects of victory. It is as difficult for modern historians to dent Zhukov's overblown reputation as it is to rescue that of British commander-in-chief Field Marshal Haig, who is still widely, and falsely, regarded as a 'butcher and bungler'. Yet Zhukov's battles were all characterized by the wanton expenditure of human life, his overruling of subordinates who were better informed of front-line realities, and his keen instinct for political advancement. His reckless squandering of more than a million lives in futile attacks on the Moscow Front in early 1942 adds up to the greatest defeat suffered not just by the Russian Army, but by any army in history.

In the summer of 1940 Stalin asked his surviving senior commanders to draft a plan for a Soviet attack on Germany. Marshal Shaposhnikov, once a colonel in the Tsarist army and now the most experienced officer left in High Command, planned a drive on Warsaw and a thrust to cut off German forces in East Prussia. Stalin rejected the suggested strategy, arguing that Hitler's objective in a Russo-German war would be the Ukraine, breadbasket of the Soviet Union, and the industrial heartland in the Don basin. Successive revisions of the invasion plan culminated in an operational scheme that would see Soviet troops defeat the German forces massed in southern Poland, then swing deep into the Balkans. Stalin's plan called for Soviet occupation of Romania, Bulgaria, Hungary and Yugoslavia. The fortifications Stalin had constructed along the 1939 border between the USSR and German-occupied Poland were to be the springboard for his great invasion of the west.

Stalin refused to give the order to invade; indeed, he did everything possible to avert a war, ordering anti-aircraft units not to fire on the increasingly blatant over-flights by German reconnaissance aircraft. Deliveries of strategic materials to Germany, one of the key features of the Nazi–Soviet Pact, were maintained so rigorously that several trainloads passed from east to west only hours before the German attack. The Pact gained Germany a million tons of feed grains, 900,000 tons of gasoline, 500,000 tons of phosphates and 100,000 tons of chromium ores. Permission to import raw materials from Iran, Romania and the Far East via the USSR was also granted and exploited. Stalin calculated that if he gave Hitler no provocation, the war could be delayed until Soviet forces were properly prepared. As it became obvious that Hitler planned to invade anyway, and every indication pointed to an invasion in the summer of 1941, Stalin still refused to take the necessary steps to prepare his forces on the frontier. They stayed deployed in an offensive posture, ready to invade the rest of Poland, although local commanders remained in the dark as to the army's intentions. There was no defensive plan in place, despite all the indications that Hitler planned war, although a highly secret committee reporting to Stalin was already thinking the unthinkable. It was working on the assumption not just that the Germans would invade, but that their forces would be able to advance deep into Russia before the Red Army could do anything about it.[7]

CHAPTER THREE

★

TO THE GATES OF MOSCOW

'Before three months have passed, we shall witness
a collapse in Russia, the like of which has never
been seen in history.'

ADOLF HITLER, 22 JUNE 1941

The German invasion forces were divided into three army groups.
Commanded by General von Leeb, Army Group North was to
advance from East Prussia, through the Baltic States and on to
Leningrad. Detaching several divisions to besiege the border fortress
of Brest-Litovsk, General von Bock's Army Group Centre was to pass
north of the Pripyat marshes, heading for Minsk, Smolensk and,
ultimately, Moscow. Field Marshal von Rundstedt's Army Group
South occupied a start line that arced from southern Poland, along the
Hungarian frontier and across Romania. Ahead lay the great plains of
southern Russia and the Ukraine – excellent tank country.

While each group had broad territorial objectives, the German
armies had not come to conquer cities. They were there to kill
Russians. Hitler and the General Staff were in complete agreement:
the Soviet forces had to be trapped and beaten in European Russia,
preferably within 250 miles of the border. Their concern was that the
Soviets might fall back deep into the Russian interior, drawing
German forces into a battle of attrition on the edge of Asia. As
Directive 21 put it, 'The bulk of the Russian army stationed in
western Russia is to be destroyed in a series of daring operations
spearheaded by armoured thrusts. The organized withdrawal of intact
units into the vastness of interior Russia is to be prevented.'

On the face of it, the German strategy looked perfectly orthodox,
following the precepts laid down by Von Clausewitz. The great
19th-century strategist had argued that the capture of great cities was
rarely decisive, but if the enemy's army was destroyed, his capital

would fall automatically; therefore, make the army the primary objective. In fact, the German High Command had no choice in the matter. An invasion on such a scale presented horrendous logistical problems. These effectively dictated the strategy, and there would be only one chance to make it work.

The Soviet equivalent of an army group was a 'front', four of which were deployed in a giant arc stretching from Finland to Romania. The North Front, commanded by Colonel-General Popov, was the smallest: it faced the Finns and the German Army in Norway. The North-Western Front under Colonel-General Kuznetsov defended the Baltic States, while General Pavlov's Western Front faced Army Group Centre. Colonel-General Kirponos's South-Western Front held the line from southern Poland and along the Hungarian border. Armies deployed opposite Romania were organized into a fifth front, the Southern, under General Tiulenev, a few days after the invasion. *Stavka* was also assembling reserve armies between Moscow and Smolensk.

Each German invasion since 1939 had opened with a devastating air attack, and the Luftwaffe showed it had lost nothing of its edge despite its losses over Britain and Greece. Over-flights before the attack had provided a good intelligence picture of the Soviet Air Force, and on 22 June the 66 air bases that were home to about three-quarters of Soviet aircraft were systematically bombed. Around 800 Soviet aircraft were destroyed on the ground, while another 400 were shot down in some very one-sided air battles. The Luftwaffe had better fighters and many veteran pilots, who soon ran up enormous personal scores.

In the first months of the invasion, the Luftwaffe found itself in an extremely target-rich environment. Indeed, its reconnaissance flights persistently identified more columns of Russian troops than its bomber squadrons could attack. Many had to be ignored while more pressing targets were dealt with. There was, incredibly, a shortage of bombs – testimony to Germany's inadequate production rates and sloppy logistic planning. The plethora of targets and the army's escalating demand for close air support ruled out any serious strategic effort by the Luftwaffe in 1941. The Soviets were allowed to dismantle whole factories and dispatch trainload after trainload of industrial plant to safety without intervention by the German Air Force. Factories old and new were able to keep working with little threat from the air.

The German Army was forced to rely increasingly on air power to compensate for its own problems. The vigorous presence of the Luftwaffe above the Russian battlefields was not the manifestation of German technical superiority it looked to be at the time. It should be recognized as a symptom of the army's weaknesses: its lack of artillery and anti-tank weapons, and the fact that only a small proportion of the army was mechanized. The Panzer formations depended on air support both to break through the Soviet defences and to defend the 'outer ring' of the lines of encirclement that they found themselves holding.[1] The Panzers needed bombers to compensate for their relative lack of organic artillery, as well as transports to deliver emergency supplies of petrol, oil, lubricants and ammunition. It was fortunate for the German Army that the Luftwaffe won air supremacy so quickly, wiping out the Soviet Air Force and freeing its assets for support of the ground war.

The massacre in the air was immediately followed by one on land. The Soviet forces were caught completely unprepared; Stalin's absolute insistence on offering no 'provocation' had left them in no position to offer effective resistance. When an incredulous Stalin finally accepted the news was true, that Hitler had broken his word and invaded, he demanded a counter-attack. Marshal Timoshenko wrote the orders and issued them that very night. All four fronts were to launch an immediate offensive, but were not to pursue beyond the 1941 border! All commanders attempted to comply, putting in at least a token counter-strike while trying to salvage something from the mess, but none managed to arrest the ferocious pace of the German assault.

Precisely why the Soviet forces were so badly prepared to meet the German onslaught has been the subject of unending debate, and whole books have been devoted to it. In the late 1980s a Soviet defector writing under the pseudonym 'Viktor Suvorov' claimed that the Red Army had deployed forward because it was poised to invade Germany. This was dismissed by the *bien pensants*, but rumours persisted and more recent (and more credible) historians have concluded he was on to something, even if he exaggerated the likely timetable Stalin was working to.

Stalin's blithe overconfidence in early 1941 can be attributed at least partially to an embarrassing failure by his intelligence sources. The Soviet General Staff appears to have credited Hitler with a far larger army than he actually had. We know now that by May 1941 more than 60 per cent of the Wehrmacht was concentrated on the Russian frontier. Stalin's agents had a very accurate idea of how many German divisions were now in Poland and Romania, but because of their inflated perception of the German forces, this amounted, in their view, to less than 40 per cent of the total. So it was a worry, but not a sign of imminent invasion.

The second reason the Red Army was wrong-footed lay in its own doctrine. German commanders were staggered and delighted in equal measure at the lack of defensive preparations they encountered in the first few weeks. In fact, the Red Army's defensive strategy was an immediate all-out counter-offensive, in some ways not unlike the French operational plan for 1914. The Red Army was deployed close to the frontier, ready to take the battle to enemy territory from the first – hence the split between north and south either side of the Pripyat marshes. The Red Army High Command stationed relatively small forces north of the marshes: even if they broke through their German opponents, they would soon find themselves in the forests and woods of East Prussia amid a defensive belt with excellent communications to the rear – where a whole Russian army was destroyed in 1914. The best place for the Red Army to attack Germany was south of the marshes, which explains the huge concentration of force in the Kiev Military District. From here, the massive Red Army tank formations could advance across the plains of southern Poland and into Germany with few major geographical obstacles to hinder their progress. Thus the Red Army found itself hopelessly wrong-footed when the invasion came. Its forces along the frontier were positioned for an attack; no defensive measures had been taken; bridges were not prepared for demolition; fall-back positions were neither scouted nor prepared; and fuel and ammunition were stockpiled far too close to the front line.

The German army groups advanced in two echelons. The Panzer divisions and motorized divisions grouped together into four Panzer groups, one each in the north and south and two for Army Group Centre. The Panzer groups cut through the front line and pressed on, trapping the Russian armies between them and the mass of infantry divisions hurrying forward in their wake. There would be no supply line to the Panzer groups; shuttling supplies forward would be impossible with so many unsubdued enemy formations in between. Each Panzer division therefore carried about twice its normal allocation of fuel.[2]

The Russian forces found themselves all but leaderless in the immediate wake of the invasion. Stalin left it to the hapless Molotov to broadcast the news that the country was at war. He avoided military responsibility too, but while Timoshenko, People's Commissar of Defence, was supposedly in charge of the army, and Admiral Kuznetsov of the navy, neither man dared make a decision without reference to the *Vozhd*, the 'leader'. Stalin ordered Zhukov to fly to the South-Western Front as 'Politburo representative', so there was not even a chief of the General Staff in place any more. The one immediate decision Stalin did take was to order the immediate evacuation of industrial plants in the western provinces of the USSR.

General von Bock's Army Group Centre had 750,000 men and was spearheaded by two Panzer corps, commanded by Generals Heinz Guderian and Hermann Hoth, respectively. Bock's friend, the former gunner officer Field Marshal Albert Kesselring, commanded Luftflotte 2. Army Group Centre faced a similarly sized opponent in the shape of

44-year-old General Dimitri Pavlov's Western Front, the Russian 3rd, 4th, 10th and 13th Armies, totalling 700,000 men (including 19,000 NKVD troops). Pavlov might have been defeated by Zhukov in the last great strategic wargame conducted before the war, but he was in many ways the archetypal young Red Army general who had survived the purges to find himself at the top of his profession. As a young soldier he had fought in the Russian Civil War, gaining both a reputation for physical bravery and rapid promotion. He commanded Russian troops sent to Spain and was made one of the first Heroes of the Soviet Union for his handling of Republican tank forces at Madrid in 1937. He had made the winning move of the Winter War, leading his corps across the frozen sea in Vyborg Bay to outflank the Finnish strongpoints of the Mannerheim Line. Zhukov rated him as a perceptive commander who understood armoured warfare.

Pavlov began the last battle of his life with more than 2,000 tanks, including 383 KVs and T-34s. For a few hours he had some 400 modern and 1,500 not-so-modern aircraft, but Kesselring's fliers made short work of them. The 29-year-old Soviet Air Force commander, Major-General Kopets, veteran of the Spanish Civil War and promoted from captain to general in three years of purges, could not bring himself to report the news to Moscow. He shot himself that night.

On 23 June Stalin ordered Pavlov to ensure that the city of Minsk did not fall to the Germans. For the first, but no means last, time in this war, a city's symbolic and political importance was allowed to take precedence over practical military necessity. Neither a transport hub nor an industrial centre of any significance, Minsk was of no real strategic importance, but Stalin was not prepared to give up the capital of a Soviet republic. It would, he told his terrified generals, be better for the Western Front to be surrounded in the city than to see it in German hands. As if that were not enough, Stalin also demanded that Pavlov counter-attack, which resulted in the complete destruction of the few units that received and obeyed the orders. One advancing Russian tank unit, however, came close to capturing 'Fast Heinz' Guderian himself, racing ahead of his troops in a car!

As the Luftwaffe rained bombs on Minsk and the Western Front broke up into fragments of organized fighters and a tide of fugitives, Pavlov was besieged by Russian generals. First the ageing Shaposhnikov, then Marshal Kulik came to clutter up his headquarters. On 27 June he was visited by the famously incompetent Party hack, Marshal Klim Voroshilov, who arrived in a gleaming limousine, shouting and swearing. These interventions by senior command were as pointless as they were predictable. After 48 hours the game was up, the capital of Belorussia (White Russia) was lost and Guderian's tanks were on the road to Moscow. Isolated units and thousands of stragglers managed to slip away before the hard-marching German infantry sealed the Minsk pocket, but 20 Russian divisions were smashed and a staggering 350,000 prisoners were taken, along with 2,500 tanks and 1,400 guns.

Army Group North was the smallest of the German groups, but it had the easiest task initially because the road network in the Baltic States was more extensive than in the regions south of the Pripyat. The defenders, Colonel-General Fedor Kuznetsov's North-Western Front, should have been prepared, however. Even under Stalin's plans for an attack on Germany, the North-Western Front was supposed to remain on the defensive, but in the Baltic States, as everywhere along the frontier, the Red Army was caught napping. In a matter of days, the Panzer divisions were through Lithuania and halfway across Latvia, reaching the River Dvina on 26 June. Soviet mechanized units found themselves out of contact with the High Command or adjacent units, and out of ammunition and fuel shortly afterwards. The Russian 8th Army fell back northwards into Estonia but the 11th retreated due east, leaving no real covering forces between them. Kuznetsov was sacked on 4 July and was lucky to escape a firing squad for such a shambolic performance. He was replaced by one of his own army commanders, General Sobennikov, with the highly competent General Vatutin as his chief of staff.

By mid-July the North-Western Front had suffered 75,000 casualties and lost 2,500 tanks and 3,600 guns; aircraft losses in this sector were more than 1,000. The most horrendous loss of life occurred on 28–29 August, when the Russian Navy evacuated more than 20,000 people from Tallinn, the Estonian capital. The operation was commanded by Vice-Admiral Vladimir F. Tributs, commander-in-chief of the Red Banner Baltic Fleet. The 66-ship convoy was covered by heavy units from Kronstadt, but it ran into a German minefield during the night. The Germans had laid more than 4,000 mines in the area and the Luftwaffe arrived to find a target-rich environment the following day. Mines and air attacks accounted for almost all the transport shipping, which was packed with soldiers. The destroyers *Kalinin*, *Artem*, *Engels* and *Skory* were all mined off Cape Juminda; the destroyer *Yakov Sverdlov* went down off Moon Island and *Volodarski* sank off Seiskari. Estimates of casualties vary from 4,000 to 12,000 personnel, but the higher totals are more widely accepted. More people died off Cape Juminda in 1941 than at Russia's far more famous naval defeat, Tsushima. In 2001 a memorial was unveiled on the Juminda peninsula, Estonia, to commemorate the thousands of people who died in the convoy battle just offshore in August 1941. A third of the ships came from the three Baltic Republics.

The navy had already lost two destroyers on German minefields in July (*Serdity* and *Smely*), as well as the *Karl Marx* to air attack on 8 August. Between July and November 1941 the Baltic Fleet lost 15 destroyers, taking it out of the equation as a surface fleet for the rest of the war. Of the battleships, *Oktyabrskaya Revolutsia* (ex-*Gangut*) was hit by German shore batteries off Kronstadt in September, then crippled by air attack while moored at Leningrad in April 1942. *Marat* was sunk by Stukas in shallow water at Kronstadt, but some of her guns remained in action through the siege of Leningrad. Reverting to her Tsarist name, *Petropavlovsk*, in 1943 (dead French revolutionaries presumably going out of fashion), she was gradually repaired and eventually refloated after the war. In contrast to his colleagues ashore, for whom the initial defeats sometimes had fatal consequences, 41-year-old Vice-Admiral Tributs emerged from the 1941 campaign unscathed, and would end the war with two Orders of Lenin and a dozen other medals, including the US Legion of Merit. The Red Banner Fleet included a large number of submarines, and their achievements in the Baltic were talked up by Soviet propagandists, who claimed they had sunk 73 ships for a total of more than 50,000 tons in 1941. The actual number of ships was three, totalling 4,849 tons. This pattern continued through the war until 1945, when two Russian submarines, the S13 and L3, would cause the worst maritime disasters in history.

In the south, the stage looked set for a more balanced fight. Field Marshal von Rundstedt encountered more determined opposition than his colleagues in the shape of Colonel-General Kirponos and the South-Western Front. This army group had been intended to lead the offensive against Germany and consisted of four armies with a combined strength of 59 divisions. On its left flank, deployed ready to invade Romania, the Southern Front had another 21 divisions. This was the main strength of the Red Army in 1941: 1.4 million men supported by 8,000 tanks and some 4,500 aircraft – more armour and planes than the entire German Army. At 49, Colonel-General Mikhail Kirponos was one of the older purge survivors. He had commanded a Red Army regiment in the Civil War and learned German operational methods at the Frunze Academy. Junior to his colleague Pavlov, he commanded a division under Timoshenko during the final offensive against Finland in 1940. After a short spell in charge of the Leningrad Military District, he succeeded Zhukov to command the Kiev Military District in early 1941.

Kirponos's opponent was the archetypal Prussian. Gerd von Rundstedt had fought on the Russian front in the First World War as chief of staff of the 86th Infantry Division. Aged 65, openly contemptuous of the Nazis and their ideology, he was the consummate German professional soldier. His army group comprised three German armies, the 11th, 17th and 6th: a total of 43 German and 14 Romanian divisions.

It was only a month since General Kirponos had been in Stalin's office, discussing plans for a pre-emptive strike into German-held

Poland. Now everything had changed; German forces were surging across the frontier and the air was thick with German bombers. So one can imagine Kirponos's reaction when he received orders from Moscow to proceed with the original invasion plan. Stalin ordered him to hold the Hungarian border, while launching an offensive into Poland, spearheaded by his mechanized corps; Lublin was to be captured by 24 June. Like Pavlov, he soon received a delegation of top brass to stiffen the sinews: Zhukov, Chief of the General Staff, and Nikita Khrushchev, Party boss of the Ukraine.

A handful of T–34s made their combat debut on 23 June. The anti-tank gunners of the German 197th Infantry Division discovered to their dismay that their 37mm anti-tank guns made no impression on them at all. The standard anti-tank gun became known as the 'door knocker'; even repeated hits had no effect on the T–34's armour. The Germans were lucky that they tended to face T–34s in small numbers at a time, and that coordination between Russian tanks and infantry was very poor. Low standards of junior leadership and lack of radios largely negated the T–34's daunting superiority in firepower, protection and mobility. General von Kleist's 1st Panzer Group faced several major counter-attacks by Soviet armour, but experience told – the veteran German units coordinated their actions while their opponents often blundered into battle with little reconnaissance, and were not supported by neighbouring formations. The Luftwaffe had achieved complete air superiority and concentrations of Soviet troops were bombed from the moment they tried to assemble.

Zhukov was summoned back to Moscow, his journey made all the more disagreeable by the news that his predecessor, General Meretskov, had been arrested and was probably under torture already. (He was, but was released and would eventually rise to the rank of Marshal of the Soviet Union.) NKVD interrogators beat false confessions out of many officers; Pavlov and his staff were made to confess to a long-standing treasonous plot, implicating their friends and colleagues. How seriously the secret police followed up such allegations depended on the prominence of the original victims and the mood of NKVD chief Lavrenti Beria. Senior commanders were not executed except by Stalin's express order, but even the relatively outspoken Zhukov was, by his own later admission, worried that he would pay the price for the Red Army's shambolic performance.

Stalin made Pavlov and his staff the scapegoats for the defeat at Minsk and they were all shot. Some were out of reach of the NKVD having already been killed or captured. Pavel Ponedelin, commander of the 12th Army, was sentenced to death in absentia. He had been arrested, but then released, in 1938. Chief of Staff of the Leningrad Military District before achieving army command, he had been taken prisoner amid the rout of his army, and survived the war to be liberated in 1945. However, he was arrested in October 1945, held in jail until 1950, then shot. Whether his Leningrad connections were enough to doom him then can only be speculated. His fate was shared by General Nikolai Kirillov of the 13th Rifle Corps, also sentenced to death after capture and arrested, imprisoned and executed with Ponedelin. The families of the victims were made to suffer too: some were executed and others were flung into labour camps. This even applied to the families of some commanders posted as 'missing' who were later discovered to have died honourably on the battlefield.

To announce that a front headquarters had been unmasked as a nest of traitors was hardly calculated to boost morale in the rest of the army. The USSR was already a paranoid society, ruled by a paranoid dictator. In a horrifying illustration of the climate of suspicion and panic that gripped the nation in the summer of 1941, it was later discovered why the 10th Army had failed to obey Pavlov's orders in June. When radio and telephone links failed, he sent two officers to 10th Army headquarters to give them verbal instructions. They were neither recognized nor believed; both were shot as 'German spies'.

Together with Timoshenko and Vatutin, Zhukov produced a new plan for Stalin's approval. It called for two sacrificial lines of defence to be held to the death, gaining time for reserves to be mustered, industry to be evacuated and autumn to set in. After berating his generals, Stalin quit Moscow for his dacha on 29 June and failed to return to the Kremlin the next day. His anxious henchmen telephoned, but got no answer. When they eventually summoned the courage and initiative to drive there, they found a very different Stalin from the combative monster they all feared. The *Vozhd* thought the game was up. In a week he had lost more territory than Tsar Nicholas II lost between 1914 and 1917. By any yardstick, he had led Russia into its worst defeat of all time, and it was far from over. Beria, Molotov, Mikoyan, Voznesensky and Malenkov arrived at Stalin's dacha with the power to change history. Foreign minister Molotov was arguably the only plausible alternative leader, since everybody hated Beria, the secret police boss. But Molotov remained doggedly loyal. Once Stalin realized they had not come to kill him, but to seek his continued leadership, the *Vozhd* took charge again. They established the State Committee of Defence, led by Stalin. From his point of view, the purges had worked: he had killed every potential rival and utterly cowed the only senior figures capable of removing him from power.

Army Group Centre made faster progress than Army Group South, reaching Smolensk by 26 July. The rapid exhaustion of both fuel and ammunition, as well as stiffening Soviet resistance on the high road to Moscow, would prevent any further advance for the moment. Meanwhile a large salient was appearing around Kiev, the USSR's third city (after Moscow and Leningrad), as German forces swept across the southern Ukraine. Stalin insisted that General Kirponos's South-Western Front continue to counter-attack, sacking his old crony Marshal Budenny for supporting Kirponos's plea for permission to retreat. Both sides could read a map, and Hitler responded to the invitation by ordering Guderian's 2nd Panzer Group (part of Army Group Centre) to drive south from the Smolensk area to encircle Kirponos's whole army group.

Hitler's decision to halt Army Group Centre at Smolensk, 250 miles short of Moscow, has often been regarded as one of the most grievous strategic errors committed by the German dictator.

Chief of the General Staff Colonel-General Franz Halder urged Hitler to press on to Moscow and ignore both Leningrad and the Ukraine. Hitler visited the headquarters of both Army Group Centre and Army Group South at the beginning of August, resorting to his usual tactic of spouting endless economic statistics when his commanders argued for resuming the advance. Ultimately he ignored them all and dispatched Guderian and his tanks to the south.

Post-war commentators have tended to side with the generals on this issue, few more stridently than former army captain and armchair strategist Basil Liddell Hart. He claimed the delay in the advance on Moscow was a fatal mistake that cost Hitler the war. However, while a German offensive towards the Soviet capital in August would obviously have enjoyed better weather than Operation *Typhoon*, which kicked off at the end of September, the argument is finely balanced. In early August, Army Group Centre was scattered across central Russia, its armoured spearheads to the fore, but infantry divisions struggling along behind. Supplies of everything except heat and Russians were running dangerously low. It is by no means certain that these exhausted divisions could have pushed on, unsupported, to victory. By the time *Typhoon* was launched, the German forces were in much better shape for their dash at Moscow, and this enabled them to defeat the Red Army in another colossal battle, inflict enormous losses and come very close to success.

Army Group South's 1st Panzer Group headed up from Kremenchug on the River Dnepr. On 16 September, the armoured pincers met, trapping four Soviet armies totalling nearly 50 divisions. The next day Stalin signalled permission to give up Kiev, but still said nothing about withdrawal of the armies caught in the trap. Possibly on his own initiative, Marshal Timoshenko sent Major-General Bagramyan to Kirponos's headquarters with oral instructions to break out. But oral contracts are not worth the paper they are written on, and in Stalin's world only written orders might enable a general to survive in these circumstances. Kirponos insisted on formal permission to retreat from *Stavka*, and that delay was fatal.

There was a fleeting chance of escape for those formations near the edge of the pocket, or those with commanders prepared to take decisions without reference to higher headquarters. As the German infantry divisions hurried to seal off every avenue of escape, several key figures broke out, including future traitor General Andrei Vlasov and future Marshal of the Soviet Union Ivan Bagramyan. Kirponos led his staff out on foot but was killed in the fighting by a German mortar bomb. According to Soviet figures, the South-Western Front had 677,000 men in late August, of whom 150,000 escaped and 527,000 became prisoners-of-war. The more commonly quoted German figure is 655,000 prisoners, a total possibly inflated by the many civilians dragged off to their deaths by the German Army at the same time. Fewer than one in six of these prisoners would survive the year.

Kiev fell on 19 September 1941. A few days later, an order printed in Ukranian and Russian was posted throughout the town by the occupation forces. It read:

> Jews of the city of Kiev and surroundings: on Monday September 29, you are to appear by 7.00am with your possessions, money, documents, valuables, and warm clothing at Dorogozhitshaya Street, next to the Jewish Cemetery. Failure to appear is punishable by death.

No one realized just what the Germans had in store, that the warm clothing would only be needed for a short walk from the trucks since everyone would have to strip naked before stepping into the pits to be shot. In 48 hours, the SS men of Sonderkommando 4a and two *Kommandos* of Police Regiment South shot 33,771 Jews in a nearby ravine at Babi Yar. Fooled until the last moment, the victims were made to strip and lie on the still-warm bodies at the top of the heap, before the guards opened fire with sub-machine-guns and pistols. Although the bodies were bayoneted too, to check no one had been missed, a few individuals escaped death, lying under other bodies until they could slip away at night.

Four *Einsatzgruppen* entered the USSR in the wake of the German Army. These 3,000 SS men were to provide internal security by combating Soviet partisan activity, but their primary purpose was to kill the Jewish population of eastern Europe. Since 90 per cent of Soviet Jews lived in towns, this was quickly accomplished, and 1.5 million people were put to death. The *Einsatzgruppen* had enormous impact on the War in the East, their strength growing tenfold during 1941. By the beginning of 1943 there were 300,000 men engaged in their genocidal mission – this at a time when the German Army was desperately under strength. The zeal with which the *Einsatzgruppen* dealt with the least hint of resistance behind the lines won them plaudits from every army headquarters. However, some junior army officers refused to cooperate with SS men who combed the prisoner-of-war camps for Jewish members of the Soviet armed forces. The commandant of a POW camp at Vinnitsa even court-martialled his deputy for handing over prisoners-of-war to the SS, but the Army High Command issued a formal instruction that soldiers were to assist the *Einsatzgruppen*: 'This order clearly states that the Wehrmacht has to cooperate in the solution of this problem.'[3] Some army units were already complying with a will. The soldiers and junior NCOs had grown up under Hitler and had no reservations about their mission in Russia. A significant minority – 29 per cent in one analysis of three front-line Wehrmacht divisions – were Nazi Party members.[4]

The Army High Command was already sliding down the moral slope, issuing the notorious 'Commissar Order' before the invasion. Soviet political officers who were captured were to be shot immediately. An OKH order of 6 May also authorized retaliation ('corrective measures') against villages in the vicinity of any partisan resistance. Worse, the order specifically exempted soldiers from the legal code for a whole catalogue of crimes: German troops literally had a licence to kill.

The German Army's reaction to the vast numbers of prisoners was in the same spirit: on 8 September 1941 OKH decreed that Soviet prisoners-of-war had forfeited all rights. Why and how was not explained, but any and all measures were now permissible. By then, nearly two million Soviet servicemen had been captured and winter was approaching. No provision had been made to deal with so many prisoners. The German generals' operational plans envisaged a succession of encirclement battles to destroy the Red Army in western Russia. They planned how they would break through the enemy front, and how they would sustain the armoured forces operating deep in the enemy rear; they conducted wargames to see how long it would take for the hard-marching infantry divisions to complete the encirclements. But no one made preparations to deal with the hundreds of thousands of Russian soldiers they assumed they would capture. While the generals could argue after the war that they knew nothing about the SS death squads gearing up to slaughter the Jewish population, they cannot be absolved of their pivotal role in the wholesale killing of Russian prisoners-of-war. On receipt of the 8 September order, some army units simply machine-gunned their captives. The majority were left in barbed-wire compounds, deprived of food and warm clothing and allowed to starve or freeze to death in conditions of indescribable squalor. The only regret ever expressed by the Nazi leadership was that this was a waste of potential slave labour. In a letter to Field Marshal Keitel in February 1942, Alfred Rosenberg wrote:

> The fate of the Soviet prisoners-of-war in Germany is on the contrary a tragedy of the greatest extent. Of the 3.6 million prisoners-of-war, only several hundred thousand are still able to work fully. A large part of them has starved or died because of the hazards of the weather. Thousands also died from spotted fever. The camp commanders have forbidden the civilian population to put food at the disposal of the prisoners, and they have rather let them starve to death.[5]

The military repercussions of German savagery would not be felt immediately, not until news of their crimes spread throughout a Russia that was no stranger to arbitrary cruelty. Despite their actions, the Germans managed to recruit several million Russians and other nationalities to fight for them in the east. How many more would have rallied to them had more humane treatment been offered has been debated ever since the war. Since the NKVD was still dealing with the burning embers of Ukranian nationalism in the early 1950s, opposition to the Soviet regime was clearly widespread. The Germans' evil crimes rebounded on them and arguably cost them the war.

The mass surrenders of 1941 demonstrated that large elements of the Red Army were no more ready to die for their country than those of France in 1940 or the Italian Army in North Africa, where 300,000 men surrendered to 30,000 British and Commonwealth soldiers. There was no folk memory of atrocity, and for a while the Communist Party had taught that German workers were allies of the Russian proletariat. Fraternization between German and Russian soldiers had been not uncommon on the Eastern Front during the First World War. Easter 1916 had witnessed scenes not dissimilar to those of the notorious unofficial Christmas truce on the Western Front in 1914. Suspicious that his armies would continue to disintegrate, Stalin ordered NKVD chief Lavrenti Beria to restore discipline. Before the men of the Red Army learned what an appalling fate was in store for anyone surrendering to the Germans, Beria had already made surrender a crime, punishable in the NKVD's usual way. Officers and political officials who had been taken prisoner were declared traitors, and their families made to suffer for their 'crime'. This had tragic consequences for many men who held out behind the lines, fought their way back and found themselves in the hands of the NKVD, branded as 'enemies of the people'.

German objectives changed in September. Although the German Army had inflicted enormous losses on the Red Army, Soviet resistance was continuing and the German forces were running out of supplies and replacements. The initial progress in the north had petered to a halt in the dense forests and swamps that barred the approaches to Leningrad. The terrain was unsuited to armoured operations, and the 4th Panzer Group – poised at one stage for a mad solo dash at the city – was reassigned to Army Group Centre. Deprived of its tanks, Army Group North ground its way to the outskirts of Leningrad in fighting more akin to the First World War than the brave new world of Blitzkrieg. Meanwhile, the Russians evacuated the factory complex that built KV-1 heavy tanks from Leningrad to the Urals, temporarily halting production.

The Red Army had suffered grievously, but was still in the field. On 6 September Hitler demanded a maximum effort to capture Moscow before winter set in. The Soviet capital was at once a political and military objective. It was hoped that the loss of the city – and the Kremlin – would demoralize the Red Army, and possibly even topple the Soviet regime. Moscow was also a key industrial centre that lay at the hub of the Soviet rail network. Political considerations aside, its loss would hamper Soviet strategic movement, logistic arrangements and military production. As usual, the Germans planned to isolate the city rather than embroil themselves in an urban battle: the 3rd and 4th Panzer Groups were to bypass Moscow to the north; the 2nd Panzer Group would advance from Tula, passing to the south and linking up with the others some distance east of Moscow.

Operation *Typhoon* opened on 2 October, and led immediately to two more battles of encirclement. Another 650,000 Red Army soldiers passed into captivity. With the 2nd, 3rd and 4th Panzer Groups concentrated in Army Group Centre, the Wehrmacht was staking everything on its dwindling mechanized units. The three groups consisted of a total of 13 Panzer divisions and seven motorized divisions, although the total tank strength was probably no more than 1,000. By this time, most motorized formations had lost more than half their vehicles. In three months of fighting, the 2nd Panzer Group, for example, had advanced across 1,200 miles of Soviet territory, and since the Germans calculated that for every mile 'conquered' combat vehicles actually drove two miles, the wear and tear on vehicles, not to mention crews, was depleting the tank regiments as comprehensively as actual battle. Nevertheless, the Panzer groups advanced rapidly, cutting off the 19th, 20th, 24th and 32nd Soviet Armies at Vyazma. The 13th and 50th Armies were encircled as the 2nd Panzer Group broke through to Orel.

There was panic in Moscow. Party functionaries raced to pack their bags as the regime implemented its emergency plan to transfer most government departments to Kuibyshev (Samara), 600 miles away on the Volga. The General Staff set up a new headquarters near Arzamas, Gorki. Stalin had his personal aircraft fuelled and ready for a quick exit. A group of NKVD officers drew up a plan and distributed the necessary explosives to blow up all factories and key buildings, ironically, exactly what Hitler said he would do if he got his hands on the city. German bombing raids on Moscow exacerbated the sense of doom and helplessness. Alexander Werth, the British correspondent, observed the stampede to the east on 16 October, the day of 'black snow' caused by so much paperwork being burned in government offices. There were riots in factories as workers spotted their bosses fleeing, and a run on the banks.[6]

The NKVD cleared its jails and interrogation centres in Moscow. Its records reveal that more than 200 prisoners were murdered on 16 October. Just as the Nazis would do as the war drew to its end, the Soviets settled accounts with their helpless 'enemies' when it looked as if their regime might not survive; the wives of executed Generals Tukachevsky and Uborevich, who had been arrested with their husbands, were shot and cast into burial pits at the Kommunarka State Farm.

On 20 October Stalin declared a state of emergency in Moscow and announced that he would be remaining in the capital. Alexander Werth witnessed the sudden change of heart in the city. The panic ended and last ditch resistance became the cry. Three factors helped Stalin decide to stand in the path of the Panzers. The first light fall of snow on the night of 6 October dusted German positions, heralding not the iron grip of winter, but the autumn rains that subsequently turned the roads into a sticky morass. Russians call this time of year the *rasputitsa* – the 'time without roads' – and it would impose a temporary halt to operations every year, along with its counterpart, the *bezdororzh'e*, the spring thaw.

Stalin could always count on the mud, but in October 1941 he could also count on the Japanese. Some 750,000 Soviet troops were stationed in the Far East, in case the Japanese generals planned further aggression there. Now Soviet intelligence sources in Japan confirmed that the Tojo government intended to launch a war against the United States, and it was too late in the year for Japan to contemplate an attack on the USSR. By mid-November some ten divisions were sent to the Moscow Front from Siberia and Central Asia. Although there was no further mass transfer of units from the Far East, the Red Army in Manchuria continued to supply a steady stream of replacements to units in the west.

The third reason for Stalin's confidence was the staggering success with which the Red Army mobilization system was creating new divisions. The Reserve Armies Administration, established in July, oversaw a massive expansion of the Red Army that compensated for the terrible losses of the summer campaign. Between July and 1 December 1941 the Red Army mobilized 143 new rifle divisions and replaced 84 rifle divisions that had been destroyed in combat. The Moscow Military District was the greatest source of recruits, supplying 26 divisions, possibly because its manpower reserves were swollen by refugees and stragglers.[7]

The industrial workforce was increased by arbitrary measures at the same time. Between July and December 1941, another million men and women were arrested and sent into the *gulag* for use as slave labour. At the same time, some inmates were taken from the *gulag* and formed into military units that were employed as suicide squads. However, in the paranoid atmosphere of the USSR, the prison camp population actually rose in the early part of the war. When the Germans invaded in June 1941 there were some 2.3 million Soviet citizens languishing in Stalin's concentration camps; a million more were arrested by December 1941 and another two million people were dragged off to the *gulag* during 1942. It was worse in the armed forces. Recent Russian figures admit that 990,000 Red Army personnel were condemned by military tribunals in addition to the unknown quantity shot out of hand during moments of crisis. A total of 420,000 men were sent to penal units during the Second World War while 444,000 were dispatched to labour camps. A truly terrifying total of 158,000 men were shot: ten times as many military executions as the German Army ordered between 1939 and 1945.

Although the fighting on the approaches to Moscow was at its height by then, the issue was delicately balanced; *Stavka* held its nerve and refused to commit the powerful reserves it had assembled. Instead, the fresh troops were held in readiness for a counter-attack.

On 7 November the first hard frost occurred and the liquid mud solidified. It was also the day that the Soviet regime traditionally held a military parade through Red Square. The central committee was astonished when Stalin calmly announced his intention to hold the parade as usual, despite the proximity of the front line and the obvious threat of air attack. It was a timely display of confidence. Stalin was scenting victory even as German reconnaissance patrols were approaching the outlying stations of the Moscow metro.

Directly the ground hardened, and the German advance resumed. In the South, Von Kleist's 1st Panzer Group approached Rostov, and Von Manstein's newly formed 11th Army swept into the Crimea, driving the Russians back on the great naval base at Sebastopol. The new industrial city of Kharkov and the whole Donbas region, economic powerhouse of the USSR, were overrun. Despite daytime temperatures averaging -5°C, and its severely depleted units, Army Group Centre battered its way towards Moscow. Guderian was able to establish his headquarters in Tolstoy's old estate. The area that is today Moscow's airport at Sheremetievo, nearer to the city centre than London's Heathrow, was the scene of heavy fighting. On 28 November, elements of the 7th Panzer Division forced a crossing over the Moscow–Volga canal at Yakhroma, and penetrated as far as Krasnaja Polyana, 15 miles north of the city. In the cold clear air, the distant spires were visible through binoculars.

Their reports generated great excitement at Hitler's headquarters, but few officers on the ground still believed they would enter the city. Unit strengths were dwindling at an alarming rate; there were no replacements; the Red Army was contesting every yard of ground with tremendous bravery and increasing military competence, and supplies were running out.

Most front-line soldiers affect a disdain for the supply services, whose dull duty it is to forward the petrol, ammunition, rations and sundry necessities for the fighting men to do what they are paid for. So the rapid breakdown of German supply arrangements during the invasion of Russia caused great irritation and the usual flurry of angry signals. But it was neither a surprise nor a cause for alarm, even if some Panzer divisions only survived Soviet counter-attacks because emergency supplies of ammunition were flown in by air. What none of the soldiers standing at the gates of Moscow realized was that they were only there by a miracle, and it could not be sustained for much longer.

The entire invasion had been conducted on a logistic con trick. As we have seen, the Wehrmacht consisted of a relatively small mechanized army and a largely unmodernized force of infantry divisions. Although only part of the army's total strength was motorized, its demand for supplies, especially POL (petrol, oil, lubricants) created a heavier logistic burden than the armies of 1914–18. Unfortunately for the Wehrmacht, the German railway network had deteriorated since the First World War: there were fewer locomotives and less rolling stock than in 1914. As the army moved deeper into Russia it would depend on the Russian rail network, which, as the Germans knew very well, was built on a wide gauge incompatible with German rolling stock. The tracks could not carry as heavy a load as equivalent German ones. Even when the rails were converted to German gauge, all the facilities, like water towers, were built for Russian engines and were too far apart for German engines. The latter were unsuited to the east anyway: their water tubes froze in the much colder winter temperatures, and most of those sent to the USSR during the winter of 1941 became immobilized.

Neither could supplies be brought forward by truck. Even the mechanized formations had no spare vehicles to shuttle back and forth between railheads: they needed every truck they had. To obtain enough trucks, the German Army had seized vehicles from all across Europe because German industry was delivering only a fraction of the quantities required.[8] In 1941 the Germans had more than 2,000 different vehicles in service, few sharing any common parts, and the situation never improved. To take one unit by way of example, in mid-1943 I Flak Corps had 260 different types of German vehicle on its strength and 120 different types of foreign vehicle. In many cases the corps had just a couple of each type. This sorry collection of second-hand vehicles compared poorly to the British, Russian and American armies, which standardized their lorries and built them in vastly greater numbers, thus keeping their units well supplied and more highly mobile. Because Russian roads were even worse than OKH planners had assumed in pre-1941 wargames, fuel consumption turned out to be 330,000 tons per month, rather than the 250,000 budgeted for. Germany only had two or three months' supply of oil in reserve and it was discovered that captured Soviet petrol was too low-grade to power German engines.

The army's head quartermaster, Major-General Friedrich Paulus, conducted a wargame in December 1940 which demonstrated that the logistic arrangements would collapse before the Germans reached the upper Dnepr. However, as the date for the offensive drew nearer, the famously professional German planners fudged the logistic plan again and again, persuading themselves that if the army could not sustain a campaign on this scale for six months, then the war would have to be won in three. Martin van Creveld's study of the 1941 campaign observes, 'The German General Staff seemed to have abandoned rational thought at this point.'[9] It eventually abandoned wargames too. By Hitler's order in early 1942 the General Staff ceased wargaming possible future scenarios and just obeyed the orders of their leader, a former corporal, as Von Rundstedt often noted.

December 1941 found the German Army tantalizingly close to Moscow, but with no prospect of advancing further. Outside the capital the thermometer sank to an average of -12°C every day, and plunged to -20° on occasion. Without winter clothing the soldiers froze. More than 100,000 frostbite casualties were reported that month, despite the men grabbing every item of clothing they could from the unfortunate civilian population. Photographs show some bizarre get-ups that looked uncomfortably like paintings of Napoleon's retreat from Moscow in 1812. Without winter equipment, heaters, special oils and lubricants, tanks and aircraft ceased to function too. Such was the chaos at the railheads far to the west, that even if the army had possessed adequate quantities of cold-weather gear, it is unlikely it could have been brought forward to the front-line soldiers who so desperately needed it.

On 5 December the Red Army counter-attacked. The temperature that day reached a high of -15°C and the snow was three feet deep. The German Army had little air support: the Luftwaffe found it was taking five hours to get a bomber airborne in these conditions. Even if it lumbered into the air, it was discovered that German aerial fuses did not function in snow that deep; the bombs just vanished into the snow without detonating. The Red Army placed greater reliance on artillery than aircraft, and its heavy guns and *Katyusha* rocket launchers functioned without apparent difficulty. The *Katyushas* were especially disturbing, with their fearsome noise and ability to deliver an enormous quantity of explosive all at once. The name, 'little Katie', came from Mikhail Isakovski's song,[10] made famous by Lidiya Ruslanova, the Red Army's Vera Lynn. Unlike Ms Lynn, Ruslanova had made a fortune from her singing and paid for two *Katyusha* batteries herself; her popularity with the army was her undoing, and Stalin had her arrested in 1948 and sent to the *gulag* for ten years. She was released after his death in 1953.

Once driven out of their positions, the Germans found it impossible to dig new trenches in the frozen ground unless they had explosives. Night-time temperatures were so cold that even the smallest villages assumed tactical importance. The dilemma was whether to try to survive in the open or seek shelter in a village that was likely to be on the Russian gunners' maps too. Roads, which were seldom of great tactical importance in western Europe's extensive road net, were relatively few and far between. Now these logistical lifelines became the focus of fierce local battles.

Konev's Kalinin Front began the Russian counter-offensive on the night of 5 December. It failed to penetrate the improvised German defences except near Kalinin itself, where the 31st Army broke clean through to find itself 20 miles behind the German front line. On 6 December, Zhukov's Western Front attacked north-east of Moscow where Panzergruppe 3 (Reinhardt) and Panzergruppe 4 (Hoepner) threatened to encircle the city. Here the Germans gave ground rapidly, uncovering the Kalinin–Moscow railway, which they had overrun. Guderian's 2nd Panzer Army fell back from Tula. The 2nd Army retreated towards Orel; three of its divisions disintegrated in the process, leaving the Russians in possession of large numbers of abandoned guns and vehicles – the acid test of victory.

The 'stars' of Zhukov's forces were celebrated by the Soviet newspaper Pravda on the front page of the edition dated 13 December: Kuznetsov of the 1st Shock Army, Rokossovsky of the 16th and Vlasov of the 20th. Hitler's commanders found the campaign less career-enhancing. Army Group South was as over-extended as the forces before Moscow, and Field Marshal von Rundstedt had authorized 1st SS Division 'Leibstandarte Adolf Hitler' to withdraw from Rostov at the end of November. When the field marshal said he would sooner resign than countermand a correct military decision, Hitler accepted his departure. On 18 December, the commander of Army Group Centre, General von Bock, was relieved of his command on 'health grounds' after arguing that his men should retreat to more defensible ground. Hitler then accepted the resignation of the

OKH chief of staff Field Marshal von Brauchitsch and appointed himself commander-in-chief instead. His arrogance and conceit really did know no bounds.

Even Hitler's earlier favourites were not spared in the round of sackings that followed. Heinz Guderian was fired and placed on the retired list. Fellow Panzer Colonel-General Hoepner counted himself lucky to receive the same treatment; he withdrew 4th Panzer Army to escape encirclement rather than obey Hitler's ludicrous order to remain where he was. Hitler demanded he be cashiered without trial, but was prevailed upon to grant Hoepner his pension. (Hoepner, who had been involved in the planned *coup d'état* in 1938 at the time of the Munich crisis, joined the subsequent conspiracy against Hitler, and was executed in the wake of the 20 July 1944 bomb plot.) Aged 69, Field Marshal von Leeb took the opportunity to retire on health grounds on 13 January 1942, handing command of Army Group North to Colonel-General Georg von Kuechler.

Hitler's gamble had failed. The Red Army had not collapsed; Moscow had not fallen; and now his generals wanted to retreat. The question was where. Drawing on his own personal experience of the Western Front in the First World War, and arguing that it would be just as cold 50, 100 or even 200 miles west of Moscow, the Führer demanded that his soldiers stand fast. That they ultimately managed to stop the Red Army that winter, and went on to smash a major Russian offensive early in the spring, apparently vindicated Hitler. Just as his insistence on the Ardennes strategy in 1940 had delivered victory, so his instinctive strategy in 1941 had triumphed despite the generals' objections. The Führer's confidence never wavered. In the wake of Japan's attack on Pearl Harbor, he declared war on the USA.

Hitler's gratuitous declaration of war on America stemmed partly from President Roosevelt's very aggressive naval policy in the Atlantic, which had already seen a number of clashes between German submarines and US Navy warships. American policy had already overstepped the strict bounds of neutrality by a generous margin, but it remains very doubtful that Roosevelt could have declared war on

Germany, especially once the USA was under attack from Japan. Hitler was not bound by treaty to support Japan's war of aggression, and in any case, Hitler had such a record of breaking agreements that one more would hardly have mattered. Hitler liked to quote economic statistics when his generals dared present him with operational plans he disliked; yet he read very selectively, and had apparently no idea just what a sleeping giant he had kicked into vengeful wakefulness. To take just one example, American factories manufactured 41,000 M4 Sherman tanks between 1942 and 1945; twice as many as the combined total of Panzer IIIs, Panzer IVs, Panthers and Tigers built in Germany. And Germany was already losing the production war with Russia. As Albert Seaton commented, 'The underlying logic of the Führer's policy towards the United States defies analysis.'

CHAPTER FOUR

★

ATTACK AND COUNTER-ATTACK

'We still need to assimilate the experience of modern war … neither here, nor today will the outcome of the war be decided. The crisis is yet far off.'[1]

MARSHAL SHAPOSHNIKOV, DECEMBER 1941

The dramatic reversal of fortunes at the gates of Moscow encouraged Stalin to make the same premature assumption of victory that Hitler and his generals had been led to by the great battles of encirclement in the summer of 1941. No matter that Zhukov had husbanded the newly mobilized and only half-trained reserves to make the Moscow counter-attack possible; that he had been supported by the majority of the Red Air Force; and that the Germans had been at the extreme end of their tenuous supply lines. Stalin ordered immediate offensives all along the line from Leningrad to the Crimea.

The attempt to break the siege of Leningrad relied on the Volkhov Front, named for the river that flows north from Lake Ilmen into Lake Ladoga. In command was another youthful survivor of the purges, 43-year-old Kirill Meretskov, a veteran of the 1st Cavalry Army from the Civil War who had served in Spain alongside Pavlov. As commander of the Leningrad Military District in 1939 he had presided over the less-than-successful assaults on the Mannerheim Line at the end of that year. In January 1941 he was sacked for a dismal performance in a wargame and replaced by Zhukov. Worse was to follow: in the wake of Pavlov's arrest, he too was seized and tortured into confessing he was part of Pavlov's conspiracy. For reasons lost in the torturers' archives, he was still alive in September 1941 and was released without explanation and restored to his rank.

The Volkhov Front was created in December 1941. On 7 January it launched its offensive and was reinforced with the 26th Army from *Stavka* reserve a week later. The 26th ploughed ahead and was re-named the 2nd Shock Army, one of four 'breakthrough' forces intended to have extra artillery to batter their way through the German defences. In the event, the 2nd Shock made such progress that it found itself in a deep salient. The Russian attacks stalled in the dense forests and the fighting reverted to positional warfare. Attacks and counter-attacks saw bunkers and trench lines change hands repeatedly, but changes to the front line only showed up on tactical maps of the smallest scale. The tables were turned in March 1942 when the German Army Group North counter-attacked at the base of the salient and encircled 2nd Shock Army. After the commander of the army fell ill, Meretskov sent his new deputy, Andrei Vlasov, to take charge of the pocket.

Vlasov, who had had some experience of breaking out of German encirclements the previous summer, was once again the victim of confused and disastrous command arrangements. He managed to establish a tenuous line of communication to the rear, but his position was untenable. *Stavka* disbanded the Volkhov Front, which had little to show for an estimated 95,000 casualties. Meretskov's heart must have been in his mouth when this, his first operation since his release from jail, went so terribly wrong, yet the army group was re-formed in June and he was put back in charge. But from April to June this left the Leningrad Front trying to run nine armies, three independent corps and two battle groups; Vlasov received neither reinforcements nor permission to withdraw. When the *rasputitsa* finished at the end of May, the Germans closed the ring again. The modern Russian official history blames the commander of the Leningrad Front, Colonel-General Mikhail Khozin, who failed to act on *Stavka* instructions issued in the middle of May to withdraw 2nd Shock. Khozin was demoted to command the 33rd Army, but later climbed back to army group command; he lived until 1979. Vlasov's men fought on until the end of June when they capitulated. Very few survived the war.

The German blockade of Leningrad continued. There was little thought of storming the city, merely bombing and shelling it and allowing the sub-zero temperatures and lack of food to do the rest. Hitler had publicly stated his intention to level the place. Although the famous railway across the ice brought in some supplies across the frozen Lake Ladoga, hunger turned into starvation in the winter of 1941–42, and more than half a million people perished. The bodies could not be buried and the city's sanitary system broke down. Only the intense cold prevented an epidemic. The local NKVD were predictably busy, enforcing 'the discipline of the revolver': the secret police executed about 5,000 people in the first year of the siege. The stubborn, determined resistance of Leningrad is little known in the west, and Stalin, who pointedly never visited the city afterwards, took care it was not even commemorated in the USSR.

The siege would eventually last for 900 days, but Stalin's response to this epic defence was to purge the Leningrad party after the war, possibly assassinating the former Party boss Andrei Zhdanov in 1948 and removing senior figures associated with him and the city. Two thousand functionaries and Party officials were sacked and around 200 executed. Lieutenant-General Alexei Kuznetzov, Chief Commissar of the Leningrad Front, was arrested in 1949 on false charges of treason and executed in 1950. (Khruschev posthumously rehabilitated him and many other victims of this purge in 1954.) The brilliant technocrat Nikolai Voznesensky, Deputy Premier and organizer of Russian industry, was another prominent victim of the 'Leningrad Affair', murdered in the back of a van in 1950.

In the Moscow area, the temperature sank to -25°C in January. The Kalinin and Western Fronts were ordered to destroy Army Group Centre, and came desperately close to doing so. The Germans reeled back, and before a coherent front line could be re-established, Russian cavalry units had penetrated far behind the lines, where they would remain a threat to German communications until the spring. Two Soviet armies, the 29th and 33rd, were cut off by German counter-attacks, forming pockets that were slowly reduced as better weather enabled German armour and aircraft to operate again.

In the harsh weather conditions, neither side managed to mount effective air attacks. The Luftwaffe had failed to seriously interrupt the evacuation of Soviet industries out of reach of German attack: the army's demand for close air support was unceasing and left no opportunity for strategic air missions. German aircraft did mount a few missions against Moscow, beginning with a major raid on the night of 21 July, when 127 bombers delivered 104 tons of bombs on the Soviet capital. The Russian response was a token bomber raid made on Berlin by 18 Ilyushin Il-4s of the Baltic Red Banner Fleet's torpedo/mine air wing on 6 August. The German raids on Moscow prompted more bombing by the Soviet long-range air force in September, but the advance of the Ostheer quickly put most Russian airfields beyond range of Berlin. A couple of night raids on a similar scale by the Luftwaffe hit a number of famous landmarks, and the Japanese embassy. The German bombers had even launched some daylight raids in the autumn, once they had fighter airfields within range, but the demands for tactical air support soon reduced attacks on Moscow to nuisance strikes by a few dozen aircraft at night. The other vital strategic target, the Soviet rail network, had been left alone too for the same reason.

The Red Air Force was conspicuous by its absence when the Germans fell back from their most advanced positions near Moscow. In December 1941 and January 1942, the Germans had very few metalled roads along which they could retreat. These highways, which the engineers worked like demons to keep clear of snow, were crowded with men and vehicles. The Luftwaffe was only able to mount a token effort to protect them with fighters. Yet they were hardly ever attacked from the air.

The Red Army's advances trapped similar numbers of German troops behind the lines. Three important 'pockets' survived, largely by aerial resupply. At Demyansk, six German divisions under General von Seydlitz held out until relieved in late March. Von Seydlitz was later to play a key role at the battle of Stalingrad, where he was captured, and became a leader of anti-Nazi German prisoners in Russia, calling on their former comrades to overthrow Hitler. He was a veteran of Germany's previous war in the east, and had been involved in an earlier battle of encirclement at Brczeziny, near Lodz, in 1914. He led a breakout from Demyansk, an epic 30-day battle of endurance that ended just as the spring thaw imposed a halt on operations. The Luftwaffe's success in sustaining these trapped forces would later be seized upon by Hitler and Göring in November 1942, when the 6th Army was surrounded at Stalingrad; both chose to ignore that Von Seydlitz's force was far smaller. They also overlooked the sorry state of Von Seydlitz's survivors. The High Command saw divisions rejoining, albeit without their heavy weapons. They could be replaced, but the mental and physical consequences of living and fighting in this frozen wilderness without nourishment, sanitation or medical facilities were harder to overcome.

Meanwhile, in the Ukraine, an offensive south of Kharkov pushed a 70-mile salient into German lines and established a bridgehead on the west bank of the Donets. An amphibious assault re-established a Russian presence on the Kertsch peninsula, held by a single German division, the 46th, while the rest of Von Manstein's 11th Army fought its way into Sebastopol. The 46th Division made repeated requests to withdraw from the peninsula, which Von Manstein turned down, sending his only reserve, two brigades of Romanian mountain troops. The Soviets recaptured the port of Feodosia in a night-time amphibious operation, threatening to cut off the 46th Division. The commander of 30th Corps, Lieutenant-General Hans Graf von Sponeck, gave the order to retreat, despite explicit instructions to stand firm. The line was stabilized at Parpach and Feodosia, the latter eventually re-taken by a counter-attack from 15 to 18 January. At the insistence of the fervent Nazi Field Marshal Walter von Reichenau, commander of Army Group South, Sponeck faced a court martial and was sentenced to death. The regiments of the 46th Division were stripped of their awards and battle honours – the only time this happened to an army formation during the war. Some accounts claim the divisional commander, Lieutenant-General Kurt Himer, was retired in disgrace, but he was still with the 46th Division three months later when he died of wounds on 26 March.[2]

The spring thaw found the German Army holding its positions some 180 miles west of Moscow, the sort of distance the Panzer spearheads had covered in less than a week in the summer of 1941. Small wonder then that Stalin concentrated his forces on the Moscow Front, in expectation of a renewed drive on the Soviet capital. On a map, the German threat looked very obvious: a salient centred on Rzhev pointed at Moscow like an arrowhead. Behind it lay the trapped Russian 33rd Army. To the north, Russian forces had driven the Germans back to Veljkiye Luki, the front line dipping south to within 60 miles of Smolensk. To the south, the Russian drive on Bryansk had been stopped well short of the city: Kursk, Belgorod and Kharkov all remained in German hands.

Casualties had been unprecedented. From the invasion to the end of November the Ostheer had suffered 743,000 casualties, of whom 200,000 were dead. By comparison, German losses in the invasions of Belgium, Holland and France were 44,000 dead and 156,000 wounded. The fighting outside Moscow from December to January cost another 55,000 dead and 100,000 wounded. Panzer divisions were lucky to have 20 operational tanks by early 1942: three-quarters of the approximately 1,000 tanks assembled for Operation *Typhoon* were lost by 4 December. The Luftwaffe had lost 758 bombers, 568 fighters and 767 other aircraft destroyed; 473 bombers, 413 fighters and 475 other aircraft were damaged.

Soviet losses were astronomical. Every mechanized corps and 177 rifle divisions had been written off. About 1,000 vehicles remained from the pre-war tank fleet of some 22,000. The defence of Moscow and the counter-attack that followed had cost nearly a million casualties. More than three million Red Army soldiers were taken prisoner in the headlong German advance of 1941.[3] By February 1942, only about a quarter of a million remained alive.

Behind the lines

Many Red Army units caught behind the German lines in the initial invasion did not surrender. Instead, they melted into the forests and swamps, to re-emerge when the German forces had passed eastwards. As early as July 1941, German commanders were reporting attacks well behind the lines, launched by cut-off units of the Red Army and local volunteers. The Partisan War had begun.

Despite its previous association with guerrilla warfare, the Soviet regime discovered a severe shortage of experienced guerrilla commanders in 1941. Stalin had executed most of the Bolshevik 'Old Guard' and there had been no preparations for resistance activity in the late 1930s. All pre-war Soviet war plans assumed a conventional war in which the Red Army would take the offensive. Stalin's future successor, Nikita Khruschev (then Party boss in the Ukraine), issued the first call to arms in June 1941, with Stalin taking up the theme of guerrilla struggle in his radio address to the nation in July.

As the German advance swept deeper into the USSR, so NKVD and Party officials attempted to organize guerrilla units in its wake. Initial attempts were not successful. In the open country of the Ukraine there was nowhere for the partisans to hide, and the local population was welcoming the German tanks with flowers. Resistance efforts foundered in the Crimea too, where the disaffected Tartar population helped the Germans hunt down the guerrillas. (This would neither be forgotten nor forgiven.) The NKVD continued its mass arrests in the Baltic Republics, but the Red Terror proved as counter-productive as later German policies. Local people anticipated the arrival of the Germans and began attacking Soviet installations.

By early 1942 the Partisan movement had yet to make a serious impact on the war. Although a central command system had been created in Moscow to coordinate the campaign behind the lines, there were probably no more than 30,000 guerrillas in the field.[4] However, a nucleus had been created. The remnants of Red Army units, in some areas reinforced by forces cut off after the failed counter-offensives in the spring of 1942, combined with Party activists and locals who had discovered the nature of Hitler's 'New Order' for themselves. The blind savagery with which the German Army treated the conquered peoples of the USSR soon alienated many potential sympathizers, and news spread of the prisoner-of-war camps, where more than two million soldiers had met their deaths during the winter.

Behind the Russian lines men and women were struggling to survive too. In sub-zero temperatures, sometimes in near-total darkness, they unloaded machine tools from rail cars and reassembled whole factories in remote areas. The success with which Soviet industry was evacuated east in 1941 was justly celebrated by the USSR as a triumph as significant as any victory on the battlefield. Indeed, it was the foundation of all subsequent victories. Iron, steel and engineering plants were shipped to the Urals, Siberia or Kazakhstan in some 1.5 million wagon-loads. A total of 16 million people went with them, labouring with grim determination to get the machines turning again. The Yak fighter factory in Moscow was dismantled and shipped to Siberia, where production resumed after just six days on site. In three months production exceeded the quotas achieved in Moscow.

The Herculean efforts of the Soviet industrial workforce enabled the Red Army to re-equip in time for the 1942 campaigns. Many German memoirs stress the overwhelming numerical and material superiority of Soviet forces, but in 1942 it was Germany that enjoyed every industrial advantage, with the factories of most of Europe at her disposal. German steel production, for example, was four times that of the USSR.[5] Nevertheless, even in the second half of 1941, in the middle of the relocation programme, the USSR built more tanks than German factories delivered in the whole year. Soviet industry delivered 4,500 tanks, 3,000 aircraft and 14,000 artillery pieces to the Red Army between January and May 1942. During that whole year, Soviet production figures would reach 24,000 tanks and self-propelled guns, 127,000 guns and mortars and 25,000 aircraft. Comparable German figures were 9,000 tanks, 12,000 guns and mortars and 15,000 aircraft. Note the yawning disparity in artillery manufacture.

The growing gulf in Soviet and German industrial production would not begin to transform the situation at the front until late 1942. Meanwhile, as the floods caused by the spring thaw began to subside, both sides prepared to take the offensive – and in the same area.

The drive south

The Soviet blow fell first. Emboldened by the Red Army's winter victories, Stalin ordered immediate offensive action to follow the spring thaw. However, Marshal Boris Shaposhnikov, Chief of the Red Army General Staff, and the Chief of the Operations Department, General Alexander Vasilevsky, both counselled caution. They argued that the winter offensives had only succeeded because the Germans were poorly equipped to fight in what had been, even by Russian standards, a very harsh winter. Come the spring, there was no reason the enemy could not repeat the lightening advances of summer 1941. These more thoughtful Red Army leaders recognized their forces still had no answer to German tactical skill and professionalism, nor the formidable striking power of the Luftwaffe. The German front line lay within 200 miles of Moscow, which the Panzers had proved they could cover in a week. Shaposhnikov and Vasilevsky wanted to dig in, to fight the enemy from carefully prepared positions and not try to take on the veteran Panzer divisions in mobile warfare. It was to be another year before this more cautious strategy would be tried to defeat a German summer offensive.

Zhukov characteristically wanted to attack the Germans head-on, on the Moscow Front, believing that by getting his blow in early he could inflict major damage before the Germans had fully re-equipped. Stalin liked the idea, but not the choice of direction. He favoured the southern sector, where Marshal Timoshenko had made two successful assaults on the German lines south of Kharkov. In January, the Soviet 6th, 57th and 9th Armies had attacked the German lines around Iszum along the northern Donets River. Ski troops and three cavalry corps exploited 50 miles further, seizing the rail junctions of Barvenkovl and Lozovaya before German reserves arrived to re-establish the front.

The resulting salient lay between two strategic objectives, the city of Kharkov to the north and the Donbas industrial region to the south. It was an obvious springboard for a future offensive. On 7 March Timoshenko's South-Western Front attacked again, north-east of Kharkov, and established a second, smaller bridgehead across the northern Donets. Kharkov was now menaced from north and south, and Timoshenko was eager to attempt a larger offensive, although efforts to deepen the north-eastern bridgehead at Stayri Saltov continued for several weeks without making significant progress. April brought the spring thaw: the roads dissolved into swamps and Timoshenko departed for Moscow to plead his case.

Two false assumptions underpinned Stalin's strategy for the spring. Firstly, the Red Army leadership unanimously expected the German summer offensive to head straight for Moscow. Secondly, his generals grievously underestimated the Wehrmacht's powers of recovery and thus the strength of the German forces overall, and in the southern sector in particular. Stalin gave his blessing to Timoshenko at a meeting in the Kremlin at the end of March, but did not give the fire-eating cavalryman all the forces he requested as they would be needed to repel the anticipated German drive on the capital.

The classified post-war Soviet General Staff study of the Kharkov theatre of operations in May 1942 laments the 'treacherous' delay by the Anglo-American forces in the summer of that year. It claims that this was a cynical betrayal by the western Allies that enabled the Germans to re-deploy their forces, thus regaining the initiative they had lost during the winter. Future premier Nikita Khruschev was the South-Western Front's Commissar at the time, and shares responsibility with Timoshenko for what happened when the Red Army launched its first major strike against a German Army no longer enfeebled by the grip of winter. So when the official history was published under his aegis, they blamed Stalin, who was safely dead at last.

The sector of the German lines selected for the Red Army's breakthrough was held by the 6th Army, commanded by one of Hitler's favourite generals, Friedrich Paulus. As a staff officer, Paulus had played a key role in planning the 1941 invasion, and only Rommel would be promoted at the same meteoric rate, from lieutenant-general to field marshal in a year. The 6th Army was the largest of the German armies on the Russian front, and the Red Army's numerical advantage for this battle was but a fraction of the odds it would enjoy by the end of the war. Even in the sectors selected for the main thrusts, the Russians had a 3:1 advantage in armour and infantry, and only 2:1 in artillery. Red Army doctrine called for a deception plan to be part of any offensive operation, yet in spring 1942, neither senior officers nor junior ranks had learned the sort of skills that would later wrong-foot their opponents. Soviet preparations involved a considerable amount of lateral movement, and the arrival of additional forces along the front did not go unnoticed by the Germans. The thaw worked in favour of the Germans, hindering Russian troop movements and channelling them along the few hard-surface roads.

The offensive began on 12 May from both salients. On the northern one, the 21st, 28th and 38th Armies found the going unexpectedly tough. German strongpoints were plentiful and well camouflaged; many escaped the preliminary bombardment and all held on tenaciously even when surrounded. The Russians were being broken on just the sort of chequerboard defences that cost the British such heavy loss of life at Passchendaele in 1917. Some units pressed on, while others became pinned down between German positions. Coordination between tanks and infantry remained poor. Most of the 19 tank brigades employed in the offensive were directly subordinate to rifle divisions, but they tended to fight quite separate battles, taking turns to attack rather than working in harmony. Although the Russian tank regiments included both KV-1 heavy tanks and T-34s, without infantry or artillery support they were knocked out in large quantities.

After two days' fighting, the northern bridgehead had been deepened to more than 12 miles at its greatest extent, but losses had been heavy. Counter-attacks by the German 3rd and 23rd Panzer Divisions brought the advance to a sudden halt, and the bulk of the

Russian armour was re-deployed to fend them off. Better progress was made in the south, where the Soviet 6th, 57th and 9th Armies struck west towards Krasnograd and Pavlograd. By nightfall on 12 May they had broken through along a 25-mile frontage and advanced up to 10 miles in places. This brought them to the Germans' secondary defensive positions along the Orel River. Steady progress continued for the next 48 hours, with one Hungarian and several German infantry divisions overrun; some Soviet units advanced 25 miles west of their start line. It all appeared to be going so well.

It could have gone even better had the South-Western Front's armoured reserve been able to take advantage of the German disarray. But the 21st Tank Corps was stuck 25 miles behind the Russian 6th Army; the 23rd Tank Corps was 12 miles behind; and the two reserve rifle divisions were between 12 and 25 miles in the rear. Timoshenko's operational plan assumed that the known German reserves would take five or six days to reach the front line, but the Germans were faster off the mark. The absence of the Soviet second echelon forces, combined with the aggressive reaction of the German reserves, ground down Timoshenko's leading units, and the Russian advance faltered.

Heavy fighting continued north-east of Kharkov from 14 to 16 May, but without any significant advances. Meanwhile, the Barvenkovo salient continued to deepen as Timoshenko's armoured reserve pressed westwards. By nightfall on 16 May a Soviet cavalry corps was in action on the outskirts of Krasnograd. Timoshenko signalled his progress to Moscow, blissfully unaware that every mile west his soldiers travelled, the deeper they were sticking their collective heads into a noose. At dawn on 17 May Panzergruppe Kleist assaulted the south-eastern side of the salient, driving hard for Barvenkovo and with every intention of cutting in behind Timoshenko's main forces. The 3rd Motorized Corps was a cosmopolitan band comprising the Romanian 20th Division, German 1st (Bavarian) Gebirgsjäger Division, 100th Jäger Division (from Vienna), 60th Motorized and 14th Panzer Division (based at Dresden) with 170 tanks. It attacked on a 40-mile front with its main effort concentrated on a 13-mile sector. The 44th Corps – four infantry divisions and 16th (Westphalian) Panzer – struck the point at which the Russian front line curved from north–south to east–west, the very corner of the salient. It says much for the sheer size of this theatre of war that even in a full-scale counter-offensive, the average frontage occupied by the 11 divisions Von Kleist committed to the operation was more than 6 miles.

The Russian 9th Army was the first victim of Panzergruppe Kleist; outnumbered nearly 2:1 in infantry and 6:1 in tanks, it was simply flattened. Its front line was penetrated by 8.00am, and at noon the 14th and 16th Panzer Divisions were up to 12 miles inside the salient. The 257th ('Bear') Division reached the Donets, a welcome sight in 30°C heat. Vehicles and men alike were covered in dust from the fine black earth. On 18 May the Germans overran the headquarters of the Russian 57th Army, which was commanded by General Kuzma Podlas. The 49-year-old former deputy commander of the Kiev Military District had been arrested in 1938 and condemned to a five-year jail term. Podlas was one of the fortunate few to be released in 1940 and restored to command. He tried to fight his way out, but was killed in action. Barvenkovo fell that afternoon. Engineers of the 101st Jäger Division lifted some 1,750 mines in one day as they battered through the Soviet defensive lines south of Iszum.

The village of Ternovaya, held by elements of the German 429th Infantry Regiment (294th Division), had been surrounded in the initial Soviet attack on 12 May. Resupplied by air – Soviet reconnaissance reports claimed by paratroops – the garrison held on until 17 May, when it was relieved by elements of 3rd Panzer Division. A counter-attack the next day left it surrounded again as the Russian 38th Army resumed its attack to draw off German reserves. Timoshenko had ordered his exhausted troops north-east of Kharkov to continue attacking in order to prevent the Germans dispatching the 3rd and 23rd Panzer Divisions to the south. Nevertheless, the Germans did switch both tank formations to the south on 21 May. Timoshenko requested reinforcements from the *Stavka*, which

Eastern Europe and the USSR 1941

Hitler's war against the Soviet Union led to the largest armies ever maintained fighting the greatest land battles yet seen. The front line would ultimately stretch for over 1,500 miles and at any one time there were close to ten million soldiers under arms. Note how the vast Pripyat marsh sits square in the path of an invader from the west. Partisan activity from 1942–44 would be concentrated in the swamps and forests shown here. Note also the pivotal importance of Moscow as the hub of the Soviet rail network.

Operation *Barbarossa* 1941

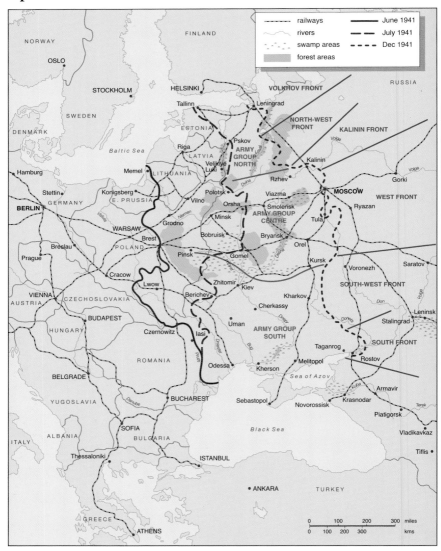

The initial pace of the German advance exceeded their wildest expectations. By August it even seemed possible that Russia might be beaten in eight weeks, as Hitler had predicted. The Baltic States and Belorussia fell quickly, the Ukraine next, and over a million Soviet troops were taken prisoner. Yet by the time the German advance ground to a halt outside Moscow, the German Army had suffered 750,000 casualties.

Stalingrad, November 1942

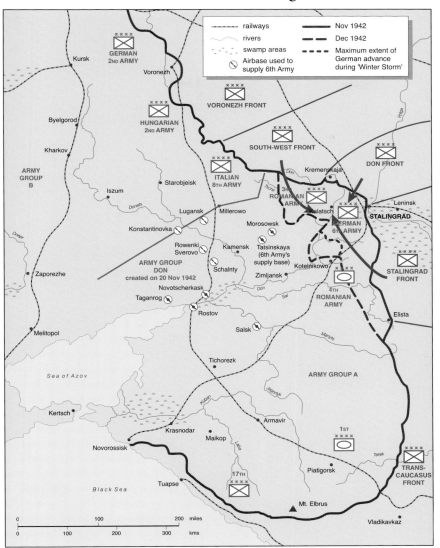

With German Panzer divisions scattered from the Moscow front to the Caucasus, the 6th Army was obliged to assault Stalingrad frontally, rather than envelop it in the traditional manner. By late 1942 the battle for the city had absorbed almost all the German units in the sector, the long flanks guarded by less well-equipped and less committed allied armies. The Soviet plan had worked.

Death of an Army

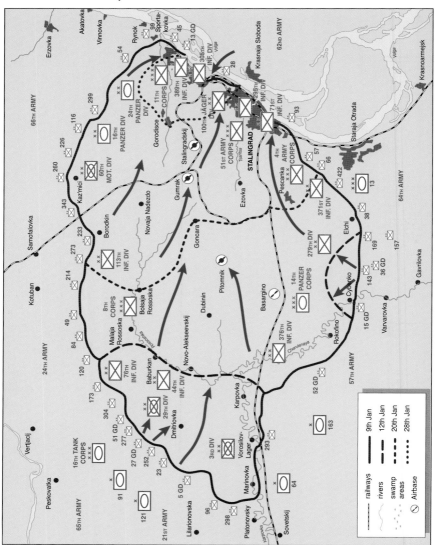

Called a 'fortress' by the German High Command, the defences of Stalingrad consisted of a line of dug-outs across the bleak steppe. The Soviets found the defenders able to conduct sharp counter-attacks as late as January, but the starvation diet and lack of ammunition led to a rapid collapse once the surrender offer was rejected.

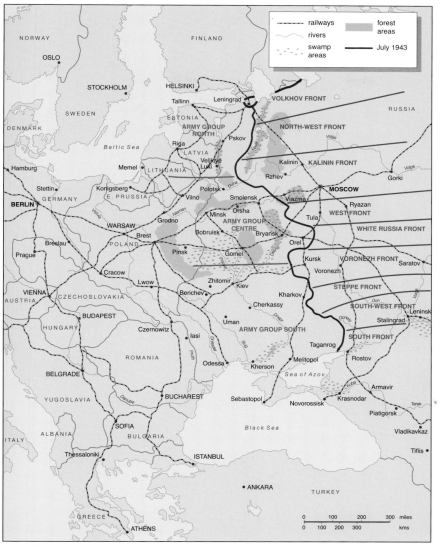

Both sides attacked in 1943. The Soviets followed up their victory at Stalingrad by pressing as far west as Kharkov, but the city was retaken during Von Manstein's celebrated counter–attack in February. The German generals then planned to attack the salient around Kursk, but the operation was delayed until July. Marshal Zhukov banked on stopping the German assault, then launching offensives of his own both north and south.

December 1943

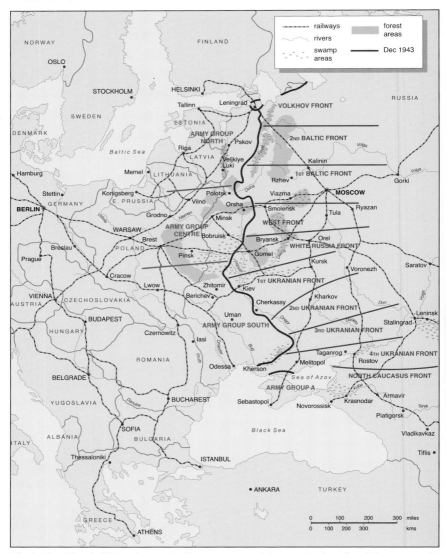

The battle of Kursk did not destroy the German armoured forces as is often alleged. Losses were far heavier during the long retreat across the Ukraine in the autumn, with large numbers of vehicles abandoned in the mud. The Soviet advance reached as far as Zhitomir before Von Manstein's counter-attacks drove them back again, but the recapture of Kiev proved impossible.

Soviet Offensives 1944

Soviet forces swept across the Western Ukraine, encountering resistance not just from the Germans, but from Ukrainian guerrillas, who in fact killed Marshal Vatutin. By the summer, the German Army Group Centre occupied a wide salient north of the Pripyat marshes. Soviet deception measures fooled the Germans into expecting another assault in the south, and the stage was set for the greatest German defeat of the war.

Endgame 1945

By the beginning of 1945 the Soviet Army was poised to conquer Germany. Hitler withdrew to a hastily prepared bunker in Berlin, still preaching victory. His generals began to ignore his orders, trying to hold back the Soviets at the cost of allowing the western Allies to overrun western Germany. By April the game was up and many German units broke contact with the Soviets to flee westwards in the hope of surrendering to the British or Americans.

granted him two rifle divisions and more armour, but these fresh formations were several days' journey from the battlefront. Even so, he seems to have misjudged the pace of the German breakthrough and was still ordering the Russian 6th Army units opposite Krasnograd, in the very nose of the salient, to continue attacking. His report to the *Stavka* on 19 May, countersigned by Khruschev, gave the impression, of course, that all was under control and that offensive efforts towards Kharkov were still under way.

On the morning of 18 May, 16th Panzer Division, divided into three *Kampfgruppen*, entered the suburbs of Iszum and cut the east–west highway that crossed the Donets at Donetsky. By 20 May the encirclement was all but complete; just a narrow neck of ground a few miles wide connected the three Russian armies with the rest of the South-Western Front. On 22 May, 14th Panzer Division beat off a series of Russian armoured counter-attacks to reach Bayrak on the Northern Donets; on the far bank lay the outposts of the 44th ('Hoch-und-Deutschmeister') Division.

Some 750,000 Red Army soldiers had taken part in the Kharkov offensive. By the end of May the battle had ended with the loss of one man in three. The encirclement and destruction of the 6th, 57th and 9th Armies struck 22 rifle and seven cavalry divisions from the Soviet order of battle, along with 14 tank and motorized brigades. Only scattered handfuls of men broke through the German cordon. David Glantz assesses Red Army losses at 170,000 killed, missing or captured, plus 106,000 wounded. Hardware losses were steep too: 650 tanks and 1,600 guns. Timoshenko was summoned to Moscow and he had good grounds for fearing for his life; in 1941 he had taken over from generals executed for defeats on a smaller scale. He was relieved of his command, but, as an old comrade from the Bolshevik 1st Cavalry Division, he retained his place in the *Stavka* and was sent to command the North-Western Front in July.

Just as the Kharkov offensive turned into a major disaster, so the Red Army lost its foothold on the Kertsch peninsula, and with it the only prospect of relieving Sebastopol. The traditional villain of the piece is Lazar Mekhlis, the Jewish Commissar assigned as *Stavka* representative to the Crimean Front. The head of the Main Political Administration of the Red Army and one of Stalin's chief henchmen, Mekhlis had played a leading role in the purge of the army, and the survivors never forgave him. He was an abrasive bully whose working relationship with Lieutenant-General Dimitri Kozlov, commander of the Crimean Front, was bad from the start. Mekhlis sacked Kozlov's highly competent chief of staff Fyodor Tolbukhin (a future Marshal of the USSR) and refused to permit any thought of defensive operations. He conducted an acrimonious correspondence with Kozlov and complained about him to Moscow. Having built a road across the frozen straits during the winter, the Russians had deployed three armies, the 44th, 47th and 51st – 260,000 men in 21 divisions – on the Kertsch peninsula by May 1942. They were supported by 350 tanks. However, attacks in March and April made little headway against Von Manstein's 11th Army. Focused exclusively on his offensive, Mekhlis forbade any digging in, never thinking that his opponent might take the offensive himself.

Von Manstein's army had had no armour when he broke into the Crimea in 1941. But Von Manstein's infantry division had advanced almost as fast as the Panzers during the invasion of France in 1940, and his lightning strike towards Leningrad in 1941 had set new records for speed of manoeuvre. With additional Romanian units to screen Sebastopol, he transferred the bulk of his army east to clear the Kertsch peninsula again. It was not much of a bulk, just five German infantry divisions and 22nd Panzer Division. The 7th Romanian Corps (8th, 10th and 19th Infantry Divisions plus 10th Cavalry Division) made up the numbers, but their offensive value was 'limited', as Von Manstein diplomatically put it. The front line ran across the narrow neck of the peninsula centred on Parpach, 15 miles north-east of Feodosia. From an initial frontage of 15 miles, the peninsula widened to about 25 miles where the Soviets' rearmost positions lay.

Air power tipped the odds. The whole of Baron von Richthofen's Fliegerkorps 8 flew in support of Operation *Trappenjagd* ('Bustard

Hunt') in which Von Manstein feinted in the north, where the Soviets had massed the bulk of their forces, then launched the 28th Light, 132nd and 50th Infantry and 22nd Panzer Division in a hook along the south coast. One battalion was landed by assault boats in the rear of the Soviet lines at Parpach on 8 May. Heavy but fake radio traffic in the north, followed by artillery barrages, helped induce Mekhlis to retain his reserves in the north. The infantry broke through, but it was not possible to exploit in depth with the armour until the following day. The Panzers beat off a Russian tank attack, but their continued advance was hampered by heavy rain, which also kept the Luftwaffe away from the battlefield. The weather cleared on the 11th, without the Russians showing any sign of reacting to the penetration of their front, and 22nd Panzer swung north to cut off about eight Russian divisions in their front line. Organized resistance collapsed and a scuttle to the rear began. Von Manstein's pursuit was relentless and Kertsch fell on 16 May. The Stukas had a field day. The roads were jammed with abandoned or knocked-out vehicles: aerial photographs taken by the Germans are reminiscent of the 'road of death' on the highway outside Kuwait in 1991. Von Manstein drove past endless columns of prisoners to meet Richthofen on a hill overlooking the straits. The beach was equally crammed with Soviet tanks and transport. Russian torpedo boats tried to rescue their men from the shore, but German field batteries and repeated air attacks drove them off. Drum fire from Von Manstein's corps artillery pulverized the last pockets of resistance and it was all over by 18 May.

Although some die-hards held out in caves for a few more weeks, the three Russian armies had ceased to exist. Five German infantry divisions and one of tanks, plus a pair of Romanian divisions, had annihilated more than 21 Russian divisions in a head-to-head fight. Von Manstein's 11th Army recorded the capture of 170,000 prisoners-of-war, 1,133 artillery pieces and 258 tanks. Mekhlis was sacked, and also lost his job as Deputy People's Commissar of Defence; Zhukov's criticism was biting, but Mekhlis was Stalin's creature and did not share the fate of his many victims. He remained a Commissar at front level throughout the war despite further clashes with senior army commanders and at least three formal censures for incompetence. Kozlov was posted to command a reserve army, but worked his way back to deputy front commander by the end of the year.

With the Kertsch bridgehead eliminated, the naval base of Sebastopol was isolated and doomed. The landward approaches were defended by giant concrete and steel fortifications, forts 'Stalin', 'Molotov', 'Siberia' and 'Maxim Gorky'. Their heavy guns duelled with German artillery until a combination of gargantuan siege guns and constant air attack silenced them. The German siege train included the 60cm mortar 'Karl' and the 80cm calibre railway gun 'Gustav'. The latter, the biggest gun ever built, was originally intended to breach the Czech Sudetenland and French Maginot Line defences. Its 7-ton armour-piercing shells destroyed a Soviet ammunition bunker under Severnaya Bay, passing through the water and 100 feet of rock before detonating inside the magazine. Its high explosive rounds weighed more than 10 tons and were used to pulverize one fort after another. Even then, it took teams of combat engineers with flame-throwers and grenades to storm the strongpoints, which were connected by underground tunnels. It was horribly reminiscent of the battle of Verdun in 1916, although Von Manstein took care to maximize the use of engineers, artillery and air power rather than squander his infantry.

The Luftwaffe flew some 23,000 sorties to deliver 20,529 tons of bombs on Sebastopol in three weeks. (By comparison, the Luftwaffe dropped 21,860 tons of bombs on the whole of the UK during the 1940–41 'Blitz'.) German artillery fired 562,944 rounds. The assault began on 7 June and by the end of the month it was clear that the end was near. Destroyers could enter the port by night, but the remorseless German advance brought their guns in line with the harbour. Submarines continued to deliver ammunition and take off a lucky few of the wounded, but the bulk of the garrison fought and died in the ruined forts, bunkers and rubble of their city. The last centres of resistance were overwhelmed in early July and 90,000 men went into captivity. Von

Manstein was promoted to field marshal by a delighted Führer. His opponent, General Ivan Petrov, was reckoned to have done a good job holding on as long as he did, and was evacuated; he was made a Hero of the Soviet Union in 1945. Of the approximately 30,000 civilians left in Sebastopol, two-thirds were deported or executed.

The Crimean campaign cost the Red Army grievously. Modern estimates suggest that the Russians lost about 150,000 men in Sebastopol and another 240,000 in the Kertsch peninsula disaster. The decision to hold the fortress to the last and to attempt its relief in the winter of 1941–42 made sense if it tied down substantial German forces, but Von Manstein was given a rather minimal force for such an undertaking. If his divisions could have been more usefully employed elsewhere, then the same argument applies even more strongly for the Red Army. The reckless expenditure of manpower in the Crimea left them with little in reserve in the summer of 1942.

As the guns fell silent at Sebastopol, Hitler moved his headquarters to Vinnitsa in the Ukraine to oversee a new and enormously ambitious offensive. Although some of his senior commanders, most notably the navy commander-in-chief Admiral Raeder, argued that Germany should remain on the defensive in Russia while attacking in the Mediterranean, Hitler's attention was focused almost exclusively on the east. That he would continue to concentrate on the Russian front, and site his headquarters in East Prussia until the end of 1944, demonstrates its overriding importance to him. It also exposes the limits of his horizons. In what was now a global war involving four continents, Hitler remained obsessed with the Eastern Front and would attempt to micromanage the campaign there, while critical events in other theatres passed him by.

Stalin's hopelessly premature offensives cost the Red Army approximately 1.4 million casualties between January and June 1942. German losses were around 190,000, or less than one-seventh of the Soviet total. Stalin and his generals had very little to show for this enormous squandering of life. Great stretches of the front line remained pretty well where it had been established in December

1941. Even where the Ostheer had been compelled to pull back, at Rostov in the far south and opposite Moscow, it had only given up a maximum of 150 miles. The conventional view is that the winter campaign left the German Army clinging to its lines, but sensing it had bitten off more than it could chew; that the failure to capture Moscow – and win the war at a stroke – made ultimate defeat inevitable. This is open to challenge. The Red Army, so badly smashed in 1941, was in a desperate plight at the beginning of 1942 and lacked the competence at every level to take on the Germans in major operations. Its regiments were filled with half-trained conscripts, commanded by junior officers who were largely making it up as they went along, and all were terrified of making a mistake that could result in their arrest. The Red Army's failure in these circumstances was to be expected. The surprise is the sheer scale of the disparity between Russian and German casualties in the first half of 1942. In this grisly battle of attrition, Germany was actually winning.

Hitler's target in 1942 was the Soviet oil industry. By seizing the oil fields of the Caucasus he intended to solve the oil shortage that bedevilled the German war machine, and deprive the USSR of its main source of fuel. The German Army would strike past the junction of the Don and Donets, seizing Rostov on one flank and Stalingrad on the other. The Volga was a vital waterway for the USSR, and the occupation of Stalingrad would block another logistic artery.

The shores of the Caspian sea lay 400 miles south-east of the front line. But to undertake this dramatic advance, the German Army had less than half the forces available in 1941. A total of 68 divisions, including eight Panzer and seven motorized divisions, would take part in the offensive. Army Group Centre retained the balance of German armour, but its divisions were at very reduced strength. The SS motorized divisions 'Leibstandarte', 'Das Reich' and 'Totenkopf' were withdrawn to France during 1942 to refit as Panzer divisions, reappearing to dramatic effect in February 1943. The absence of an armoured reserve in late 1942 would prove critical. Across the whole front, 3.25 million German soldiers faced a Red Army calculated by

German intelligence at five million strong. In fact, its strength was closer to six million.[6] While the Soviet mobilization had conjured up 488 divisions in 1941 and would create another 134 during 1942, the German Army had no reserve other than its garrisons in western Europe. To bulk out the numbers, Hitler pressured his allies into contributing nearly three-quarters of a million personnel.

Germany's allied forces varied in motivation, training and equipment, but all were notably inferior to regular German soldiers. Such reliance on second-rate troops, who could not be replaced, reveals just how Hitler had raised the stakes. This was an 'all or nothing' strategy. The Romanians had already contributed heavily, suffering some 98,000 casualties in the battle for Odessa in 1941. This expended the best of their peacetime-trained formations and a terribly high proportion of their officers. For the 1942 campaign they deployed no fewer than 24 divisions, a maximum effort they could not repeat. The Italian expeditionary force of three divisions sent to Russia in 1941 had suffered badly in the winter, lacking cold weather clothing and equipment. Nevertheless, Mussolini expanded it to become the Italian 8th Army: ten divisions with a total strength of 229,000 men and 1,100 guns in April 1942. An infantry corps and an Alpine corps (with its supply column of 20,000 mules) were added during the summer, the latter earmarked for the Caucasus Mountains. Hungary was pressured too, and its divisions reinforced its rather token contribution to Hitler's war of conquest to make a full army of ten divisions (2nd Army). Even Slovakia dispatched fresh troops – its motorized division would end the year very far from home, on the Kalmyk steppe with Panzergruppe Kleist. This was the first and only year of the war in which Germany's allies made a significant numerical contribution to the Russian front. By January 1943 most of these men would be dead or in Soviet prison camps.

The Luftwaffe concentrated almost its entire strength on the Eastern Front for the summer campaign. Against a Soviet air arm that was reduced to 5,000 aircraft and unable to seriously interrupt German aerial missions, the Luftwaffe had a total of more than 4,000 aircraft of which about 3,000 were deployed to Russia. In June 1942 the Luftwaffe had the following aircraft on the Russian front: 1,237 bombers, 369 dive-bombers, 278 Me-110 twin-engine fighters, 1,253 Me-109 fighters, 486 recce aircraft, 529 transports and 112 sea planes.

The original German plan called for Army Group South to be divided into two army groups (A and B) after Hitler sacked Von Bock for the second time on 15 July. (He had been restored to command in early 1942.) Army Group B, commanded by the 62-year-old former cavalryman General Maximilian von Weichs, was to advance into the bend of the Don River, then drive on Stalingrad as one half of the traditional pincer movement. Army Group A, led by Field Marshal Wilhelm List, comprising 1st Panzer Army, 17th German and 3rd Romanian Armies, would form the other pincer. List was ordered to take Rostov before linking up with Army Group B in another battle of encirclement on the approaches to Stalingrad. With the Red Army driven back to the Volga, hopefully with heavy losses, Army Group A would then swing south and east to occupy the Caucasus oil fields. Dividing Army Group South into two was all very well if they could coordinate their actions but, as usual with the Nazi command structure, so much had to be referred back to Hitler. There was little liaison between the different German army groups, and the division of Army Group South into two was a recipe for confusion. Had Von Bock remained in charge of a united Army Group South, the subsequent disaster would probably not have been on quite such a drastic scale.[7]

July saw such rapid German advances that the Soviet official history tried to explain this as a deliberate strategy to draw the Germans on to defeat. The fact that future premier Khruschev was Chief Commissar of the South-Western Front, and that the commander of the Southern Front was later his Minister of Defence, may not be unconnected with this. However, like many other 'feigned retreats' in history, this was nothing of the sort. The South-Western Front (Timoshenko) and Southern Front (Malinovsky) had 1.3 million men in 68 divisions and six tank corps. They also had a copy of the German plan for *Fall Blau* (Operation *Blue*), recovered from a crashed German aircraft on 20 June. Nevertheless, they retained large forces in the Don bend on the line of the Rivers Tschir and Tsimla as the German spearheads, delayed by petrol shortages, approached.

Paulus's 6th Army succeeded in trapping the Russian 62nd Army and 1st Tank Army in a double envelopment, crossing the Don behind the Soviet forces. Timoshenko's and Malinovsky's Fronts both collapsed with catastrophic losses, possibly more than 350,000 or twice as many as thrown away in the Kharkov débâcle earlier in the year. More than 2,000 tanks were lost too. There would have been many more prisoners if the Germans had not run out of petrol; they had only ten Panzer or motorized divisions operating across a frontage of 400 miles.

One minor Russian success went unnoticed in the shadow of this catastrophe, but was to have great importance in November. Russian troops managed to cling to a small bridgehead on the west bank of the Don, south of Kremensk. Meanwhile, on the Central Front where Stalin had expected the blow to fall, Zhukov launched an offensive north of Orel, inflicting heavy casualties on 2nd Panzer Army. The impatient Führer ordered Army Group A to take Rostov and advance along the eastern coast of the Black Sea while Army Group B was to detach 1st and 4th Panzer Armies. While this armoured force struck at Maikop, Grozny and Baku, the rest of Army Group B continued towards the Volga. The speed of the Russian collapse in the south arguably helped the Red Army in the long run since it encouraged Hitler in his belief that he could capture both Stalingrad and the Caucasus at the same time. Tougher resistance might possibly have allowed saner counsels to prevail and led to the Germans settling for more achievable objectives.

The 4th Panzer Army was soon returned to Army Group B, supporting the German 6th Army, which reached the outer suburbs of Stalingrad on 23 August. The honour of breaking into the city fell to the 79th Panzergrenadier Regiment, which captured the northerly suburb of Spartanovka just before midnight. Hitler's army had reached the Volga.

Had 4th Panzer remained with 6th Army in July, it might well have been able to seize the city then, but by the beginning of September it was clear the Russians were determined to hold Stalingrad. Unlike the previous summer, in July 1942 the German Army no longer had enough armoured forces to bypass the city on either side and cut it off. It was going to have to make a frontal attack.

At the same time, Russian resistance in the Caucasus slowed the advance of Army Group A. Hitler sent General Jodl to investigate Field Marshal List's lack of progress, only to have his own instructions quoted back at him. The stifling heat of the Ukranian summer did not make for cool tempers. In an incandescent rage, Hitler sacked List and announced that he would command the Army Group personally. List, 62, who had commanded the German 12th Army in France and the Balkans, was pensioned off and did not serve again. (List was one of several German officers sentenced to long jail terms at Nuremberg who found that their early release on health grounds gave them a new lease of life; he died in 1971.) Hitler was so furious with the rest of his generals that he refused to take his meals with them at Vinnitsa. As for the hapless Jodl, he was to be replaced by that rising star in the Nazi firmament – the hitherto undefeated commander of the 6th Army, General Friedrich Paulus, whose men were fighting their way into Stalingrad.[8]

★

CHAPTER FIVE

VERDUN ON THE VOLGA: THE BATTLE OF STALINGRAD

'Stunned, we stared at our situation maps on which menacing thick red lines of encirclement and arrows showed enemy attacks … We have never imagined a catastrophe of such proportions to be possible.'

JOACHIM WIEDER, CHIEF INTELLIGENCE OFFICER, GERMAN 8TH ARMY CORPS

The battle of Stalingrad cost more lives than any other battle of the Second World War. The Germans and their allies suffered 800,000 casualties, while Russian losses were 1.1 million. It was the turning point of the war. The Wehrmacht was defeated so catastrophically that not even Goebbels' propaganda machine could conceal the extent of the disaster. Most families in Germany lost a relative or friend at Stalingrad. The invasion of Russia had been sold to the German people as a defensive measure as much as a campaign for 'living space'. According to the Nazi view, German soldiers were advancing into Russia to protect western European civilization against Bolshevism. Military reality and Nazi myth converged in the wake of Stalingrad. The war of conquest was now a struggle for survival.

The enduring image of Stalingrad is that of the desolate, frozen city that became the tomb of the German 6th Army. Yet the pitiless fighting that consumed most of Paulus's command took place across the snow-covered steppes to the west. It was only after Panzergruppe Hoth's relief effort failed and the airstrips were overrun that the final battle for the city began. And a significant proportion of the casualties had occurred before the first snows fell, in house-to-house fighting that lasted from mid-September to mid-November. The Russians suffered even more grievously as their newly mobilized infantry divisions, led by inexperienced officers, tried to halt the advance of some of the most battle-hardened professional soldiers in the world. The German 6th Army had been fighting for two years, and, if some veterans were beginning to wonder if they would ever get any leave, the army had justified pride in its unbroken run of victories. Between July and November 1942, the Red Army suffered 323,000 killed or missing, and 319,000 wounded in and around Stalingrad, together with 1,426 tanks and more than 12,000 guns.

For the first time the German Army was unable to simply sweep past a city, leaving the defenders to surrender – its standard procedure in 1941. With the much depleted armoured force already fully committed, the army was compelled to fight its way into an urban area, defended with desperate courage by Russian soldiers with the Volga (and Stalin) at their backs. Reports of the army's low morale, the panicked evacuation of Rostov and the stampede back to Stalingrad had perturbed Moscow. *Ni Shagu Nazad!* ('Not a step backward!') was the theme of Stalin's Order 227 read out to Red Army units on 28 July. Draconian disciplinary measures were enforced, with a reported 13,500 soldiers executed that summer and many more consigned to newly created *Strafbats* (penal battalions). These suicide units were employed as human mine-detectors or to spearhead assaults: spectacular acts of bravery were required to win transfer back to a regular regiment. Casualties averaged six times that of a normal infantry unit. About 25,000 Russian soldiers found themselves in the penal battalions during 1942, but the total increased to 178,000 the following year. Until September 1943 most rifle divisions included a battalion of *Strafniki*; after that they were concentrated at army level and fed into assaults as appropriate.

Reaching the Don on 23 July, the German Army cut the last rail line between Moscow and Stalingrad, condemning Russian reinforcements to long road marches or rail journeys via central Asia. However, the whole German offensive was being conducted from a single low-capacity railway, so both sides were fighting at the end of a tenuous supply line. In October, when the 6th Army was locked in bitter street fighting in the city, most of its horse transport was withdrawn. There was no sense wasting valuable train capacity on forage for draught animals for an army that was no longer moving. Still, Paulus was confident, giving his blessing to a commemorative patch that his men would wear after the victory: the German eagle presiding over a gigantic grain silo – the scene of intense fighting in September – with the legend 'STALINGRAD' emblazoned across the top.

Formerly the city of Tsaritsyn, Stalingrad had received the name of the Soviet dictator to commemorate the Bolshevik victory there during the Civil War, a victory ascribed to the genius of Iosif Vissarionovich. The name had a magnetic effect, drawing Hitler to insist on the capture of a city he did not need, and Stalin to sacrifice hundreds of thousands of men to defend it. Hitler's original view had been simply to stop Russian river traffic and not to get involved in a fight for the city. As he confessed to his old Nazi cronies at Munich's Löwenbräukeller on 8 November, 'I don't want a second Verdun.'

The city hugged the west bank of the river for nearly 15 miles, but, with a population of 445,000 in 1939, it was smaller than Rostov. However, in the late summer of 1942 it was crowded with refugees from the German advance. At the heart of the city lay three large manufacturing complexes: the Red October steel works, the Barrikady ordnance factory and the Stalingrad tractor factory, which actually manufactured T-34 tanks. All three became centres of resistance. To attack the tractor factory in mid-October required the combined efforts of four German divisions with extra engineer battalions, equipped for bunker fighting with flame-throwers and explosive charges, assaulting on a frontage of less than 5,000 yards. The city centre was defended by the Russian 62nd Army with some 54,000 men, 900 guns and mortars and 110 tanks.[1] The German 6th Army had 25 divisions, with more than 100,000 men committed to the battle for the city, supported by some 2,000 guns, 500 tanks and Fliegerkorps 8, the latter providing more than 1,000 sorties a day.

The battle for the city began in earnest on 13 September. The German 295th, 71st and 94th Infantry Divisions and 29th Motorized

Division, supported by 14th and 24th Panzer Divisions, launched an all-out attack which overran the low hill (height 335 feet) where the Soviet 62nd Army's headquarters had been located. The railway station was taken and the 71st Division advanced far enough to bring the Volga landing stage under fire. With German outposts on the Volga, it looked as if General Anton Lopatin, commander of the Russian 62nd Army, was right – the city was going to fall. But Lopatin had been transferred 48 hours earlier. In his role as political trouble-shooter, Nikita Khruschev took charge and appointed Vasili Ivanovich Chuikov to replace him.[2]

Once a teenage Bolshevik officer in the civil war, Chuikov was the archetypal Red Army general. Son of a peasant farmer, he obeyed Stalin's orders without question. British officers encountered him after the war as commander of Soviet forces in Berlin. His drinking binges were the stuff of legend, and woe betide the junior officer who crossed him the morning after. Chuikov survived the purges to command a rifle corps by 1938 and the 9th Army in 1940. A dismal performance in Finland saw him consigned to China as the Soviet military attaché, something that Soviet histories of the Second World War would gloss over for the next 50 years, because Chuikov redeemed himself at Stalingrad. His army (redesignated 8th Guards in April 1943) subsequently fought all the way to Berlin, and it was his headquarters that accepted the German surrender on 2 May 1945. With Khruschev's accession, Chuikov became a marshal in 1955 and did not retire until 1971. He was buried with great ceremony at Volgograd (Stalingrad) in 1982. The 8th Guards Army, due to be disbanded after the Soviet withdrawal from eastern Europe, was reprieved by President Yeltsin. The defenders of Stalingrad had not been forgotten.

The German assault brought the front line to within half a mile of Chuikov's new headquarters in a bunker by the Tsaritsa. He committed his last reserve of 19 tanks, ordering the commander to hold or be shot (he was killed in his T–34) and summoning the 13th Guards Division, then assembling on the east bank of the Volga. The Guards ran a gauntlet of machine-gun and artillery fire to establish a bridgehead from which they made a succession of sharp counter-attacks. Committed piecemeal, the target of repeated Luftwaffe air strikes, the Guards Division suffered terribly, but the German advance stopped.

In ferocious house-to-house fighting, most of the city's wooden buildings were destroyed, leaving the soldiers to fight over rubble, through cellars and among the giant industrial complexes that resisted the heaviest bombardment. Because each assault left the attackers so disorganized, short of men and ammunition, counter-attacks often succeeded, and the same objective could change hands repeatedly. The railway station captured by the Germans on the morning of 14 September was retaken within an hour, but stormed again by the Germans the same morning, only to be recaptured by the Russians in the afternoon. Casualties were appalling. The 13th Guards Division arrived nearly 10,000 strong, but only a few hundred men were still in action by the time 2,000 replacements arrived a month later.

Chuikov's army bled to death, fighting on in an ever-shrinking bridgehead. Chuikov was forced to relocate his headquarters again, this time in open trenches half a mile north of the Red October landing stage. Engineers dug bunkers, unaware nearby oil storage tanks were still full; their ignition during an air raid nearly immolated the entire staff. Drafts of replacements were fed in, just enough to keep the units operational, although divisions were often reduced to little more than battalions. The 92nd Rifle Brigade (naval infantry from the Baltic and Northern Fleets) arrived on 17 September with the 137th Tank Brigade. Major counter-attacks just north of the city failed to relieve the pressure, the German 6th Army smashing each one in turn, barely pausing in its effort to storm the city.

The trap is set

Paulus flew to Vinnitsa for a meeting with Hitler on the eve of the September offensive. He was confident then, and remained convinced he could take the city almost to the moment the great Soviet counter-attack began in November. The very same day, Zhukov and Rokossovsky presented their own plan for a full-scale counter-offensive, aimed at encircling the German 6th Army. The fate of Paulus's army was being plotted before it had even begun its assault on Stalingrad. Zhukov and Rokossovsky foresaw how the battle for the city would soak up battalions, regiments, whole divisions – and that the main body of the 6th Army would be sucked into the maelstrom, leaving its long flanks guarded by second-rate units.

As the German offensive ran its course in the summer of 1942, the Red Army had continued to grow. The staggering casualties of 1941 had been almost completely replaced by the spring of 1942. The replacement divisions were untrained men with unfamiliar weapons led by novice officers, and were all but annihilated in the futile offensives between January and June. However, while they fought and died, another 40 divisions were mobilized in early 1942 and were able to train harder and longer before going to the front. Three more tank corps were added to the Soviet order of battle between May and November 1942. Rather than feed the new formations into battle as they assembled, the Red Army created a powerful reserve. With this new force, Zhukov and Rokossovsky planned not just to cut off the Germans in Stalingrad, but to push all the way to the Black Sea coast and amputate Army Group A. A third, and potentially the most decisive, blow would fall simultaneously on Army Group Centre, thus smashing the entire Ostheer.

Army Group A had driven rapidly into the Caucasus, conducting a 1941-style Blitzkrieg across the Kuban during August. The Soviet naval base at Novorossisk was overrun, and Maikop fell, although not before the oil installations were blown up by the Russians. The advance continued across the baking steppe, temperatures topping 50°C. Ahead lay the mountains of the Caucasus, visible for miles as a line of cloud on the horizon. On 21 August a team from the German 1st Mountain Division planted the German flag on Mount Elbrus, at 18,481 feet the highest mountain in the Caucasus. Fighting their way through the mountain passes, the men of 49th Mountain Corps entered the sub-tropical forest surrounding Sukhumi.

Some 200 miles east, the Russian forces protecting the oil fields around Grozny had been driven back to their last line of defence, the River Terek. At the end of August Panzergruppe Kleist seized the first of several bridgeheads across the river. Meanwhile, elements of the 16th Motorized Division had driven to the outskirts of Astrakhan on the Caspian Sea. The strategic objectives of Baku and Tiflis were tantalizingly close, but Army Group A was 600 miles south of Stalingrad and had outrun its supply lines. Bringing forward the replacements, ammunition and equipment for the last push took most of October. In a final attempt to break through, Kleist renewed the assault on 1 November, the 13th Panzer Division penetrating to within a few miles of Ordzhonikidze before a Soviet counter-attack forced it to withdraw or be encircled.

The German offensive at Stalingrad continued, long after General von Weichs, commander of Army Group B, begged Hitler to call it off. In public speeches Hitler committed himself to taking Stalingrad. German soldiers had reached the Volga, he said, and no power on earth could shift them from it. In a situation briefing at his headquarters on 2 October, he told the High Command that 'world opinion and the morale of our allies' demanded the capture of Stalingrad. Paulus regrouped his forces and stockpiled ammunition, then struck on 14 October, aiming at the tractor and Barrikady factories. For two weeks the fighting raged day and night, with German combat engineer teams spearheading each assault with flame-throwers and explosive charges. Tanks surrounded by infantry protection teams fired into Soviet strongpoints at point-blank range, and Stukas appeared above Stalingrad every morning, bombing with great precision. By November only 10 per cent of the city remained in Russian hands, the ruins of the tractor factory were finally captured and Chuikov's army was split in two.

The 6th Army gathered itself for a final effort before winter. On 11–12 November it attacked the Red October steel works with nine divisions. By this stage in the battle, front-line rifle companies were reduced to 30 or 40 men. The 6th Army had only 180 operational tanks.[3] The same night, German intelligence repeated its warnings about Russian armies massing along the 180-mile front held by Romanian, Italian and Hungarian forces. These allied formations were far less well equipped than German units; for instance, the Romanian divisional anti-tank units had horse-drawn 37mm guns, weapons that had proved unable to stop T-34s during 1941. Their field guns were a mixture of old Austrian and French weapons for which there were no ammunition stocks available in the German logistics system. The Romanian infantry divisions were trying to hold frontages of more than 12 miles each.

Halder's diaries chronicle the Führer's retreat into fantasy that autumn, an escalating practice of denial that would culminate in his withdrawal to the Berlin bunker in 1945, still transmitting orders to non-existent armies to march to his rescue. News that Russian tank production now exceeded 1,200 vehicles a month produced a spectacular tirade – but no change in policy. (The truth was even grimmer: Soviet tank production exceeded 2,000 tanks per month in 1942.) Halder was himself sacked in October, with his successor, General Kurt Zeitzler, also urging a withdrawal from Stalingrad, and equally to no avail. However, the idea that Hitler ignored clear warnings of the forthcoming Soviet offensive should be treated with caution.[4] In fact OKH had little indication of what was to come. Gehlen's team had identified a threat to the 6th Army's northern flank and had moved the 48th Panzer Corps to cover it. Consisting of 22nd Panzer Division – 45 operational tanks – and the 1st Romanian Tank Division – 40 Czech R-2 tanks – this was all that was available. The Germans never realized the attack would be on such a scale, and there was no hint that the Russians would attack to the south of Stalingrad too.

Three Soviet fronts (South-Western, Don and Stalingrad) with a combined strength of 1.1 million men, 894 tanks and 12,000 guns, began the great winter offensive on 19 November. At Stalingrad itself, the dawn was barely perceptible, the gaunt silhouettes of the ruined tower blocks hidden in the fog. The gloom never lifted, and in the afternoon came the first heavy snowstorm. The city and the surrounding steppe were about to be engulfed in the terrible, virtually Arctic winter. The initial bombardment of the thinly stretched German front was supplemented by the thunderous roar of 100 multiple-rocket launcher batteries, never before used in such quantities. More than 1,200 Soviet aircraft had been deployed to support the fronts. The sudden concentration of Russian fighters and the onset of severe weather ended the Luftwaffe's domination of the Stalingrad area.

The Russians swept through the Romanian and Italian armies, Luftwaffe field divisions, security units and other formations dotted along the south bank of the Don. The encirclement was completed on 23 November, when the two Russian spearheads met at Kalatsch. The Russians did not know it, but they had trapped more than 300,000 German and allied troops in the Stalingrad pocket. The entire 6th Army was there, the bulk of 4th Panzer Army; 20 divisions belonging to four army corps and a Panzer corps. There were 13 infantry divisions, three Panzer divisions, three motorized divisions, a Luftwaffe flak division, field artillery regiments including two *Sturmgeschütz* assault gun battalions, a dozen combat engineer battalions, a Croat regiment attached to a Jäger division, construction units, medical services, elements of the Reich labour service, the 20th Romanian Infantry and 1st Cavalry Division, as well as survivors of the Romanian forces who had escaped eastwards into the pocket. Thousands of Russian *Hilfswillige* – civilian service personnel who had volunteered or been press-ganged into most German divisions by 1942 – were also present, but as they never appeared on official ration strengths, their dreadful fate is practically unrecorded. If Hitler had had his way, there would have been even more men in the pocket. As the Russian pincers closed on 23 November, 48 Panzer Corps found itself in a sea of Russian troops and surrendering Romanians. Army Group B ordered it to break out of the encirclement and withdraw to the River Tschir, which it managed to do. Hitler was so furious he had the commander of the operation, Lieutenant-General Heim of 14th Panzer Division, arrested and flung into prison without trial. Heim, who had won the Knight's Cross in August 1942, languished in Moabit prison until April 1943.[5]

The encirclement caught the 6th Army without its winter clothing; this was at the army's supply depots of Tatsinskaya and Morosowsk, outside the perimeter. Once again German soldiers would have to endure sub-zero temperatures, wearing standard uniforms padded with newspaper and straw. And the army had food and fuel for only a week. Paulus signalled Army Group Don on 22 November:

> Fuel will soon be exhausted. Tanks and heavy weapons then immovable. Ammunition situation strained. Food provisions sufficient for six days. Army intends to hold remaining area from Stalingrad to Don. Supposition is that closure of the South-Western Front succeeds and adequate provisions will be flown in.

Damaged equipment was blown up in expectation of an immediate order to break out. The corps commanders were adamant that the army should fight its way back to German lines. Hube (14th Panzer Corps), Heitz (8th Corps), Jänicke (4th Corps) and Strecker (11th Corps) argued bitterly with Paulus and his chief of staff, who insisted that they obey Hitler's orders to 'dig in and wait for relief from outside'.[6]

Although a defensive front was quickly established facing west, there were no real defensive positions on the open steppe. The troops entrenched themselves as well as they could in the frozen earth and snow, but the expression 'Festung Stalingrad' ('Fortress Stalingrad') that appeared on one of the earliest OKH orders gave 6th Army staff officers their first clue that the High Command had no idea of local conditions. From the very beginning of the Stalingrad disaster, the 6th Army staff officers suspected the worst while the front-line troops remained confident. Hitler had ordered them to hold on. Soon they were told, 'Manstein will get you out.'

The Demyansk pocket had held out the previous winter because the Luftwaffe had been able to supply the men inside, albeit at great cost in aircraft: 265 Junkers Ju-52s.[7] Now Reichsmarschall Göring made his fateful promise to supply Stalingrad. Without reference to his staff officers, in complete ignorance of the 6th Army's requirements and the Luftwaffe's transport capabilities, Göring told Hitler he could supply Paulus's men by air. The Reichsmarschall's reputation had been in tatters since May; RAF Bomber Command's 1,000-bomber raid on Cologne, and subsequent heavy raids, made a mockery of his bombastic pronouncements that Germany would never be bombed. Göring knew Hitler wanted to hold the city: by promising the Luftwaffe could make it possible, he sought to redeem his position within the Nazi hierarchy.

The major airfields from which the operation was to be mounted, Tatsinskaya and Morozovskaya-west, were more than 100 miles from the pocket. Eleven *Gruppen* of Ju-52s and Ju-86s, comprising 600 aircraft, operated from Tatsinskaya, and 400 from Morozovskaya-west, soon supplemented by Heinkel He-111s. A *Gruppe* of Focke-Wulf Fw 200s and Ju-290s flew from Stalino, while gigantic Messerschmitt Me-323s and Gotha 242s made the journey from Makeyevka in the Ukraine. Fighter cover was essential and a handful of Messerschmitt Bf-109s from the Udet wing flew into Stalingrad to operate from Pitomnik, the best airstrip inside the pocket.

Aircrew were pulled off training to fly transports to Stalingrad. Nazi Party leaders generously donated the services of their personal aircraft and their hitherto pampered crews. It was dangerous enough to fly in such savage weather conditions: snow storms could reduce visibility to zero in an instant, and icing was a constant menace. New Russian fighters, especially the La-5, were much more capable of intercepting the lumbering Ju-52s in clear weather; and since the transport planes' routes were quite predictable, the Russians established dense concentrations of anti-aircraft guns. Running this gauntlet cost the transport squadrons dearly. More than 1,000 aircrew died. Aircraft losses were 266 Ju-52s, 42 Ju-86s, 165 He-111s, nine Fw 200s, five He-177s and one Ju-290. And it was followed by a similar massacre of German transport aircraft over Tunisia – 'Tunisgrad' as it was dubbed. When Field Marshal Milch was belatedly sent to rescue the situation in mid-January 1943, he discovered a situation of utter chaos at the airfields supplying Stalingrad. Ground crew had no proper quarters and were trying to work on aircraft parked in the open in temperatures of -30°C. They did not know the cold-start procedures required in such conditions, unsurprisingly as the men Milch inspected had just been transferred from North Africa. These and other problems left only 15 out of 140 Ju-52s operational, 41 out of 140 He-111s. Only one of the 20 famously temperamental Fw 200s was airworthy.

Although Pitomnik was the best airstrip inside the pocket, it was not equipped for night operations and daytime flights soon became prohibitively dangerous. Two weeks after the encirclement, under the personal direction of the Red Army's air chief, General Novikov, the fighters were shooting down nearly half the lumbering transports heading for Stalingrad. From mid-December flying was largely restricted to nights or cloudy days, but the weather often closed in on the airstrips, preventing any flying at all. On the other hand, the airlift was practically suspended for the first week of January, when clear skies left the transports nowhere to hide. Even daytime landings were hazardous, and crews began to drop supplies by parachute instead. Towards the end, the 6th Army was so short of petrol it could not gather and move heavy containers, so supplies piled up around Pitomnik while men starved to death only a few miles away.

The 6th Army's artillery and armoured vehicles were practically immobilized by the lack of fuel, although some reserves were hoarded for a breakout. There were no stockpiles of food and hunger turned to starvation as the weeks slipped by. The bread ration was 8oz a day for men in the front line, and half that for the rear echelon. The steady slaughter of the remaining transport animals provided another 8oz of horseflesh, supplemented by 1oz of cheese and 1oz of butter: an utterly inadequate diet for men fighting in extreme cold.

The sacrifice of the Luftwaffe's transport groups brought the 6th Army a daily delivery of about 100 tons of supplies for the duration of the siege, although during the first weeks it was only 60 tons or so – enough for a single division. The 6th Army had requested a minimum of 500 tons per day, and even that was a grotesque underestimation as Paulus, a career staff officer, knew very well when he made it.[8] The figure of 500 tons actually refers to the absolute minimum supply requirements of Von Seydlitz's 51st Corps, which he had calculated at 400 tons of ammunition alone, per division per day; a figure which would double in case of heavy combat. Even on half-rations and with light combat, 51st Corps needed 598 tons (295 Ju-52 loads) per day, or 990 tons (495 Ju-52 flights) in case of heavy fighting.

The barest minimum quantity of supplies required by Paulus's troops was about 1,500 tons per day. So the idea that the Luftwaffe could sustain the beleaguered army was not just unlikely, it was absolutely impossible – it would have been impossible even if there had been no Russians in the way! Several senior officers protested, including Fiebig (8th Air Corps) and Pickert (9th Flak Division). Richthofen (Luftflotte 4) wrote in his diary, 'The 6th Army believes it will be supplied by the air fleet ... Every effort is being made to convince the army that it cannot be done.' Other Luftwaffe officers assumed that all they were trying to do was deliver as many supplies as possible before the 6th Army broke out. Yet the German High Command persisted in maintaining the myth that aerial supply could keep the 6th Army operational. Perhaps like Hitler they pinned their faith on the conqueror of Sebastopol, the apostle of Blitzkrieg who had planned the Ardennes breakthrough in 1940, Germany's newest field marshal, Erich von Manstein.

Operation *Winter Storm*

Von Manstein assumed command of Army Group Don on 26 November, signalling Paulus the same day with a promise to do everything to get him and his men out. Only 48 hours earlier he had sent a signal to OKH, agreeing with Von Weichs's judgement that 6th Army must break out at once because it would run out of fuel by the time a relief force could be assembled. But Hitler intervened, telephoning Von Manstein in the middle of the night to reject his proposals for an immediate breakout operation. Hitler insisted that the 6th Army remain in the 'fortress', which it would continue to defend. Von Manstein was equally adamant that he be given command of Army Group A as well as Army Group Don, and be granted freedom of action to fight the battle as he saw fit. The Prussian field marshal was reduced to bargaining with the Bohemian lance-corporal for enough units with which to effect a rescue. If not Army Group A, then how about 1st Panzer Army? The most telling moment in the conversation came when Von Manstein asked Hitler what Army Group A was doing, strung out across the Kuban all the way to the Caucasus. Hitler told him it was there to seize the Baku oil fields, which, he said, were crucial to the continuation of the war; Von Manstein returned to the attack, requesting command of both army groups and a free hand, promising the Führer all the oil he wanted after the battle was won. Silence was the stern reply; then a blank refusal to cede an inch of ground: there was to be no mobile battle, just static defence while Von Manstein organized a relief column to Stalingrad. The city, Hitler claimed, would be the springboard for a new offensive in summer 1943 which would see German forces advance through the Caucasus and link up with Rommel's army in Africa. The Afrika Korps had of course been in headlong retreat since the end of the Alamein battle on 4 November; Von Manstein might not have known the full extent of the disaster, but his commander-in-chief certainly did. Hitler terminated the call. Von Manstein left the room without saying a word.

It took two weeks to stabilize the front and muster enough forces to make a serious attempt. Colonel-General Hoth, commander of 4th Panzer Army, received the 23rd Panzer Division, hurried back from the Caucasus, and the 6th Panzer Division, transferred by rail from France, followed by 17th Panzer Division detached from Army Group Centre.

Before examining the German operations intended to rescue the 6th Army, it is important to remember what was happening in the north. Many books have been written on the Stalingrad campaign that fail to mention an even larger battle that took place at the same time, which had profound consequences for Paulus and his men.[9]

Germany's biggest and most powerful army, the 9th, commanded by Walther Model, was fighting for its life in November 1942. The story of Stalingrad cannot be told without reference to the battles around Rzhev that embroiled 23 German divisions (six of them Panzer divisions) in ferocious defensive actions. The battles around the Rzhev salient ruled out the transfer of significant German reserves to help rescue the men trapped in Stalingrad. When the German High Command reviewed the Stalingrad situation map, it was at all times conscious that another army was also engaged in a life-or-death struggle. Model was the definitive glassy-eyed fanatic, and if he said he could spare no reserves, the situation had to be grim indeed.

The small town of Rzhev is the uppermost major settlement on the Volga River and had remained in German hands since 1941. A sizeable minority of its people had been taken to Germany as forced labourers; and the Germans had established a prison camp there. The salient's shape derived from the failure of the Soviet offensive in this sector during January–February 1942, and the ultimate liquidation of the encircled Soviet survivors during Operation *Seydlitz* in July 1942. Zhukov regarded the Rzhev salient as too dangerous to ignore. He viewed it as an obvious platform for a German offensive that could capture Moscow. When the great Soviet winter offensive for 1942 was planned, two major strikes were decided upon: Operation *Mars* would crush the Rzhev salient; Operation *Uranus* would amputate the 6th Army. Both had follow-on operations scheduled: *Jupiter* was the name for an offensive that would take Soviet forces from Rzhev towards Smolensk, while *Saturn* would round off Operation *Uranus* by driving all the way from Stalingrad to Rostov.

Operation *Mars* was scheduled to begin on 28 October, once the weather was cold enough for ice to have formed across the region's streams and lakes. The freeze came late that autumn, so Zhukov postponed until 25 November so his tanks could cross minor water features without bridging equipment. Seven armies, including

83 divisions, took part in the operation: more than 800,000 men and 2,350 tanks. The German salient projected some 150 miles north from Viaz'ma. Rzhev lay at the north-east tip of the salient, where the German front line had reached the Volga. A little more than 100 miles to the west of Rzhev, the front line ran north-east to south-west either side of the small town of Belyi. Both towns were the scene of fierce fighting that lasted from 25 November (the day before Von Manstein arrived to take command of the Stalingrad relief effort) to 15 December (as Hoth's Panzer Corps got within 50 miles of the 6th Army's positions).

Forty miles south of Rzhev the German front line was held by the 34th Panzer Corps. On 25 November the Soviet Western Front's 20th and 31st Armies launched strong infantry and tank forces against the well-constructed German defensive positions. Enjoying odds of more than 5:1, the Soviets attacked across open ground; thick fog and snow showers handicapped their artillery bombardment, which left many German heavy weapons positions unobserved. The German 102nd Infantry Division beat off three divisions of the 31st Army supported by about 100 tanks, mowing down wave after wave of infantry which surged forward through the snow. The 20th Army's attack did not gain much ground either, and by the end of the day the snowfields were littered with knocked out tanks and thousands of bodies. One Soviet division succeeded in crossing the frozen Vazuza River to establish a bridgehead around two fortified villages it stormed on the west bank. The Western Front's commander was a shaven-headed 45-year-old general, Ivan Konev. He started his Soviet career as Commissar aboard an armoured train in the civil war, and had been promoted to front command from the 19th Army in 1941. Stalin replaced him temporarily with Zhukov at the end of that year, which left him in a permanent state of competition as to who could be the more ruthless. Their rivalry would colour the very last battles of the war, but all that lay very far in the future. Now the two men bullied their subordinates to smash through the German lines along the Vazuza River. The plan called for three corps to be passed through the gap created by the 20th Army on D+1, and they insisted on sticking to the schedule despite the tiny size of the bridgehead.

The German positions were anchored on the small villages that dotted the floodplain of the Vazuza. Fortified for all-round defence, they held out even when the Soviet forces bypassed them. On 26 and 27 November heavy concentrations of Soviet forces, infantry, tanks and cavalry squeezed into the sector and forced their way west. The German strongpoints they bypassed caused a great deal of trouble. Their direct fire of machine-guns and mortars took a constant toll of the attackers, and they called in successive artillery bombardments and (weather permitting) air strikes. The result was carnage. By dusk on 28 November the Soviet assault in this sector had broken down completely, and the Germans were mounting sharp local counter-attacks to relieve some of the villages. German casualties were heavy, especially among their infantry, but Soviet losses were far worse.

One reason advanced as to Zhukov's determination to punch through south of Rzhev was that the offensive was going according to plan on the other side of the salient. About 120 miles south-west of Rzhev the armies were fighting on reversed fronts, with the Soviet armies attacking eastwards from the swamps west of Belyi. On 25 November, the Soviet 41st Army broke through German defences south of Belyi; the next day, the 1st Mechanized Corps (including 224 tanks) exploited through the gap, its progress hindered more by the lack of roads in this extensively forested region than by enemy action. However, the 41st Army proceeded to mount some very Zhukov-style frontal attacks on Belyi while the mechanized corps was eventually struck by a major German counter-attack – three Panzer divisions from Army Group Centre's reserve.

The Soviet 41st Army fell into a classic German trap. In a miniature version of what was to befall the German 6th Army, the Soviets crammed their men into the battle for Belyi, sparing few units for flank protection. Despite severe winter weather conditions, the 1st, 12th, 19th and 20th Panzer Divisions were concentrated in this sector by 7 December, and, in a deft winter Blitz, armoured forces attacked from both sides of Belyi to surround the 41st Army. This drove Zhukov to order another round of unrelenting attacks on Rzhev, either to soak off the German reserves or possibly because this was his default setting to meeting defeat. On 11 December the 20th and 29th Armies, including the 5th and 6th Tank Corps, attacked out of the Vazuza bridgehead. In a classic instance of what often happens when you reinforce failure, the Soviets lost 300 tanks in two days of futile headbanging. The Germans noted that many vehicles in this second wave had not been whitewashed for winter camouflage, but had come straight from the factories in olive green. They might as well have painted target rings on them.

Model's counter-attack left some 40,000 Soviets trapped around Belyi, and for all Zhukov's swearing down the telephone at his subordinates, the attacks on the other side of the salient did nothing to save them. On the night of 15–16 December, just as the German relief effort at Stalingrad slowed to a halt, the Soviets blew up their heavy weapons, abandoned their vehicles and charged back towards their own lines on foot. Most got through, but the hundreds of tanks and guns they left behind testified to the complete failure of Zhukov's offensive. The 1st Mechanized Corps lost two-thirds of its 12,000 infantry and almost all its tanks.

Russian soldiers called it the 'Rzhev meatgrinder'. The Soviet 20th Army lost 58,000 out of 114,000 men; overall losses approached 500,000 dead, wounded and missing. *Fremde Heere Ost* estimated Russian tank losses at 1,700 – more than the number of tanks allocated to the Stalingrad offensive – and they were right. German losses were approximately 40,000, and were heaviest among the infantry battalions facing the initial impact. Zhukov's meatgrinder cost the Red Army more than ten men for every German casualty: a ratio that even Soviet manpower reserves could not sustain.[10] Few commanders in history have kept their heads, let alone their jobs, after such a fiasco; but Stalin retained both Zhukov and Konev, recognizing perhaps that neither had any political ambition. So the battle at Rzhev was airbrushed out of history, barely mentioned in Soviet sources, which focused on the dramatic events unfolding at Stalingrad.

Army Group Centre was eventually able to dispatch the 17th Panzer Division to Von Manstein's aid, but the most obvious, if far distant, source of reinforcements was also denied. The substantial German forces in the west had been on high alert since 8 November when an Anglo-American army landed in North Africa: Operation *Torch*. German forces in the occupied zone of France were immediately ordered to take control of the Vichy state and seize the French battlefleet at Toulon. Only after the danger of an amphibious invasion of southern France had passed were the armoured formations released to the Eastern Front. Of course, Hitler and OKW had no idea that the British would succeed in postponing the invasion of France into 1943 and finally to 1944, despite the US Army's wish to engage the Germans as soon as possible and America's mistrust of Britain's Mediterranean strategy. From the German perspective, the attack on North Africa appeared to be a prelude to an attack on southern France.

It is important to recognize, as Hitler often did not, that the Russian front did not exist in a vacuum, but was part of a world war between coalitions of varying cohesion. Hitler left his headquarters at Vinnitsa in the Ukraine on 7 November and spent the next couple of weeks in his mountain retreat at Berchtesgaden. He departed the Ukraine knowing that his favourite general, Erwin Rommel, had been decisively beaten, even if he would not admit this to his generals in Russia. The day after Hitler left, the Allies landed in North Africa, sealing the fate of Axis forces in Tunisia and Libya; on 11 November he ordered the occupation of Vichy France. Then on 19 November came the news from Stalingrad. Yet Hitler did not return to the 'Wolf's Lair' for another four days. Crisis follows crisis and the Führer remained on his lonely mountaintop, perhaps for the first time sensing his own ultimate defeat.

Hoth began the Stalingrad rescue mission on 12 December. It was planned to unfold in two stages: Operation *Winter Storm* would punch through the Soviet encirclement to link the defenders of Stalingrad to the rest of the German Army; then in Operation *Thunderclap* the 6th Army would escape westwards along the corridor carved by Hoth's Panzers. It was the latter which posed the greater difficulty. Much of the 6th Army's horse transport had been withdrawn in October, and there was too little fuel inside the pocket for the army's trucks, let alone tanks, to take part in a full-scale breakout. Fuel would have to be flown in, yet aerial deliveries were not even sufficient to maintain stocks at their existing levels. Von Manstein knew this within days of taking charge, and it makes nonsense of his suggestion in *Lost Victories* that Paulus should have ordered *Thunderclap* without Hitler's permission. The 6th Army was stuck. Every day it held out saw its meagre supplies depleted further, steadily diminishing its chances of escape. An immediate flight to the west the moment the Soviet pincers met at Kalatsch might have saved the 6th Army, but Hitler would probably have sacked any officer ordering the breakout before the operation could have been accomplished.[11] On the other hand, General Jänicke and others believe the Führer would have retrospectively endorsed a decision to escape, as he did on later occasions.

The 6th Panzer Division began the relief attempt with 160 tanks, but 23rd Panzer had only 40 operational tanks on 18 November. The 17th Panzer Division had 60. Despite facing substantially larger Soviet forces, Hoth's 57th Panzer Corps fought its way forward about 30 miles in 12 days of intensive fighting. On the morning of 17 December, the 23rd Panzer Division captured two crossings over the River Aksay, bringing it within 45 miles of the 6th Army's perimeter. Then came the crushing news: a new Soviet offensive (Operation *Little Saturn*) had opened north-west of Stalingrad. The Soviet South-Western Front attacked the Italian 8th Army and Romanian 3rd Army along the River Tschir, destroying them utterly. Italian losses in this German disaster are often overlooked, but they suffered disproportionate mortality in the Russian prison camps: 28,000 out of 49,000 Italian prisoners-of-war would die in captivity. With the front broken open, powerful armoured formations thundered towards the vital airfields/supply depots at Tatsinskaya and

Morosowsk. Major-General Badanov consciously drove his 24th Tank Corps far ahead of its supply columns, expending his command in order to seize Tatsinskaya, which his tanks overran on 24 December. Hitler's attempt to micromanage the battle from his headquarters in East Prussia contributed to the ensuing disaster. He forbade General Fiebig to evacuate the airfield as requested on 23 December, permission being granted only as shells fell on the runway. Although 108 out of 180 Ju-52s escaped, struggling to get airborne with visibility down to 2,000 feet, all the ground equipment was lost. Badanov's exhausted troops were driven off a few days later by a German counter-attack, but they destroyed the depot completely.[12]

Von Manstein was obliged to detach 6th Panzer to deal with the new threat, leaving Hoth to battle on alone. Grinding through the Soviet lines had reduced the *Panzergruppe* to just 35 tanks. The sound of the fighting could be heard from within the pocket. The 6th Army prepared its three strongest divisions to attack at Karpovka as soon as Hoth's troops were within 20 miles – there was not enough fuel for a longer advance. Starting with the Volga Front, the encircled army planned to retreat south-west, units leapfrogging back with the army's remaining 100 armoured vehicles providing flank protection. Behind Hoth's battered spearhead the Germans assembled a supply column (2,300 tons capacity) to give 6th Army the ammunition and fuel it needed. Inside the pocket another column stood ready to take out thousands of wounded and sick, then return carrying 4,000 tons of supplies.

On clear nights, Hoth's soldiers could see flares on the distant horizon, rockets arcing high above the Stalingrad perimeter. But the relief effort was faltering. On 19 December, with the Soviet breakthrough along the Tschir menacing the airfields, Von Manstein ordered Paulus to prepare to launch not just *Winter Storm* but *Thunderclap* as well. 'Development of the situation may compel us to expand the mission' was how the enigmatic last section of his signal began. The 'fortress area' – even he slipped into OKH wishful thinking – was to be evacuated sector by sector.

The order was not given. Conscious that the 6th Army had so little fuel left, that it would soon be compelled to abandon its vehicles and guns, neither Von Manstein nor Paulus would take responsibility for the breakout, an operation that would have seen the remains of the army try to fight its way across 30 miles of open steppe with nothing but rifles and shovels, abandoning their sick and wounded comrades to the enemy. Yet there can be no doubt that this superhuman task would have been made with exceptional determination, and as several of Paulus's officers said at the time, better to escape with six divisions than lose all 20. The British correspondent Alexander Werth visited Stalingrad immediately after the battle. He observed:

> Judging from the Germans I saw in Stalingrad over six weeks later, they must still have been in reasonably good condition around 20 December; they had by then been encircled for less than a month, and were not yet anywhere near real starvation. They also said they were 'full of fight' at the thought of Von Manstein about to break through to Stalingrad. Even in January, those still in reasonably good condition fought with the greatest stubbornness during the Russian liquidation of the Cauldron.[13]

Von Manstein and Paulus conferred by teleprinter on 19 December, the necessarily stilted exchange creating enough ambiguities to fuel post-war arguments about who was to blame for the ensuing disaster.[14] For part of the month, the two commanders could speak by means of a new radio with scrambler device, and Paulus pleaded to be allowed to break out; Von Manstein refused to order him to do so, but did say he would back him up if he acted unilaterally.

The agonizing at German headquarters was ended by General Rodion Yakovlevich Malinovksy and the Soviet 2nd Guards Army on Christmas Eve. Although Stalin berated his commanders for not immediately liquidating the pocket, the Red generals won the argument. The Soviet reserve was not flung against the city, but attacked the rest of Army Group Don. The Germans had recaptured

Tatsinskaya airfield from the survivors of the Soviet 24th Tank Corps, but the Russians took it back again shortly afterwards. By 31 December, Hoth's relief force had been driven back beyond its start line and the German defensive front along the Don had collapsed. The Russian offensive had blown a gap more than 200 miles wide, and the entire German army group in the Caucasus was in danger of being cut off.

The 6th Army was doomed. Several officers shot themselves. An understandable – but unedifying – scramble took place among the Nazi leadership to extract friends and relatives from Stalingrad before it was too late. Albert Speer tried and failed to get his brother out. Aircrew landing at Pitomnik in mid-January had to resort to their personal weapons to fight off attempts to storm the aircraft. Now that the boot was on the other foot, General Chuikov could afford to appreciate the formidable fighting qualities of the 6th Army, noting in his account how 'up to the end of December, they continued to live in hope and put up a desperate resistance, often literally to the last cartridge. We practically took no prisoners, since the Nazis just wouldn't surrender. Not until after Von Manstein's failure to break through did morale among the German troops begin to decline very noticeably.'[15] Discipline was maintained with the same savage methods the Soviets had already resorted to. The unassuming, softly spoken Paulus had 364 of his men shot for cowardice in just one week; 18 more than Field Marshal Haig had executed in the British Army during the whole of the First World War.

All able-bodied men in the pocket were combined into 'fortress battalions'. The Luftwaffe ground personnel, flak crews, clerical staff and all rear echelon services took up rifles instead. The rapid exhaustion of medical supplies left the sick and wounded to suffer in the most revolting conditions, their numbers overwhelming the medical staff. Dysentery and typhoid fever swept through the starving units and dressing stations alike. There were some 50,000 wounded men in the pocket. Thousands had reached the field hospital at Gumrak only to be stacked into unheated freight cars at the railway station. The novel *Forsaken Army*, written by a survivor, describes how medical teams let the badly wounded freeze to death overnight rather than prolong their agonies in the hellish dressing stations. Standing orders forbade leaving the wounded to the enemy, so, as the perimeter contracted under steady Russian pressure, aid posts were cleared and the casualties moved into the city.

———

Paulus rejected an offer to surrender on 9 January and directed that flags of truce were to be fired on in future. The next day the Russians attacked the western perimeter, where the defences, such as they were, stretched across the bare steppe. The perimeter was penetrated by tanks after a concentrated artillery barrage and, in temperatures of -30°C, the German survivors fell back towards the city itself. There was no intermediate defensive line, nothing on which to build a new position. Pitomnik airbase was overrun on 16 January, leaving the small strip at Gumrak the 6th Army's only contact with the outside world.

The renewed Soviet offensive overran the Hungarian 2nd Army in the Don Bend, destroying it in a series of battles around the small town of Voronyets. This was the blackest day in the history of the Hungarian Army: of the 270,000 men in the Hungarian forces there, 130,000 were killed, captured or posted missing. The Hungarians had significantly fewer anti-tank guns and artillery pieces than equivalent German units, and their First World War *Schwarzlose* machine-guns were prone to stoppages. Nevertheless, their own commander-in-chief, Gusztáv Jány, called them cowards; words that were thrown back at him in 1946 when he was tried and executed by the newly installed Communist regime. The Russian breakthrough in the Hungarian sector led to the capture of many of the airfields from which the Stalingrad airlift was being mounted. By mid-January 1943 the nearest German-held airfields were more than 200 miles from the city.

On 3 March 1943 the Nazi propaganda magazine *Die Wehrmacht* carried a colour painting on its cover, showing a determined band of German soldiers led by General Karl Strecker preparing to make their last stand in the snow-covered ruins of the Stalingrad tractor factory.

The reality was terribly different. The German forces in Stalingrad suffered about 60,000 casualties in December and another 100,000 in January. On 22 January, Gumrak – the last airfield – was overrun, and a last Heinkel He-111 took 19 wounded soldiers to safety, although its elevator was riddled by Russian ground-fire as it took off. The Luftwaffe had evacuated 34,000 wounded during the siege, but that left tens of thousands of men to wait for death in conditions of indescribable horror. In the final days of Stalingrad, 6th Army signalled Army Group Don that it had so little food left, rations were no longer to be given to the wounded. The tiny quantities of sustenance available went only to the surviving fighters, who continued to resist until the end, inflicting heavy losses on their attackers and even delivering counter-attacks until 25 January.

Paulus capitulated on 30 January. The 6th Army had been split in two by the final Russian attacks, and Strecker's 11th Corps, holding the tractor factory and Barrikady ordnance works, held out until 1 February. Its commander made one last radio call before surrendering. A party from Strecker's headquarters broke out of the city as it fell, as did elements of the 71st Infantry Division and an unknown number of little groups. A few were observed by German aircraft, but were all swallowed up on the vast frozen steppe, never to be seen again. German aircraft flying over the city on 2 February could see no sign of movement among the ruins.

CHAPTER SIX

★

THE CORRELATION
OF FORCES

'This war will be won by industrial production.'

STALIN

In early February 1943 the survivors of the 6th Army crossed the Volga at last, but as prisoners, not conquerors. An estimated 91,000 men were still alive when Paulus surrendered, but the majority were extremely ill. Paulus himself had dysentery, which helps explain his lassitude in the final weeks. Red Army intelligence had grossly underestimated the size of the force trapped in the pocket, and the Russians were astonished at the sheer number of men they had captured. They housed them in prisoner-of-war camps at Beketovka and Krassno-Armiensk, which were swept by epidemics. As many as half the captives died from typhus, spotted fever and dysentery in the next few months – as did a number of Red Army medical staff trying to stop the spread of disease. Fewer than 6,000 men from the 6th Army would survive to return to Germany.

Hitler recognized that the Stalingrad disaster threatened the very foundations of his regime. He insisted that Paulus must fight on, and promoted him to colonel-general, then to field marshal. He refused permission for the 6th Army to surrender. As late as Christmas, there were plans to fly in fresh battalions of infantry in the hope the army could hold out until the spring. These plans were abandoned when the Soviet offensive in late December thrust the front line so much further west. After the last pockets of resistance had been overrun, Hitler summoned the Nazi Gauleiters to Berlin, to prepare them for the news of the fall of Stalingrad. Goebbels' propaganda machine went into overdrive. He had already been reduced to faking a Christmas broadcast from the 6th Army. The radio message 'from 6th Army on the Volga' was recorded in Germany. His ministry also intercepted the last letters from Stalingrad, rightly fearing they would expose the sickening realities of *Festung* Stalingrad. Three days' mourning were declared and the radio stations played '*Götterdämmerung*' and the soldiers' lament '*Ich hatt' ein' Kamaraden*'.

The beginning of 1943 is a convenient moment to pause the narrative and examine how the German and Soviet forces compared in terms of equipment, tactics, operational methods and morale, and the economic base which sustained them – what Marxist military theorists call 'the correlation of forces'. German accounts of the Eastern Front have left us with an enduring image. Hordes of Russians bludgeon their way west, relying on sheer weight of numbers to overwhelm the Wehrmacht. There is considerable truth in this picture, but it is by no means the whole story.

In sheer quantities of manpower, the Red Army outnumbered the invaders by a good margin in 1941. However, it lost so heavily in the first five months of the war – the Germans took more than three million prisoners by December 1941 – that even its rapid mobilization barely kept pace with the losses. During 1942 the Red Army expanded at an incredible rate, but its casualties in the first half of that year were catastrophic. From mid-1942 it began to develop a significant numerical advantage, one that escalated enormously in late 1943 as Germany deployed more men in the west to resist the Allied liberation of France. Then the great Soviet summer offensive of 1944 tore the heart out of the Ostheer.

German casualties in Russia were far higher than anticipated from the early days of the invasion. The Ostheer expended German manpower faster than it could be replenished by the Wehrmacht's replacement system, even while winning its famous victories in 1941. The reserve pool was depleted so quickly that emergency measures had to be instituted. Exempt occupations were redefined, which released enough men for another five divisions; some internal security units were transferred from Germany to the front line, and one battalion was detached from each of the 23 divisions still in western

Europe at the end of 1941. Rather than reinforce the exhausted units on the front line, the army created new formations, so although the total army strength in Russia increased in terms of numbers of divisions, overall manpower totals declined. In 1941 there were 3.2 million troops in 136 divisions; in 1942 there were 2.7 million men in 179 divisions. By early 1942 the Germans had lost a million men in Russia. It was only by calling up the next classes of conscripts early, substituting slave labourers for German farm workers and other expedients – as well as demanding more divisions from Germany's allies – that the Ostheer found sufficient strength for the 1942 offensive. Hitler's lunge to the Caucasus was not only a gamble; he mortgaged the future to pay for it.

Many German divisions lost more than their authorized strength on the Russian front, just as they had on the Western Front in the First World War. The 18th Panzer Division, for example, had a 100 per cent turnover in enlisted men and 173 per cent in officers between June 1941 and the division's disbandment in October 1943. The famous 'Großdeutschland' Division suffered 100 per cent casualties between summer 1942 and its retreat to the Dnepr in September 1944 and lost twice its authorized number of officers in the process.[1] The division suffered even heavier losses, nearly 17,000, in the first four months of 1945. Junior officers in the German Army suffered disproportionate casualties from 1941 onwards; so bad that an infantry subaltern's chances of returning home in one piece from the Russian front compared unfavourably with those of a U-boat crewman or a fighter pilot. Command of companies frequently devolved on non-commissioned officers. Even the NCOs, the backbone of the German Army, were disappearing much faster than they could be replaced. The speed with which units were eaten up in battle on the Russian front has led to claims that the German infantry's morale was sustained more by Nazi fanaticism and fear of the Russians than by loyalty to their comrades.[2] However, both the Allied armies and the Germans suffered even higher rates of attrition in Normandy. Casualties in Russia were severe because they took place over a prolonged period, but there is no reason to suppose that the sources of combat motivation were any different for the Ostheer than for their comrades fighting in North Africa, Italy or France.

Total German Strength on All Fronts (Millions)

Date	Total	Army	SS	Luftwaffe	Navy
1941	7.3	5.2	0.16	1.5	0.4
1942	6.7	5.75	0.19	0.19	0.57
1943	9.48	6.55	0.45	1.7	0.78
1944	9.42	6.51	0.6	1.5	0.81
1945	7.83	5.3	0.83	1.0	0.7

German Army, Air Force and Navy Casualties 1939–45 (Millions)[3]

Killed in action	1.8
Killed through other causes	0.19
Wounded	4.3
Missing in action	1.9
Total	8.19

The USSR had more than twice as many men of military age as Germany, although nearly a third of the total Soviet population found itself behind enemy lines by the end of 1941. Mobilization was brutally quick: new divisions were assembled and pushed into the front line in a matter of months. Rifle battalions were filled out with older men, so teenagers served alongside men in their thirties and forties. As the Red Army began to reconquer Soviet territory, all available men were swept into the front-line units as replacements – creating the paradox that in 1944–45, long-serving units were sometimes full of very inexperienced soldiers.

The Red Army could not have managed without the crucial assistance of Soviet women, even if this was deliberately played down after 1945. Two million female personnel served in the armed forces. They provided most of the medical staff, from base hospitals to front-line infantry companies, three-quarters of the gunners in anti-aircraft batteries defending the cities, and many radio operators, including those of the partisan and special forces raiding teams. Some even served as tank crew and snipers. The presence of women in the front-line units inevitably led to sexual relationships, with varying degrees of consent. Many an officer had a female radio operator/medic/typist to share his bed. Wives left at home were often right to fear the worst. It was all theoretically against regulations, but life was short and pleasures all-too-fleeting. Marshal Rokossovsky had a daughter by his mistress, Lieutenant Galina Talanova, a medical officer he met when he commanded the 16th Army in late 1941. She stayed with him throughout the war, and he remained in contact even after he returned to his wife and other children in Moscow in 1945.

Soviet Army Front Line Strength 1941–45 (Millions)

Jun 1941	Nov 1941	Dec 1941	Nov 1942	Jan 1944	Jun 1944	Jan 1945
4.7	2.3	4.2	6.1	6.1	6.5	6.0

Soviet Army Losses 1941–45 (Millions)

Killed in action	6.8
Died in German captivity	2.7
Wounded	15
Sick	3
Total	27.5

The battle of the factory floor

The Red Army's greatest quantitative advantage lay in its vastly superior numbers of tanks, aircraft and (above all) artillery. This was not because the USSR enjoyed greater economic resources, but because its war economy was far better managed than Germany's. Despite conquering so much of Europe, the Nazi regime signally failed to exploit this industrial windfall for military production. In 1943 Germany produced about four times as much steel and three times as much coal as the USSR – after all, in 1941 it had conquered the Donbas where more than half of Russian coal was mined. Nevertheless, the Russians built 33 per cent more tanks, 50 per cent more aircraft and vastly more heavy artillery pieces. The ratio tilted sharply in favour of the Soviets during 1943–44, despite the managerial genius of 36-year-old Albert Speer, who trebled German war production in three years.

Germany's most serious economic weakness was its lack of oil resources. As early as 1941 the Luftwaffe was using its reserve fuel stocks to sustain current operations, but the fuel shortages that were to dog both army and air force towards the end of the war played little part in the critical campaigns of 1942–43.

Like an army, an industrial workforce fights on its stomach. German agriculture was sustained by the use of slaves, predominantly Polish and Russian/Ukranian teenagers and children. On Soviet farms, the ceaseless manpower demands of the front and the factories left women, children and the elderly to wrest a living from the unforgiving climate. Even a high proportion of the draught animals were taken by the army, so women had to haul the ploughs themselves. Their unsung efforts meant Russia had just about enough to eat. The daily ration for industrial and rural workers in the USSR was a quarter of the German ration, and a fifth of the British.[4]

Germany had been preparing for war throughout the 1930s, and the German victories in 1940 brought the industrial resources of most of western Europe under their control. By the time Hitler attacked Russia, half the German industrial workforce was working on military orders – a greater devotion to military production than that achieved by the USA in the Second World War. By every indicator of economic strength, Germany should have outproduced its opponents, enabling the Wehrmacht to face not just the Red Army but the western Allies' invasion of France with every confidence. Had German industry been as well organized as the German Army, the Allies would not have enjoyed such crushing superiority by 1944. Yet until 1943, even the much smaller British economy was outbuilding Germany in aircraft and warships, and closely matching its production of guns and tanks. By squandering its economic advantages in the first half of the war, the Nazi regime lost the battle on the factory floor. Competing and overlapping bureaucracies, inconsistent procurement policies and not a little corruption among the Nazi elite deprived German soldiers of the weapons and equipment they so desperately needed.

German and Soviet Production Figures (Millions of Tons)

	1941	1942	1943	1944	1945
Coal					
Germany	246	258	269	281	–
USSR	151	75	93	121	149
Steel					
Germany	31	32	35	35	–
USSR	18	8	10	12	12
Oil					
Germany	6	7	–	–	–
USSR	33	22	18	18	19

The war in the air

Germany used air power to devastating effect against Poland in 1939, and against Britain and France in May 1940. Indeed, it was only in the air that Germany had any superiority; in numbers of men, tanks and guns it was outnumbered. All the more astonishing then that German aircraft production remained virtually static between the outbreak of war and 1941. Throughout the Battle of Britain, the British built more aircraft than the Germans. German bureaucrats displayed no sense of urgency once the French aircraft industry fell into German hands. Capable of manufacturing 5,000 aircraft per year, even using its relatively labour-intensive methods, French factories produced a mere 2,500 aircraft for Germany in four years of occupation – equivalent to just 10 per cent of its potential output. The post-war reputation of German efficiency is confounded by the incompetence with which

Nazi agencies managed their conquered territories. A giant slice of Soviet industry was captured by the Germans, but achieved only 10 per cent of its pre-1941 productivity under German rule. Agricultural yields in German-occupied Russia were so low – just 50 per cent of pre-1941 levels – that not enough food was produced to feed both the population and the German Army. So the civilians starved. For all Hitler's talk of exploiting the east, Germany received more from Russia during the period of the Nazi–Soviet Pact than it did after seizing most of European Russia. At its greatest extent, German-occupied Russia comprised about 850,000 square miles and 65 million souls, yet occupied France yielded seven times as much in terms of food and minerals.

Meanwhile, the Soviet aircraft industry was stepping up production. French manufacturer Louis Breguet had visited the Soviet factories in 1936, noting that 'With ten times as many personnel employed as the French, the Soviet industry is producing 20 times as many aircraft.' And the Germans knew it – a delegation of Luftwaffe officers was taken around Russian factories in April 1941. Their report, according to Field Marshal Milch, was suppressed by Göring.

Aircraft Production 1939–45 (Thousands)[5]

	1939	1940	1941	1942	1943	1944	1945
Germany	8	10	12	15	25	40	7
USSR	10	11	16	25	35	40	21
Britain	8	15	20	24	26	26	12
USA	6	13	26	48	86	96	50

Totals by Type for the Luftwaffe

Messerschmitt Bf-109	33,000
Focke-Wulf Fw 190	6,600
Heinkel He-111	7,300
Junkers Ju-88	14,700
Junkers Ju-188	1,100
Dornier Do-17/217	3,000
Heinkel He-177	1,100

The production figures conceal a second weakness of the German air arm. Under the blasé incompetence of Hermann Göring, the Luftwaffe failed to develop a new generation of aircraft to replace the 1930s designs with which it won its early triumphs. Great time and effort were expended on disastrous projects like the Messerschmitt Me-210 twin-engine fighter, several manufacturers amassing fortunes but not actually delivering any new aircraft. Although some designs like the Junkers Ju-88 twin-engine bomber proved remarkably versatile, incremental improvements in veteran machines like the Messerschmitt Bf-109 were not enough to match the completely new fighters of the Allied air forces.[6] Corruption, ineptitude and the confusion of rival agencies competing for Hitler's favour left German pilots flying inferior aircraft, and the German Army without air cover.

Once the Allied heavy bomber offensive against Germany gathered pace in 1943, with the first daylight raids by the Americans supplementing RAF Bomber Command's nocturnal onslaught, German production priorities changed. German bomber production dwindled as every effort was made to build more fighters. Anti-aircraft batteries were concentrated around Germany's industrial cities, tens of thousands of guns and millions of rounds of ammunition that would otherwise have been on the front lines.[7] The current Russian school history of the Second World War presents the western Allies' strategic bombing campaign as a key factor in reducing German strength on the Eastern Front. The threat of an invasion of France drew most German bombers to the west at the end of the 1943, and to Italy where further amphibious assaults tempted Hitler to counter-attack.

German Operational Bombers 1943–45[8]

	Oct 43	Dec 43	Feb 44	Jun 44	Oct 44	Dec 44
Norway	16	15	15	17	–	73
E. Front	358	238	138	326	97	79
W. Europe	459	695	429	184	123	7
Italy	285	–	189	–	–	–

The Luftwaffe did make a few raids on Soviet industrial targets in 1943, but this was a local initiative by Luftflotte 6. A series of night attacks were made in June 1943 against the tank and engine plants at Gorky, the synthetic rubber factory at Yaroslavl and several petrol refineries. To put these operations into context, a total of 168 Heinkel He-111s took off to attack Gorky on 3 June 1943: 149 aircraft attacked and dropped 234 tons of bombs. Eight days later RAF Bomber Command attacked Düsseldorf with 693 bombers, delivering 1,968 tons of bombs in 45 minutes.

Senior Luftwaffe officers discussed transferring most of their bomber strength to strategic missions on the Eastern Front, but their deliberations became irrelevant as the front line was shunted westwards that summer, leaving most Russian industrial centres beyond the range of German bombers. In any case, the Luftwaffe was being overwhelmed by the army's incessant demands for intervention on the front line. The German Army had come to depend on tactical air power as a substitute for heavy artillery, and as a primary element in its anti-tank defences. The escalating requirement for close air support missions that had been such a marked feature of the 1941 Blitzkrieg had never stabilized. As one veteran Luftwaffe commander put it, 'Even during quiet spells, the army command insisted on the constant commitment of air power against enemy targets within the battle areas in order to conceal their own weaknesses in point of numbers and weapons.'[9]

As ground attack became the Luftwaffe's primary mission, aircraft and weapons were modified accordingly. It was not just the German Army that experimented with new equipment during the battle of Kursk. The Luftwaffe introduced the Henschel Hs-129 twin-engine anti-tank aircraft, armed with 30mm guns. The Junkers Ju-87 Stuka dive-bomber also sprouted cannon. A 37mm gun pod was added under each wing to create a formidable 'tank buster', in which Hitler's favourite airman, Colonel Rüdel, would destroy more than 500 tanks. Attempts were even made to fit a Pak 40 75mm anti-tank gun to a Ju-88.

Although these flying anti-tank guns looked spectacular, the standard aerial anti-tank weapon was the SD-4-H1, a 9lb bomblet, of which 78 were carried inside a 1,100lb bomb case. The Germans had learned that 550lb or heavier bombs needed to score a direct hit to knock out a tank. This was difficult to achieve, but a 'shotgun' blast of hollow-charge bomblets, each powerful enough to blow through the thin top armour, produced much better results. They were delivered primarily by Ju-87 Stukas, provided the skies were clear; if the cloud base was under 1,500 feet, the Stukas could not attack: they needed that minimum altitude to pull out of their vertical dive.

In 1943 the Luftwaffe had a total strength of 6,000 aircraft, of which about half were on the Russian front. Its intervention on the battlefield was enormously important, sometimes providing relatively minor operations with extremely powerful support, as with the attack on the Soviet bridgehead south of Novorossisk in April. This involved just three German divisions, but their objective was precision-bombed by no fewer than 511 Ju-87 Stukas on 17 April and by 296 Stukas two days later. Air support was vital at the battle of Kursk, and even in the ensuing defensive battles that lasted into 1944, the Luftwaffe succeeded in making 1,000 sorties a day above critical sectors of the front.

Soviet factories built staggering numbers of aircraft and the Red Air Force lost them in equally dizzying amounts. Production figures for the war by type were:

Fighters and Fighter Bombers

Yak 1	8,700
Yak 7	6,400
Yak 9	14,600
Yak 3	4,100
La-5	9,900
La-7	5,800

Bombers

Pe-2	10,600
Il-2	36,000
Il-4	6,800
Pe-8	93

The Pe-8 was Russia's four-engined heavy bomber. Like the Luftwaffe, the Red Air Force abandoned any thought of strategic bombing, and the fact that it built so many Il-2 ground attack planes shows where priorities lay. Soviet losses were on a scale unmatched by any other wartime air force:

	1941	1942	1943	1944	1945
Total strength	29,900	33,000	55,000	68,100	58,300
Combat losses	10,300	7,800	11,200	9,700	4,100
Non combat losses	7,600	4,300	11,300	15,100	6,900

The proportion of non-combat losses is worth noting. The Red Air Force lost nearly 25 per cent of its total strength in accidents in 1941. Non-combat losses still accounted for 20 per cent two years later in 1943, slightly more than it lost in action. In 1944 61 per cent of the 12,700 Russian fighters lost were as a result of accident, not combat, rising to 62 per cent in 1945, in both cases a far greater number than were lost in battle. Manufacturing standards and pilot training were sacrificed in the determination to get as many aircraft into the sky as possible.

British and American aid was also important in the air. The following totals of aircraft were supplied for the war:

Aircraft Supplied

Supermarine Spitfire	2,800
Hawker Hurricane	1,300
Bell Airacobra	4,700
Curtiss P-40	2,100
A20 Boston	3,000
B-25 Mitchell	900

The German Panzer formations had achieved their great victory of 1940 by concentrating almost their entire strength on a narrow front in northern France. Divided among three army groups for the invasion of Russia, and with subsequent diversions of strength to North Africa, Italy and France, Germany's armoured forces would never achieve such a concentration of strength again. Between July 1942 and March 1943, the Ostheer's monthly strength returns show an average of about 2,500 tanks in Russia, of which some 1,500 were operational at any one time. During the same period, a total of 2,426 replacement tanks were shipped from Germany, 1,031 of them in the first three months of 1943 when the SS Panzer Corps was transferred from France for the Kharkov battle (see Chapter Seven).

German industry produced just enough tanks to replace the losses in Russia, but the Soviet tank forces increased rapidly as the relocated tank factories worked around the clock. In January 1943 German tank strength in the east peaked at 2,803[10] of which 1,475 were operational. The Germans also had 500 *Sturmgeschütz* assault guns. They faced a total of 8,500 Russian tanks and assault guns in five 'tank armies', backed by another 400 in *Stavka* reserve, and 4,300 in training commands and non-operational formations.[11] Assault guns and tank destroyers accounted for about a third of German armoured vehicle production from 1941 to 1945, but only about a sixth of Russian production.

Labouring under the most arduous conditions, the Soviet industrial workforce – half of which was female by 1942 – forged a mighty weapon that would strike the fatal blow against Nazi Germany: the tank armies. In the critical year of 1943, during which the Russian Army still faced the overwhelming majority of the German forces, the Russians lost four tanks for every one German tank destroyed, but the factories more than made up for those losses.

When Hitler invaded Russia the German Army's main battle tank was the Panzer III of which 5,500 were built until production ceased in 1943. A total of 6,800 Panzer IVs were built, and a further 6,000 Panzer V Panthers. These formed the main body of the Panzer divisions, although the 1,400 Panzer VI Tigers had an impact out of proportion to their numbers.

Total German Tank Strength (All Fronts) 1943–45[12]

	Jan 43	Jul 43	Jan 44	Jul 44	Jan 45
PzII	1,000	200	400	450	n/a
PzIII	2,950	1,300	900	800	510
PzIV	1,100	1,400	1,700	2,400	1,800
PzV Panther	0	450	1,200	2,250	2,150
PzVI Tiger	60	260	410	670	280
PzVI Tiger II	0	0	0	60	190

German Tank Losses (All Fronts)

	1943	1944
PzIII	2,633	220
PzIV	2,396	3,103
PzV Panther	493	2,803
PzVI Tiger I	291	788

Total Armoured Vehicle Production

	1940	1941	1942	1943	1944	1945
Soviet	2,794	6,590	24,446	24,089	28,963	15,419
German	2,200	5,200	9,200	17,300	22,100	4,400

Soviet production after 1941 concentrated on just four types of armoured vehicle: the KV-1 heavy tank, the T-34 medium tank and the T-60 and T-70 light tanks. The latter were accepted as an unsatisfactory expedient, used to fill out the tank battalions in 1942–43. In that period most tank battalions used a mixture of T-34s and T-60s, with the light tanks making up a third of the unit's total strength. T-34 production figures dwarfed those of any other wartime tank except the American M4 Sherman. They were:

Total T-34 Production

1942	12,600
1943	15,700
1944	3,700

From 1944 production switched to the T-34/85, of which 11,000 were completed in that year, with another 18,300 in 1945. Production totals for the light tanks were 4,500 T-60s in 1943; 4,900 T-70s in 1944 and 3,300 in 1945, mostly completed as SU-76 assault guns. Russian factories built 19,000 self-propelled guns from 1942 to 1945. An additional 1,200 or so self-propelled guns were created by fitting 76mm guns onto captured German tank chassis, mainly Panzer IIIs and StuG IIIs.

If the enormous disparity between Soviet and German production was bad enough in 1942 (a ratio of more than 2.5:1), it is important to note that the situation never really improved. The figures cited above – and usually given as 'tank' production in most reference books – actually include all manner of self-propelled guns, ammunition carriers, self-propelled anti-aircraft guns and other specialist vehicles. The totals for tank, self-propelled gun and assault gun production alone are far lower:

German Late-war Tank Production[13]

1943	1944	1945
11,667	13,109	1,836

The Panzer divisions were hopelessly outnumbered. Nevertheless, they and the German anti-tank gun batteries exacted a very high price, destroying nearly 2,000 Soviet tanks per month in the first half of the war, and more than 1,000 a month in 1944.

Russian Tank Losses

1941	1943	1944
22,600	22,400	16,900

Of these, about 66 per cent were destroyed in action: the rest were lost to mechanical breakdown. Soviet figures reveal that of tanks knocked out in battle, 10 per cent could be repaired by the unit, 15 per cent could be repaired at Russian factories, and

75 per cent were beyond repair, generally with their crews killed or wounded.

A tank – and in most cases its crew – had a life expectancy of about six months between leaving the factory and destruction in battle. German memoirs often describe the tactical ineptitude of Russian tank units, mostly traceable to hasty training and inexperience. Russian tanks tended to move slowly and cautiously. Drivers preferred to travel along the crests of hills, where they were easily spotted and knocked out, rather than using a covered approach. The T-34 had a significant speed advantage over almost all enemy main battle tanks, but Russian crews rarely exploited this, and did not move between firing positions fast enough. Slow, ponderous formations of T-34s often suffered grievous losses, blundering into ambushes or, by poor choice of approach, exposing themselves to long-range fire by 88mm guns that could penetrate their armour from a mile or more.

The Russians subordinated almost every aspect of weapons design to the dictates of mass production. They standardized wherever possible, and concentrated on two main types of tank (the T-34 and KV-1), a handful of artillery pieces, one principal rifle and one primary sub-machine-gun. The latter typifies the Soviet approach: the PPSh-41 looks ugly and feels poorly balanced when you pick it up, and its accuracy is unexceptional. On the other hand, the inside of its barrel is beautifully chromed so it is not corroded by mercury-primed ammunition that will function at -50°C. It is strong enough to batter down doors or enemy soldiers without damaging the weapon, and it keeps firing in snow, sand, grit or mud. As for accuracy, as one German veteran commented, in close-quarter battle 'one should shoot first and aim later'.

The T-34 tank was crudely finished too; its turrets were rough-cast. It had wide tracks to reduce their ground pressure and give better grip on snow or muddy surfaces. Its cross-country performance was superior to the Panzer III or IV. There was no turret floor, and the loader's life was a hazardous one as he (or she) scrambled around for ammunition, ducking to avoid the breech of the 76mm gun. In this respect, the T-34 is arguably more of an assault gun than a main battle tank, and its armour protection, while superior to that of the German Panzer III, was soon trumped by the next generation of German anti-tank weapons. Its tracks were not rubber-clad: this, and its unmuffled diesel, made it one of the loudest tanks ever to rumble into action − in its own way a formidable psychological weapon, like the Stuka dive-bomber's siren. It had one disadvantage, in that the engine needed about 30 minutes to warm up, giving audible warning to the Germans that the T-34 was on its way. It also had a strange feature, possibly installed to satisfy some ideologue's belief in the superiority of Communist Man on the offensive: the T-34's gas pedal is set so that the driver puts his foot to the floor to stop, and eases up the pedal to accelerate. If the driver is incapacitated and lets his foot off the pedal while the machine is in gear, the tank trundles off at top speed − hence the numerous reports of T-34s crashing into each other, and sometimes their opponents. The occasional collision with a German tank might have been a suicide-ramming of the sort claimed by Soviet propagandists, but most were the result of installing one of the most important parts of any vehicle backwards.

Although improved by the substitution of an 85mm gun for its 76mm weapon, the T-34/85 was still greatly inferior to the famous German Panzer V, or Panther. Introduced in 1943, the Panther had a superb ballistic shape, a high-velocity 75mm gun, a powerful engine and, by 1945, even infrared sights. The first examples were flung into battle at Kursk, before troop trials could be conducted, and the Panther proved superior in tank-on-tank engagements, knocking out T-34s at more than 3,000 yards. Unfortunately, fuel pump failures and motor breakdowns − there had not been time to run the engines in − put about a third of them out of action after just a few days' fighting. The Panther was a magnificent design, with frontal armour superior to that of the Tiger, and sufficient to stop even the

122mm round fired by the IS-2. Its Maybach HL 230 engine, developing 700 horse-power, gave it greater mobility than the Panzer IV, and it cost half as much as a Tiger tank. The Panther became the main battle tank of the German Army in 1944–45, with nearly 6,000 produced by the end of the war. However, the production rate of a few hundred per month was dwarfed by the output of the Russian factories: T-34s were coming out of Tankograd (Chelyabinsk) at a rate of nearly 2,000 a month.

In April and May 1944, production of the famous Panzer VI, the Tiger tank, peaked at 100 vehicles per month. With its 88mm gun, thick armour, and wide tracks for good cross-country performance, the Tiger trumped any other tank on the battlefield, but it had a desperately short range, which led some infantrymen to prefer to be supported by the more common *Sturmgeschütz*, which did not disappear to refuel just when it was needed most. The Tiger was also too heavy for German Army bridging equipment and permanent bridges tended to collapse under its weight, further reducing its operational effectiveness. Just 1,354 were manufactured in total, which represents less than 5 per cent of German tank output in the war. It was the tendency of Russian (and British and American) troops to identify every Axis tank they saw as a Tiger that helped build the legend. It was big, it looked the part, and its 88mm gun could penetrate the frontal armour of a T-34 or a Sherman at up to a mile.

To compensate for its lack of armour, the German Army improvised an incredible variety of tank destroyers, which were issued to the anti-tank battalions of Panzer and Panzergrenadier divisions. Obsolete French and Czech tanks formed the basis for many conversions. The turret was removed and a more powerful anti-tank gun substituted in an open mounting with limited traverse. German tank chassis were used too, some to create formidable tank killers with enclosed fighting compartments, low silhouettes and powerful guns. Production totals of the main types were as follows:

Type	Total
Panzerjäger I (47mm gun on Panzer I chassis)	132
Marder II (75mm gun on Panzer II)	1,217
Marder III (75mm gun on Skoda THNP-S/Panzer 38(t))	799
Hetzer (full conversion of Panzer 38(t) with enclosed fighting compartment)	2,500
Nashorn (88mm gun on Panzer IV chassis in open compartment)	473
Panzerjäger Tiger (P) Elefant (88mm Pak 43 on Porsche Tiger chassis)	90
JagdPanzer IV (75mm gun on Panzer IV chassis in enclosed compartment)	1,000
Jagdpanther (88mm gun on Panther chassis in enclosed compartment)	382
Jagdtiger (128mm gun on Tiger II chassis)	77

The Germans also developed a bewildering variety of self-propelled guns, mounting field guns and howitzers on just about every type of tracked vehicle they had captured from the French in 1940. The introduction of so many types of vehicle, all in small quantities, made their logistic difficulties even worse, but it was a case of improvise or die. Some were used only for indirect fire, but others, like the *Brummbär*, were designed for direct support of the infantry. Production totals for the main types were as follows:

Type	Total
Schwere Infanterie Geschütz 33 (150mm howitzer on Panzer I chassis)	370
Wespe (105mm howitzer on Panzer II chassis)	700
Hummel (150mm howitzer on Panzer IV chassis)	750
Brummbär (150mm howitzer on Panzer IV in enclosed compartment)	313
Sturmtiger (380mm rocket projector on Tiger I chassis)	10

Often used in a similar role, and as a substitute tank, the Germans also came to rely on the *Sturmgeschütz* assault gun. Almost as many of these were built as all the other conversions combined. Pre–war plans called for each infantry division to receive a six–gun battery of assault guns which mounted a short 75mm gun on the hull of a Panzer III, but there were only three or four such batteries ready for the 1940 campaign. By 1941 there were eight 28-gun battalions and a number of independent nine-gun batteries in service. A total of 642 *Sturmgeschütz* IIIs (with 75mm L/24) built between 1940 and 1942 were still in service in July 1942 when production switched to a new version with the 75mm L/48, offering much greater anti-tank capability. The short-barrelled StuG III disappeared during 1943, but assault gun battalions with the 75mm L/48 were widely employed, one or two being attached at corps level. Favoured divisions – especially the SS Panzer and Panzergrenadier formations – had integral *Sturmgeschütz* battalions. Production totals were as follows:

Type	Dates	Total
StuG III (75mm L/24)	1940–42	822
StuG III (75mm L/48)	1942	699
StuG III (75mm L/48)	1943–44	3,000
StuG IV (105mm L/28)	1943	300
StuG IV (105mm L/28)	1944	900

In 1943 Germany built 2,663 StuG IIIs and they seemed to have lasted longer at the front. Between September 1943 and May 1944 the Ostheer had more operational StuGs than tanks: average tank strength was 433 vehicles, and average assault gun strength was 661. Why the *Sturmgeschütz* provided so high a proportion of the armoured forces is not clear, but it was more mechanically reliable, having no turret to go wrong, and German doctrine called for the StuGs to operate only with close infantry support.

The Russians appreciated the value of self-propelled anti-tank guns too, introducing three dual-purpose assault gun/tank destroyer vehicles in the summer of 1942. The SU-76 combined a 76mm gun in an open mounting on a T-60 or T-70 light tank chassis, while the

SU-122 was a 122mm howitzer on a T-34 chassis. The self-propelled gun regiments created late that year had four four-gun batteries of SU-76s and two batteries of SU-122s, also with four guns each. In early 1943 the regiments were reorganized and consisted of either 21 Su-76s or 16 SU-122s. The first SU-152 (152mm guns on a KV-1 chassis) regiment was ready for the battle of Kursk that July. Some SU-122s carried 122mm guns rather than howitzers. The SU-85 and SU-100 carried 85mm and 100mm anti-tank guns respectively and were intended to counter the new German heavy tanks. Production totals were as follows:

Type	Total
SU-76	14,000
SU-85/100/122	4,000
SU-122/152	5,000

By mid-1944 each Russian tank and mechanized corps had one light, one medium and one heavy self-propelled gun regiment, and there were many independent SP gun regiments, 241 of them by 1945. Light regiments had five batteries, each of four SU-76s; medium regiments had four batteries, each of four SU-85/100/122s; and heavy regiments had five batteries, each of two SU-122/152s.

Britain provided the USSR with military aid, at a fearful cost in sailors' lives. The relief effort began on 1 August 1941 when HMS *Abdiel* delivered mines to the Soviet Northern Fleet. The Royal Navy escorted convoys of Allied merchant ships through the Norwegian and Barents seas to Murmansk and Archangel. The arrival of German surface units, from destroyers to heavy units like *Admiral Scheer*, *Scharnhorst* and eventually *Bismarck*'s sister ship *Tirpitz*, as well as a substantial number of U-boats, led to a new naval war in the world's most dangerous waters. These convoy battles are a story in themselves.[14] Some British leaders like Field Marshal Lord Alanbrooke doubted their value, believing the sacrifice of men and matériel was unjustified from

Britain's point of view. It was certainly unappreciated by the Communist regime at the time. Soviet leaders took their cue from Stalin and kept up a steady stream of ungrateful invective. They criticized the rate of delivery, which reached 4,000 tanks in 1942 from Britain and America, equivalent to 16 per cent of Soviet production for that year. The Russians affected not to understand the fearsome difficulties of fighting a convoy through the Arctic in the teeth of Luftwaffe air attack, U-boat assaults and occasional sorties by German battleships. Obstructionism and official indifference in the Arctic ports was accompanied by complete paranoia about contacts between British seamen and Russian civilians. Liaisons of any sort were discouraged, and when love did flourish in this very cold climate, the Russian government's response was invariably to arrest the women involved.

Between 1941 and 1945 Britain and America supplied the following totals of weapons and equipment. Three-quarters of British aid was shipped across the Arctic Ocean, whereas most US aid was dispatched via Iran or the Pacific. Britain supplied 5,218 tanks,[15] 7,411 aircraft, 4,932 anti-tank guns, 473 million rounds of ammunition, 4,338 radio sets, 1,803 radar sets, ten destroyers and one battleship. The USA supplied 7,537 tanks, 14,795 aircraft, 51,503 jeeps, 375,883 trucks, 1,981 railroad locomotives, 11,155 railroad wagons, 2.6 million tons of gasoline, 3.7 million tyres, and 345,735 tons of high explosive. The latter may have been the most important, filling the millions of shells that the formidable Red artillery used to pound German defensive positions to oblivion during 1943–45.

Stalin and his commanders knew they were being ungenerous. Perhaps it stuck in the throat to accept aid from the very Allied powers (and in the person of Winston Churchill, the very same leader) that had landed military forces at the same ports – Murmansk and Vladivostock – in 1919 to crush the Bolsheviks in the Russian Civil War. The great tank armies with which the Red Army broke the back of the Wehrmacht in 1944 depended on American trucks to carry their supplies of fuel and ammunition. Their artillery and supporting weapons, as well as accompanying infantry, also relied on US trucks for their mobility. By 1944 between two-thirds and three-quarters of the Red Army truck fleet was made in the USA.

Allied tanks were quickly introduced to Russian armoured units. The first British tanks were in action as early as January 1942. However, since half the Allied tanks supplied to the Red Army arrived in 1944–45, the critical battles of 1942–43 were fought almost entirely with Soviet vehicles. Those tanks that did arrive were distributed widely: in the summer of 1943, a quarter of all Russian tank brigades had some Allied tanks on their strength. British tanks had narrow tracks, unsuitable for snow or mud, but were prized for their excellent engines, which outlasted those of Soviet tanks, making them ideal for training. Soviet tanks were not built to last; they were usually destroyed in battle before their engines gave out. However, low standards of production and maintenance led to heavy losses from mechanical breakdown, especially during 1941–42.

For the sake of simplicity, the Soviets asked the British to supply only Valentine tanks from 1942, and the production line was kept open solely for the Red Army – all 1,388 Valentines built in Canada were shipped to Russia. The total number of British tanks supplied to the Red Army was thus 3,900 Valentines, 1,100 Matildas and 300 Churchills. American tanks were disliked by Russian tank crews because of their petrol engines and horrific tendency to catch fire and incinerate the crew.[16] Just as British tank crew dubbed the American M4s the 'Ronson' – after the cigarette lighter advertised to 'light every time' – so Russians christened the M3 Lee tank the 'coffin for seven comrades'. America supplied 1,400 M3 Lees and 4,100 M4 Shermans, fitting the latter with diesel engines at the Russians' insistence, since diesel fuel does not explode like petrol.

The addition of several hundred thousand American trucks gave the Red Army's armoured forces new strategic mobility. At the same time, the Wehrmacht found itself relying more and more on draught animals. It may be one of the most prosaic and unglamorous determinants of the conflict, but one of Germany's critical weaknesses during the Second World War was its inability to make as many trucks as its enemies. Although production increased steeply during the war, it did not match that of British factories. In its first year of war, the United States built 620,000 trucks compared to Germany's 58,000: a 10:1 advantage that would prove General Sherman's point about the folly of declaring war on a nation of mechanics.

As time went on, Germany's tanks, trucks and self-propelled guns were concentrated in a few elite units which spearheaded every offensive or rushed to block each Soviet attack. Meanwhile, the rest of the German Army underwent a demoralizing process of 'de-modernization', fighting an increasingly well-equipped enemy with much the same weapons as their fathers had on the Western Front between 1914 and 1918. German infantry divisions had more automatic weapons than their First World War equivalents, but fewer field guns. From 1942 many divisions were reorganized with six battalions rather than nine, but although their firepower was augmented with extra machine-guns and mortars, especially captured Russian 120mm weapons, Germany was unable to substitute technology for manpower. German artillery relied on experienced forward observers and well-trained crews to deliver 'time-on-target' concentrations of fire that partially compensated for their numerical inferiority. Against comparatively inexperienced Soviet artillery units, this worked well, certainly until mid-1944, but in time the Russians learned their profession. Meanwhile Germany failed to solve its production problems and German tactical air power had become no more than a memory.

Even the Panzer divisions were not immune to this process, and their experience was arguably the more traumatic as heavy losses in their tank regiments left some of them little more than motorized infantry brigades with a dozen or so tanks in support. Only a few weeks after the invasion of Russia the 18th Panzer Division had just 12 operational tanks left. By November 1941 Panzergruppe Guderian had no more than 150 tanks out of the 1,150 it had employed since 22 June. Many Panzer and Panzergrenadier divisions endured a horrific cycle of attrition that saw them reconstituted after near-annihilation, only to be overwhelmed again. One of the most telling images of 'de-modernization' shows an SS armoured column in action in the streets of Budapest in 1945. At a time the Russian tank armies were filled out with IS-2 heavy tanks and T-34/85s, even the SS are reduced to driving into action in ex-Italian L6 light tanks – obsolete death traps.

The SS evolved into a state within a state. Starting as simply one of the armed wings of the Nazi Party, it grew into an army, industrial conglomerate, internal security agency, eugenics breeding system, and, above all, perpetrator of the Holocaust. Its military role on the Eastern Front became crucial, with the SS armoured divisions 'Leibstandarte', 'Das Reich', 'Totenkopf' and 'Wiking' playing the leading role in both Von Manstein's counter-attack at Kharkov and the last great German offensive at Kursk. The political clout of the SS ensured these divisions secured the lion's share of new equipment, and their authorized strengths were larger than those of their Wehrmacht equivalents.

The SS more than trebled in size from 1942 to 1944, but of the 450,000 SS men serving in 1943, only a small proportion were in the well-known Panzergrenadier formations. Only one new SS division (9th 'Hohenstaufen') was formed in 1942, and that did not see active service until early 1944, when it was committed to Poland.[17] The combat record of the elite SS Panzer formations was excellent by any standards; however, there was a widespread conviction within the German Army that these ideological shock troops suffered excessive casualties through foolhardy displays of National Socialist ardour. Worse, the diversion of so many troops to 'ethnic cleansing' was especially perverse in the face of Germany's manpower crisis. By 1943 there were more men serving in the *Einsatzgruppen* than were lost with the 6th Army at Stalingrad. Towards the end of the war, only 50 per cent of the enlisted SS personnel were German; 25 per cent were ethnic Germans from conquered Europe and the rest were foreign volunteers.

Power politics among the Nazi leaders led to further profligate use of German manpower. Rather than transfer some personnel to the army as was suggested at the end of 1942, Göring insisted on following Himmler's example in having an army of his own. He formed 20 Luftwaffe 'field divisions', which were raised and trained in considerable haste and confusion before being dispatched to the Russian front. Consisting of two regiments of three battalions, with a total authorized strength of 9,800, they were poorly trained and required a steady infusion of officers and NCOs from the regular army to keep them operational. Again, German Army officers were appalled at how these divisions sustained unnecessary losses because their bravery was not allied to tactical proficiency.

The Partisan War

In the summer of 1942 Himmler appointed his adjutant SS-Gruppenführer Knoblauch as chief of the Reichsführer-SS command staff, with special responsibility for countering the Soviet partisans. The army's nine security divisions, formed of six or seven battalions of old soldiers and equipped with obsolete weapons, were clearly inadequate to police the occupied territories. Although the combined strength of these units, the *Einsatzgruppen* and the *Ordnungspolizei* (regular police), exceeded 100,000 men by the end of 1941, they had more than 850,000 square miles to control. In August 1942 the term 'partisan' was replaced by 'bandit' in SS documents, signalling an even more brutal phase in an already ghastly campaign of terror and counter-terror. Mass killings of civilians in retaliation for attacks on the German forces – 100 hostages shot for the death of one German – were supplemented by indiscriminate slaughters. Many anti-partisan operations led to high body counts with disproportionately few weapons captures; for example, 6,000 'partisans' reported killed and 480 weapons recovered. German losses might be less than half-a-dozen; sometimes there were none. These were outright massacres, without regard to the age or sex of the victims. Children as young as ten were regularly tortured and shot as spies. Scenes of hideous brutality by German soldiers, regular army as well as SS, were documented in nauseating detail on their personal cameras. Atrocities were photographed out of pride, not as protest. Army headquarters had to repeat orders to stop men sending their photos home.

The Russian Revolution and the Civil War had seen some hideous acts of cruelty by Russians against so-called 'class enemies' of their own nationality and other ethnic groups. The Jewish population of Kiev had endured a terrible pogrom at the hands of the White Army.[18] So the peoples of the occupied territories were not slow to respond to German atrocities, and they began executing captured Germans in the most revolting ways imaginable. During 1942 the partisans began to conscript people into their ranks, and sometimes resorted to terror tactics against the population too, forcing men to join them by holding their families hostage. At the same time the Germans began to round up able-bodied men and women for forced labour in the Reich. Under this chilling policy, children under 15 years of age had to be abandoned and left to starve when villages were evacuated. This simply stampeded more people into the forests, swelling the ranks of the guerrilla bands that grew to more than 100,000 strong by the end of the year. As in 1941, the open spaces of the Ukraine were least affected by partisan action, while about half the guerrillas were established in the trackless forests of Belorussia.

Elements within the German Army and SS favoured the recruitment of local troops to counter the partisan threat. Hitler was adamantly opposed to the idea of Russians wearing German uniforms, but other national groups, like the Cossacks, were acceptable to him. Nevertheless, more than a million Russians did serve in the German Army. The service troops that made up to 10 to 20 per cent of divisional strengths were supplemented by an eventual total of 176 *Osttruppen* battalions – 150,000 men by mid-1943. Some 180,000 men were recruited into the UNS (Popular Self-Defence Corps) in the Ukraine for security operations. Many *Osttruppen* units were transferred to France and Italy on Hitler's orders, stimulating the desertion that their removal from Russia was supposed to prevent. The UNS and Russian auxiliary police units retreated westwards from 1943 as the Germans were driven back, many of their personnel being absorbed into the SS. Himmler's farcical obsession with pure 'Aryan stock' diminished as the future looked bleaker. Initially unable to admit he was recruiting Russians – a people he had publicly labelled 'racial inferiors' – he called many of his Russian units 'Ukranian' and suddenly became very supportive of the idea of a discrete Ukranian identity.

Perhaps the most notorious Russian unit that fought alongside the Germans was the so-called Kaminski brigade, or 'RONA' (*Russkaya Osvoboditelnaya Narodnaya Armiya*: Russian Peoples' Liberation Army). This began as a locally raised militia in the small town of Lokot, south of Bryansk, at the end of 1941. After Soviet partisans assassinated its leader, the town mayor, command fell to one of his deputies, 38-year-old Bronislav Kaminski, an engineer born in St Petersburg to a Polish father and German mother. He had fought in the Red Army during the Civil War but had been arrested in 1937 and sent to the *gulag* for five years, probably just because his parents were foreign. He had only just been released and returned to his home in Lokot when the war broke out. Hardened by his time in the labour camps, and understandably anti-Communist, he set himself up as a warlord. Kaminski recruited more men and scavenged for abandoned Red Army weapons. His men fought the Soviet partisans and kept road and rail routes open for the Germans. Several German officers were attached for liaison purposes, but his force remained all-Russian. Kaminski's men took part in a major anti-partisan sweep in June 1942 in the forests north of Bryansk. The size of the operation testifies to the scale of the partisan threat in this sector, involving as it did a tank regiment from 5th Panzer Division, elements of two German regular infantry divisions and one Hungarian division, a total strength of more than 6,000 men. Kaminski's unit was divided among the German battalions, to act as local guides, translators and interrogators. The body count tells its own story: 2,600 partisans were killed, 498 captured and 12,000 civilians seized for slave labour; the German battle group lost 58 killed and 130 wounded.

Kaminski expanded his fiefdom, re-opening churches and schools and supporting private industry. He pressed the Germans to make his rule official. They did not, but were happy for him to exercise considerable independence provided he kept the partisans away from the road and rail net. Kaminski tried to create a Russian National Socialist Party, which attracted little interest. He renamed his followers the 'Russian Peoples' Liberation Army'. The sort of men who joined him can be easily imagined from TV footage of the Balkan militias in the 1990s. The partisans attempted to subvert some of his men and no doubt managed to place double-agents in Kaminski's little empire, just as Tito's guerrillas infiltrated locally raised pro-German units in Yugoslavia. Kaminski's discipline problems accelerated in the summer of 1943, once it was plain that Germany was losing the war. Nevertheless, Kaminski's forces took part in a succession of anti-partisan operations in 1943, again divided among battalions provided by German and Hungarian infantry divisions with some Panzer and Panzergrenadier support.

In autumn 1943 Kaminski had to abandon his little empire as the front line moved inexorably west. Together with an estimated 10,000 men and 40,000 camp followers, he retreated into Belorussia, where his militia continued to serve alongside German units against the partisans there. In July 1944 the brigade was incorporated into the SS as Waffen-Sturm-Brigade RONA and Kaminski was appointed Brigadeführer. Gottlob Berger, head of the SS main leadership office and a close ally of Himmler, planned to use Kaminski's troops as the basis for a Russian SS division, 29 Waffen-Grenadier Division der SS. Together with the equally unsavoury Dirlewanger Brigade, a unit of violent criminals led by a convicted paedophile, Kaminski's militia undertook further anti-partisan operations during 1944. These missions were characterized by heavy loss of life among the civilian population and relatively few weapons captures. In August Himmler created an *SS-Kampfgruppe* commanded by SS-Gruppenführer Heinz Reinfarth that included a 1,700-strong detachment from Kaminski's followers, the Dirlewanger Brigade and various SS police and paramilitary units.

It is often said that Kaminski's behaviour scandalized even the SS, as they crushed the Warsaw Rising with acts of cruelty so abominable that even the Nazis noticed. The Russian SS men certainly spent much of their time looting abandoned buildings and raping hospital patients – possibly including two German servicewomen. However, the senior SS commander in Warsaw, Obergruppenführer von dem Bach-Zelewski, withdrew Kaminski's rabble from the fighting, not for raping, murdering and stealing, but because their combat record was one of diabolic incompetence. And in any case, Himmler had decided to concentrate all his renegade Russians into former Soviet general Andrei Vlasov's hands. Kaminski was summoned to a conference at Bach-Zelewski's headquarters in Lodz, where he was shot by the SS. His followers were told he had died in a partisan ambush and were incorporated into Vlasov's Russian Liberation Army (ROA) later in the year.

That the German forces could recruit more than a million Russians to their colours despite all the atrocities and the deportations suggests that the Nazi racial policies brought about their own defeat. Many senior figures – even Goebbels, by 1943 – came to believe that had the Germans behaved with even a modicum of humanity, a great many Russians would not just have accepted German rule but actively fought alongside the German Army against the Communist regime. Of course, by the time Goebbels came around to this view, it was too late. Soviet citizens knew exactly what kind of rule they could expect if Germany won the war. And after two years of being encouraged to commit all manner of cruelties on 'Bolshevik sub-humans', casual brutality had become so ingrained in the Ostheer that units transferred to other fronts would sometimes lapse into old habits – as massacres of Allied prisoners in the Normandy campaign and the Battle of the Bulge demonstrated.

By mid-1943, when the Partisan War was at its height, approximately 250,000 partisans were in the field, with perhaps 500,000 men (army, SS, police and security units) ranged against them. On the eve of the battle of Kursk, and again as the great summer offensive of 1944 began, the partisans launched concerted attacks against rail communications. This exacerbated German logistical difficulties and tied down even more personnel guarding the trains, bridges, water-towers and other facilities. After 1945 it was claimed that the partisans killed tens of thousands of German soldiers, and played a decisive part in the Soviet victory, but OKH sources record only about 15,000 casualties attributable to the guerrillas. Compared to the enormous body-counts racked up on some counter-guerrilla sweeps in Belorussia, this ironically reinforces the impression that such operations were as much concerned with 'ethnic cleansing' as the pursuit of military objectives.

Given the suspicion with which Stalin's secret police regarded anyone who had been the wrong side of the lines during the war, millions of Soviet citizens had a keen personal interest in exaggerating their own contribution to the war. There are obvious parallels with the exponential rise of resistance groups in France after June 1944. In fact, the partisans did not play a decisive role, although they did divert large numbers of second-grade troops to security operations, and certainly undermined German efforts at several critical points. Some areas of northern and central Russia effectively remained in Soviet control despite being behind the German lines. Luftwaffe maps showed in red those areas over which it was dangerous to fly and suicidal to land. As an eventual Soviet victory looked likely, so these areas expanded. Yet the Baltic States remained free of partisan activity, as did all of the Crimea except the mountains along its southern shores. The steppes of the Ukraine gave little cover for guerrilla bands, and attempts to initiate partisan action there were defeated. Although powerful guerrilla bands were formed in the Ukraine, they were fighting for independence and vigorously resisted the Soviet Army in 1944 – they even killed Marshal Vatutin – and they carried on the fight well into the 1950s.

The defeat of the German 1942 offensive revealed the limitations of Blitzkrieg. It did not have universal application. The substitution of air power for artillery, and the mechanization of a dozen divisions had enabled Germany to beat France. But the events of 1940 were as much the consequence of French political and military errors as anything else. The German Army staked everything on another rapid victory in 1941, and, when this failed, tried a second Blitzkrieg in 1942, this time aimed at economic as much as political objectives. Enormous distances were covered in both campaigns, but the German Army could not effect a truly strategic breakthrough. Its great battles of encirclement were not, proportionately, as significant as the complete rupture of the Allied front achieved in 1940. The ratio of 'force to space' was simply inadequate. Having failed to deliver a knock-out blow, the German Army found itself embroiled in a *Materialschlacht* very like that of 1914–18; but rather worse. In the First World War Russia sent soldiers into battle without rifles, hoping they would pick up weapons discarded by casualties. This time, Russia was outproducing Germany.

Accustomed to short, victorious wars, German soldiers were neither physically nor psychologically prepared for this return to trench warfare. They were used to living in centrally heated barrack blocks, not squalid holes in the ground.

> Despite the heavy emphasis on marching, hiking and field exercises, there had been entirely too much stress laid upon nearly a 'peacetime' type of garrison life which bore little resemblance to the stark and foreboding realities of life on the Eastern Front ... In Russia, German troops were required to live for long periods of time in the open, in all kinds of weather, often in vermin-infested bunkers or redoubts where clothing changes could seldom be made ... The German soldier and airman, resting on an impressive string of victories, was soon provided with a number of startling surprises in Russia, almost all of them bad.[19]

The battlefield performance of the Red Army improved by fits and starts, not least because Stalin ordered operations beyond its abilities in both 1941 and 1942. The great strengths of the Soviet military were concealed at first by a combination of over-ambitious offensives that produced sharp defeats, and the enduring legacy of the purges: inexperienced officers and a culture of fear that discouraged initiative. Yet the operational philosophy of the Red Army was far more realistic than that of OKH. From mid-1942 it matched its resources to the scale of the front. It emphasized artillery firepower, integrating aerial bombing with the artillery fire-plan, primarily in counter-battery work, attacking German gun positions and employing its tank formations to exploit to great depth. As soon as Soviet factories had provided the tools, the Red Army put its pre-war theories into practice. The result was the 1944 offensive, Operation *Bagration*, in which the Soviet Army attacked and destroyed the main body of the German Army, effectively winning the Second World War before the Allied divisions landed in Normandy had managed to break out from the beaches. However, the improvements in Soviet military performance were at army and army group level; the tactical performance of most Soviet battalions, brigades and divisions remained lamentable, primarily because high losses meant high turnover in personnel. Few men lived long enough to gain experience, and those who did were usually promoted.

Eighteen months earlier, as the fight for Stalingrad ended and the Soviets tried to bounce the German Army out of Kharkov, Zaporezhe and the Dnepr crossings, the ultimate triumph of the Russian Army lay in the future. At the beginning of 1943, the overwhelming majority of the German Army was still concentrated in Russia, and as the Soviet South-Western Front was about to discover, it was still, man-for-man, battalion-for-battalion, the most deadly military instrument in the world.

★
THE LAST BLITZKRIEG

'Anyone who speaks to me of peace without victory
will lose his head, no matter who he is.'

ADOLF HITLER

Just a week after the surrender of Stalingrad, Soviet armoured forces
thundered across the open steppe south of Kharkov and headed for
Zaporezhe, a key crossing point across the Dnepr. It was also the site
of a gigantic hydro-electric plant, recently repaired by AEG to provide
power to neighbouring factories and coal mines. The Russians were
racing against time: the spring thaw would soon impose a halt to
mobile operations. As the snow fields melted, the roads would become
swamps, as would the surrounding fields, making soldiers' lives even
more miserable than usual – supplies could not come in, nor wounded
men be taken out, as fighting continued in a sea of mud.

In fact, the weather was not the only menace looming over
the Red Army's Voronezh and South-Western Fronts. In Zaporezhe,
Field Marshal von Manstein had taken charge and was planning a
counter-stroke that would confirm his reputation as one of the
greatest commanders of the Second World War. But first he had to
confront the Führer.

Hitler had already dispatched his Praetorians to rescue the Eastern
Front. The SS Panzergrenadier divisions 'Leibstandarte' (92 tanks), 'Das
Reich' (131 tanks), and 'Totenkopf' (121 tanks) formed the SS Panzer
Corps – and 'Wiking' Division was already in action south of Kharkov.
The SS were ordered to hold Kharkov, which would have suited the
Russians who were preparing to bypass the city and snap up any
garrison at their leisure. On 14 February, the SS abandoned Kharkov,
local resistance fighters sniping at their rearguards as they departed.

Kharkov was the first major Soviet city to be recaptured from the
Germans. Predominantly Ukranian, with a population of 900,000 in

1940, its heavy industry – tank and tractor factories – had been evacuated in 1941. Occupied for 18 months by the Germans, its fate provided chilling evidence of what German rule meant for ordinary Russian and Ukranian people, let alone for Jews. The Red Army estimated that only 350,000 people remained in Kharkov in early 1943. Many people had managed to flee the city when the Germans took over, but the whereabouts of the rest were uncertain at first. It was soon established that more than 100,000 young men and women had been deported to Germany as slaves. Almost as many, the old and the very young especially, had died of malnutrition, hypothermia and related conditions. Most deaths occurred during the winter of 1941–42, but the enduring food shortage had contributed to another sharp rise in mortality in the four months before liberation. About 30,000 individuals were spared the horrors of the starvation winter. The Germans killed 15,000 Jews and another 15,000 Communist Party members, Soviet officials, intellectuals – most of the teachers at the university – and prisoners-of-war shortly after they took over.

The German occupying authorities created a desperately transparent 'Ukranian' regime in Kharkov, seeking to divide the Ukranians from the Russians. A local Ukranian police force was established: the usual band of looters, racists and psychopaths who graced many a German-occupied city in eastern Europe during the Second World War. The *Burgomeister* himself was a Ukranian collaborator, who fled Kharkov with his fellow Quislings, mistresses and booty as the Red Army approached. As in the Reich itself, Nazi rule did not just bring the worst elements in society to the surface, it empowered them. Men who belonged behind bars were instead given uniforms and guns. In Kharkov the schools were shut down, but the black market flourished. Luxurious restaurants catered for the Germans, who helped themselves liberally to everything from watches to women.

The brief return of Soviet administration to Kharkov was marked by several characteristic features that would appear on a distressingly greater scale in 1944 as more Soviet territory was recaptured. With sinister congruence, the NKVD occupied the former Gestapo headquarters and used the basement torture chambers for the same purpose. Letter boxes were added to the outside of the building so the citizens of Kharkov could denounce collaborators – or settle old scores that might have little to do with the occupation. Again, the war and the Nazi/Soviet political systems had a deeply corrosive effect on humanity. British correspondent Alexander Werth saw former prisoners-of-war from a camp outside the city among the beggars seen near the market. Most of their fellow prisoners had died of starvation before the camp was 'liberated', but neither the Red Army nor the people of Kharkov would feed them. They were regarded with callous indifference, except by the NKVD, which treated them as spies or traitors.

Their tragedy anticipated a greater manifestation of Stalinist evil that would follow the final victory. In May 1945 Stalin ordered 100 prison camps to be built by his armies in Germany and Poland, into which were driven hundreds of thousands of bewildered Soviet soldiers who had survived capture by the Germans.[1] Most were catapulted from German prison camps to Soviet ones, and thence to the *gulag*. Only about one man in five ever returned home. Former prisoners-of-war and their families remained second-class citizens after the war, discriminated against in their employment and housing and subject to endless petty humiliations. They were not formally rehabilitated until 1994.

Hitler was so furious at the continuing success of the Soviet offensive that he flew to Zaporezhe himself, where the conference was held to the accompaniment of the distant rumbling of Russian guns. According to Goebbels' diary, he intended to dismiss Von Manstein, but in the event he listened to his general's cogent explanation of the situation and his proposals for a counter-stroke. The stage was set for one of the most famous counter-offensives of the war, Von Manstein's 'backhand blow', a master-class in armoured warfare that would be taught in NATO staff colleges for years to come.

Lieutenant-General Popov's 'mobile group' of four Soviet tank corps continued to attack, although it was at the extreme limit of its supply lines and very short of fuel and ammunition. Elements of the 25th Tank Corps were within 10 miles of Zaporezhe, but Popov's tank corps had only 53 operational tanks between them.[2] In the First World War it was accepted that no army could fight effectively more than 95 miles from its railheads, although this distance would be extended substantially by the Red Army in 1944, thanks to its huge fleet of American trucks. Popov risked everything to reach Zaporezhe before the spring thaw. It was worth risking his entire command, because if he succeeded he would cut off all German forces between the east bank of the Dnepr and the Black Sea.

Von Manstein was allowed to conduct a mobile battle instead of the sort of static defence the Führer tended to insist upon. The over-strength SS formations were backed by five Panzer divisions (3rd, 6th, 7th, 11th and 17th), as well as the 'Großdeutschland' Division (95 tanks). Popov's communications were being monitored by Luftflotte 4, which learned of his logistic problems and concentrated its efforts against the Soviet spearheads. As the weather improved, the Luftwaffe supported Von Manstein's counter-attack with up to 1,000 sorties per day. Popov's units were pounded by Junkers Ju–88s with little interference from the Soviet Air Force. On 19 February the 2nd SS Panzer Corps struck the flank of the Soviet 6th Army from Krasnograd; SS 'Das Reich' exploited through the gap and overran the 4th Guards Rifle Corps. On 22 February, the 48th and 57th Panzer Corps cut through towards Pavlovgrad to create a double envelopment. The SS Panzer Corps led the advance back to Kharkov, which it recaptured with a frontal attack in mid–March. Soviet losses were estimated at 23,000 men, 615 tanks and 354 guns, although many soldiers abandoned their vehicles and equipment to escape back to Russian lines. Only 9,000 prisoners were taken. Von Manstein noted that the extreme cold led to troops congregating in the villages rather than maintaining any real cordon, so troops determined to break out could. Given their likely fate in German hands, it is hardly surprising that they risked freezing to death as they hurried through the snow towards the Russian lines.

At the height of the Donets campaign, Army Group Centre was under attack too. Since the spring thaw spread from south to north, operations here went on for several weeks before the mud arrested progress. Air power was again vital in stabilizing the front, and although Veljkiye Luki could not be saved, the Soviets were prevented from breaking through to Orel: on 18 March the Luftwaffe destroyed 116 Russian tanks. The Soviet offensive was halted, but only after it had driven a deep wedge into the German front. This unsightly bulge – the Kursk salient – was immediately earmarked for destruction by the German High Command. Eliminating it would drastically shorten the frontage German forces had to defend, and would remove the obvious platform for the Soviets' summer offensive.

The incredible recovery in the Wehrmacht's fighting power, from the Stalingrad débâcle to the triumphant return of the SS to Kharkov, was a profound shock to Stalin. There is some evidence that the Soviet leader toyed with offering a compromise peace to Germany, using Swedish diplomats as neutral intermediaries.[3] The deal apparently involved a return to the borders of 1914, not those of 1941. However, it is more likely that Stalin allowed such rumours to circulate as a means of applying pressure to the western Allies, to make them bring forward plans for the long-anticipated Second Front, the liberation of France. Stalin's creation of the National Committee for Free Germany and the League of German Officers was an insurance policy intended to lay the ground for a military coup in Berlin. If Hitler was not prepared to negotiate, then perhaps his generals would be more open to reason. However, those senior German commanders contemplating action, like Field Marshal von Kluge, who gave his blessing to two attempted assassinations of Hitler in 1943, sought to make peace in the west in order to continue the War in the East. Ironically, this fantasy would later be shared by many senior Nazis as the Red Army approached the frontiers of the Reich.

Of course, Hitler had no thoughts of compromise. Resorting to increased doses of dubious medicines containing strychnine and atropine, prescribed by his sinister physician, Dr Morrell, the Führer spoke of destiny and final victory. The rock upon which German strategy rested – or foundered – was Hitler's 'unconquerable will'. Anything that might weaken this, such as the clinically accurate intelligence assessments of Colonel Gehlen's *Fremde Heere Ost*, was simply ignored.

The battle of Kursk

Strategies for 1943 were guided by the fact that the Soviets still enjoyed a 2:1 advantage in manpower, and an overwhelming superiority in artillery and tanks. In the spring of 1943 comparative strengths on the Eastern Front were as follows:

	German	Soviet
Men	2.7 million	6 million
Tanks	2,209	12–15,000
Field guns	6,360	33,000[4]

Nearly half the German infantry divisions were reduced to six battalions, with their artillery batteries cut to three guns. Reinforced on the eve of the Kursk offensive, the Ostheer would have about 2,500 tanks, of which 90 per cent were operational. The Russians' front-line tank strength hovered around 8–10,000, with large quantities of vehicles either in reserve formations or training. Since few Russian tank crew survived the loss of their vehicle, the Red Army had to provide new crews with replacement tanks. The daunting quantities of Soviet guns had now received American trucks to tow them, substantially improving their mobility.

The numerical odds against Germany were grim, but, despite the winter campaign of 1941–42 and the utter disaster of Stalingrad, the battle of attrition was by no means one-sided. The German Army in the east was stronger in the spring of 1943 than it had been a year earlier, despite the loss of large allied contingents. While the Soviet manpower reserves were double those of Germany, the casualty ratio had remained well above 2:1 in Germany's favour; even during 1943 it averaged 4:1, so if the war were no more than an attritional slogging match, the Germans were actually set to win. Similarly, Soviet tank production was more than double that of Germany's, but the loss ratio was more than 3:1 in the Germans' favour. Other things being equal, the Russian steamroller would grind to a halt first. In this context, Stalin's tentative peace proposals did not sound so unreasonable, and if the Germans had not committed such appalling atrocities from the instant they crossed the frontier, a compromise stemming from a military stalemate would not have been inconceivable.

In January 1943 Hitler did at least accept there was no possibility the German Army could take Moscow. Field Marshal von Kluge presented plans for a phased withdrawal of Army Group Centre, shortening the front to a more rational and defensible length, and enabling him to create a proper mobile reserve. The operation lasted throughout March 1943, and by the time it was completed the frontage Von Kluge's armies occupied had been reduced from 340 to 110 miles. Rzhev, epicentre of such fierce battles in 1941 and 1942, was finally abandoned. Nearly 200,000 Russian civilians were evacuated too, a minority who were now compromised by their collaboration with the Nazis, and the overwhelming majority who were seized as slaves and dispatched to German factories.

The last great German offensive in Russia took place that summer, around the small town of Kursk, which gave its name to the most famous tank battle in history. Plans for an attack on Kursk were first discussed in March 1943, as the spring mud imposed its annual pause on operations. After recapturing Kharkov, Von Manstein had launched the SS Panzer Corps onwards, retaking Belgorod on 18 March just as the rivers flooded and the roads liquefied. On 12 April the next operation was given the name *Zitadelle* and scheduled for mid-May, as soon as the ground dried out.

The attack on Kursk was to have been followed by a German offensive in the north, code-named Operation *Parkplatz*, which was intended to take Leningrad by storm. Given the extraordinary losses suffered by the 6th Army at Stalingrad in October 1942, it is astonishing that Hitler still had any appetite for warfare in built-up areas. Nine divisions were earmarked to join Army Group North for the assault, although Field Marshal von Küchler signalled that he had enough siege artillery in place and would not require more. In the event, the failure at Kursk and the Soviet breakthrough at Orel led to the cancellation of the attack. The siege of Leningrad, which had already cost the lives of more than a million people by 1943, would not be lifted completely until 1944.

The summers of 1940, 1941 and 1942 had belonged to the German Panzer forces, driving all before them in France, the Ukraine or to the foothills of the Caucasus. So the decision to cut off and overrun the Soviet forces in the Kursk salient did not appear unduly ambitious, given the scale of previous Blitzkriegs. Senior German officers were divided on the issue, but many had been uncomfortable with what they regarded as a foolhardy and overambitious plan to invade France in 1940. This time the voices urging caution included General Heinz Guderian, who thought it would be more prudent to remain on the strategic defensive, husbanding the armoured forces for the day the British and Americans landed in western Europe. With North Africa lost, it was only a matter of time before the western Allies came ashore, in Italy, southern France, the Balkans or – as the US Army still hankered to – in northern France. The British bomber attacks on Germany had suddenly increased in power, and the Americans were assembling another heavy bomber force in Britain, this one committed to daylight raids.

Was the traditional summer tank offensive the correct response to a fast-changing strategic situation? Again, Hitler's limitations as a strategist are clearly revealed. Poring over maps of the Kursk salient while British and US troops prepared to land in Sicily, Italian generals plotted a *coup d'état* to take their country out of the war; the 'Battle of the Atlantic' ended in defeat with U-boat losses at an unsustainable level; and Allied strategic bombing grew from a noisy nuisance to a serious threat to the heart of the Reich. While Hitler did not ignore these issues, he remained focused on the tactical minutiae of army operations in Russia, perhaps because it was something he understood and could influence. Moving a tank battalion here or an infantry division there had immediate and tangible effects, and postponed facing up to an ever-bleaker strategic situation. Hitler refused to be drawn on his long-term aims when, as happened from time to time, a senior officer tried to get some sense of the overall plan. The army groups in Russia fought in surprising isolation from each other; Hitler's behaviour was more calculated to divide and rule than to coordinate operations across the whole theatre of operations.

The first operational order for *Zitadelle* called for Army Group Centre, commanded by Field Marshal von Kluge ('*Kluger Hans*' or 'clever Hans', as his staff nicknamed him) to attack the north flank of the salient. Von Kluge's offensive would be undertaken by the German 9th Army, which included 12 infantry and four Panzer divisions; Kampfgruppe Esebeck (two Panzer divisions), with 5th and 8th Panzer Divisions in army group reserve. The 2nd Army would hold the face of the salient with just two corps of three infantry divisions each. Field Marshal von Manstein's Army Group South would assault the southern flank with the 4th Panzer Army, comprising ten infantry, four Panzer and five Panzergrenadier divisions; plus the re-constituted 6th Army, including one Panzergrenadier division, and the nine divisions of Armeeabteilung Kempf.

The attack was postponed several times to allow the new battalions of Tiger tanks and the first Panthers to take part. The idea that an offensive involving millions of men fighting across a battlefield half the size of England could be determined by a few hundred new tanks shows touching faith in technology. The 147 Tigers performed well, but the 200 Panthers were reduced to 50 by the end of the second day. Their engines had not been run in, and inevitable mechanical problems dogged 39th Panzer Regiment for the duration of the battle. It fell to those workhorses of the Wehrmacht, the Panzerkampfwagen III and IV, to provide the bulk of the German Army's tanks at Kursk. The 16 Panzer and five Panzergrenadier divisions taking part in Kursk included a total of 115 Panzer IIs, 844 Panzer IIIs, 913 Panzer IVs and some 300 StuG III assault guns. SS 'Das Reich' even had 25 captured T-34s.

Delaying the attack gave the Russians ample opportunity to fortify their positions in the salient, and they did so with typical thoroughness. Prodigious quantities of mines were laid – more than 1,800 per mile – and up to eight successive lines of defences bristling with anti-tank weapons awaited the German onslaught. This could not be disguised, even by an army famed for its camouflage abilities. By early May, many of those German generals initially in favour of a summer offensive were having second thoughts. Aerial photographs showed ominous lines of upturned earth, dug-in gun positions and evidence of increased troop levels. Von Manstein thought the moment had passed; an assault the moment the ground was suitable might have worked, but not now the enemy was so obviously prepared. Even the combative Model had cold feet. On the other hand, Von Kluge was so enthusiastic he challenged Guderian, whom he openly loathed, to a duel, after one particularly heated discussion about *Zitadelle*. Significantly, the Soviet High Command was already planning its own offensive against the Orel salient on the assumption that the German attack on Kursk would be defeated. The odds were certainly unfavourable to the Germans:

	German	Soviet
Men	600,000	1.2 million
Tanks and assault guns	2,750	3,500
Guns and mortars	10,000	25,000
Aircraft	2,000	2,700

Estimates of the German ground forces range from 435,000 to the more usually quoted 900,000. The higher figure includes German forces which, strictly speaking, did not take part in the Kursk fighting, such as six divisions of the German 9th Army engaged in the fighting around Orel which began a week after Kursk, but which were not involved in the original German offensive. The commonly quoted figure of 1.3 million Soviet troops is the sum of the Central and Voronezh Fronts' ration strength, as understood after the war, but recent Soviet sources put this at nearer to one million.[5] However, this total does not include the 5th Guards and 5th Tank Armies of Konev's Steppe Front, which were brought forward to block the southern thrust of 4th Panzer Army. Konev's front had one airborne and nine infantry divisions, plus five mechanized corps and a tank brigade including 1,500 tanks and self-propelled guns. Its total strength was about 500,000 but only part of the Steppe Front counter-attacked at Kursk: the rest took part in the subsequent Soviet offensive. This suggests that about 600,000 German soldiers were attacking 1.2 million Soviets in the battle for the Kursk salient.

On the northern side of the salient the German 9th Army, commanded by Colonel-General Model, faced the bulk of the Soviet Central Front under General Konstantin Rokossovksy, a half-Polish former Tsarist officer who had been very fortunate to survive his arrest in 1938. Beria's torturers broke several of his ribs, knocked out nine of his teeth, shattered his toes with a hammer and pulled out his fingernails. Still refusing to confess he was a Polish spy, he was subjected to mock executions then shipped to a Siberian *gulag* camp. On 22 March 1940 he was unexpectedly freed and rehabilitated. Whether it was the dismal Russian performance in Finland or the signs of renewed trouble with Japan that triggered his release no one knows, but Timoshenko had no hesitation in giving him back his old job as commander of a cavalry corps. Promoted to command the new 9th Mechanized Corps, Rokossovsky survived the Kiev encirclement in 1941, his candid account of that disaster proving too much for the Soviet regime as late as 1984.[6] He led the 16th Army during the defence of Moscow with great skill and was promoted to command the Bryansk Front. In September 1942 he was transferred to command the Don Front, retitled the Central Front in February

1943 – and had been preparing to defend the Kursk salient for nearly four months. Rokossovsky was one of the very few men, and probably the only general, that Stalin referred to by his patronymic (Konstantin Konstantinovich); even Zhukov was addressed as 'comrade'.

The Germans had so telegraphed their intentions that Rokossovsky was able to order a bombardment of Model's start line two hours before the German offensive began. Nevertheless, the German artillery opened fire at 4.30am. It was a short but intense bombardment, planned for maximum shock effect, with the Luftwaffe joining in after 40 minutes with 730 aircraft from Luftflotte 6. The ground forces commenced their assault under cover of both air and artillery bombardment. Accounts of the battle of Kursk have often focused on the new heavy tanks employed by the Germans. Model's assault was led by the most exotic combination: 89 *Elefant* assault guns of schwere Panzerjäger Abteilung 656, together with the 31 Tigers of schwere Panzer Abteilung 505 were used to spearhead the assault, supported by the 45 *Brummbär* assault guns of SturmPanzer-Abteilung 216.

The *Elefant*, also known as the *Ferdinand*, was an assault gun based on the chassis of the unsuccessful contender for the Tiger heavy tank project. When Henschel's design was chosen for production, Porsche used the components of its prototypes to create a 65-ton tank destroyer with an 88mm PAK 43 in the fighting compartment. Capable of knocking out any enemy tank at up to 3,000 yards and protected by nearly 8 inches of frontal armour, impervious to enemy fire, it was a formidable vehicle. However, its engine was not powerful enough; its sluggish top speed of 18mph and poor acceleration made it better suited to defensive operations – in which the survivors would excel later in the year.

Designed in the wake of Stalingrad, the *Brummbär* ('Grizzly Bear') or *SturmPanzer IV* was intended to support combat in built-up areas. It combined a Panzer IV chassis with an armoured fighting compartment on top, fitted with a stubby 150mm howitzer in a limited traverse mounting. Its 83lb shell would demolish enemy-held buildings at point-blank range, while its stout frontal armour kept out enemy anti-tank rounds.

Most of the German Army relied on horse-drawn transport columns throughout the Second World War. Although the Panzer divisions grabbed the headlines, the bulk of Hitler's divisions moved no faster than their fathers in 1914, or Napoleon's men in 1812.

German field police stage an arrest for the camera, somewhere behind the lines in the summer of 1941. Hundreds of thousands of Russian troops were cut off by the speed of the German advance. Some managed to evade capture and join the growing bands of partisans in the forests.

This machine-gun team was part of the Italian 8th Army, destroyed during the Russian offensive in November 1942. Italian prisoners-of-war suffered a disproportionately high mortality rate in captivity.

A Panzer III tows a *Sturmgeschütz* assault gun out of a snow drift in early 1942. From just a few batteries in 1941, assault guns went on to form a significant proportion of German armour on the Russian front.

Bodies lie on the pavement as the German bombardment of Leningrad continues. Modern estimates suggest that over 900,000 people died in the siege of the city, which continued from 1941 to 1944.

Russian volunteers (*Hiwis*) serving with the Germans during the battle of Kharkov, spring 1942. By 1943 German infantry divisions in Russia officially included 2,000 such men; 176 separate battalions of *Osttruppen* were also raised by 1944.

Russian ski troops on sledges towed by (left) a T-26 and (right) a T-60 light tank. On their own, ski troops lacked firepower because it was difficult to move mortars and machine-guns across the snow.

Both sides made use of captured tanks, the Germans painting outsized crosses on their T-34s to avoid a 'blue-on-blue'. On the same principle, this *Sturmgeschütz* captured by the Russians is now smothered in red stars and patriotic slogans.

Ice encrusts the deck gun of a German U-boat operating out of Norway against the British convoys sailing to Murmansk. Despite Russian ingratitude at the time, lend-lease supplies were very important to the Red Army, especially for the supply of trucks and high explosive.

A T-34/76, arguably more of an assault gun than a genuine main battle tank, but a crucial weapon nonetheless. Russian factories built over 30,000 of them: more than the sum total of German tank production during the Second World War.

SS troops in Kharkov in their new winter combat gear, March 1943. Unlike the 6th Army at Stalingrad, cut off from its winter clothing, the troops involved in Von Manstein's counter-attack were properly equipped for cold weather operations.

Soldiers from one of the 20 Luftwaffe field divisions, small infantry divisions established by the German Air Force to the despair of the overstretched army. In 1942 Hermann Göring was still sufficiently powerful to insist on creating his equivalent of Himmler's Waffen-SS rather than cede manpower to the army in Russia.

Two soldiers from the ill-fated 6th Army seen in Stalingrad before the fall of winter and the Russian counter-attack that surrounded them. Of the 100,000 or so men who survived the battle to surrender in February 1943, fewer than 6,000 were still alive when they were released 12 years later.

SS troops outside Kharkov in March 1943. Temperatures remained so low that it was difficult to survive overnight in the open. This made even the smallest village worth fighting for.

One of the 300 Churchill tanks supplied by Britain to Russia: this knocked-out example is serving as a table for SS-Sturmbannfuhrer Vincenz Kaiser's command post. Commanding the 3rd Battalion of 4th SS Panzergrenadier Regiment, 'Der Führer', he wears the Knight's Cross, awarded to him on 4 June 1943.

A command post belonging to SS 'Das Reich' during the battle of Kursk. The Russians claimed to have destroyed 2,952 German tanks during the battle, but German records show the permanent loss of 537, and these were replaced within a month.

Tank-riding infantry were a common feature of the great Soviet offensives in 1944. The US supplied Russia with 375,883 trucks, but it remained an iron law that no army ever had enough of them.

This battering ram of new heavy tanks made the initial penetration. Only one of Model's Panzer divisions, the 20th, took part in the first day's fighting: the other five were ready to pour through once a gap had been blown in the Soviet defences. The *Elefants* suffered from a lack of defensive machine-guns, a problem the *Sturmgeschütz* battalions had already addressed, and lost some of their number to Soviet infantry anti-tank teams. Many of the Tigers were disabled by mines, and their commanders complained that they were asked to do too much. However, Model's plan worked. The battalions of heavy tanks led the infantry through the first line of Soviet field works, and smashed the Soviet counter-attack into the bargain. On 5 July, Model's 9th Army advanced about 4 miles against the Russian 13th Army. The Russian 2nd Tank Army, ordered to recapture the original front line, counter-attacked the next day, but it suffered such terrible losses that Rokossovsky sacked its commander, Lieutenant-General Rodin. Rokossovsky ordered the surviving Russian armour to be dug in among the defensive positions and not to attempt to fight a mobile battle.

Now the Panzer divisions poured into the gap, ready to slash through the remains of the defences and break into open country. Between the small towns of Ol'hovatka and Ponyri, ten infantry and four Panzer divisions battered their way forward, but although the Germans captured part of both towns, they could not wrest them completely from the defenders. Fighting from deep entrenchments practically impervious to artillery fire, the Russian infantry kept firing, reducing German infantry companies to mere handfuls of men. Although the German tanks were knocking out impressive numbers of Soviet vehicles, they were suffering steady attrition themselves, especially track damage caused by land mines. Soviet engineers laid another 6,000 mines on Rokossovsky's Front during 6 July alone. They rarely knocked out German tanks, but often put them out of action for vital hours. Prodigious quantities of ammunition were expended, German veterans remembering the unceasing fire of the Soviet artillery. And although the Soviet Air Force was losing heavily in the battles overhead, Soviet fighter-bombers persisted in making low-level sorties against German artillery positions, coming in under the German radar coverage and attacking before they could be intercepted.

On 7 July, Model committed the 2nd and 18th Panzer Divisions, feeding in the 4th Panzer Division the next day. Rokossovsky responded by bringing up 9th Tank Corps. Attack and counter-attack followed, hour after hour, in the baking heat of the steppe. The German 292nd Infantry Division, in action near Ponyri, identified 11 discrete Russian counter-attacks against it on 8 July alone. Each afternoon the atmosphere grew thick until the clouds finally burst and saturated the bloody field. Model halted his forces on the 9th, then resumed the offensive on the 10th, making the last minor gains, but his army never did break into the open. After a week of intensive fighting, day and night, his divisions had advanced only another couple of miles by 12 July when he suspended offensive operations because of the Soviet attack on the Orel salient, Operation *Kutuzov*, which forced Army Group Centre onto the defensive. The ground won at such bitter cost was abandoned as Model turned his forces to help 2nd Panzer Army face the new threat.

The southern arm of the German pincer at Kursk was provided by Army Group South, which had more armour than Army Group North: 13 Panzer and Panzergrenadier divisions, including the SS Panzer Corps, as well as the 200 Panther tanks of 39th Panzer Regiment. The 'Großdeutschland' Division and the SS divisions 'Leibstandarte', 'Das Reich' and 'Totenkopf' each had a company (13–15 tanks) of Tigers, while schwere Panzer Abteilung 503 had 45 Tigers. The army group was supported by 1,100 aircraft assigned to Fliegerkorps 8.

Field Marshal von Manstein, the planner of the Sedan breakthrough and recent victor at Kharkov, conducted his assault differently from Model, attacking with massed armour from the very first hour. The 4th Panzer Army under the veteran tank commander Colonel-General Hoth broke into the Soviet defences north-west of Belgorod under cover of an equally short but sharp artillery bombardment. The Soviet 6th Guards Army could not stop the onslaught, and the Germans advanced up to 6 miles through the Soviet defences. General Vatutin, commander of the Voronezh Front, brought forward the 1st Tank Army (6th and 31st Tank Corps) with both his reserve Tank Corps (2nd and 5th Guards), a total of more than 1,000 tanks to block the approaches to Obajan.

The city of Belgorod lies on the west bank of the Donets, and was just within German lines at the southern neck of the Kursk salient. The German Armeeabteilung Kempf (six infantry and three Panzer divisions plus three assault gun battalions) had succeeded in bridging the river and establishing a bridgehead, but the forewarned Soviet artillery battalions delivered an intensive barrage just as the Germans tried to break out. Nevertheless, German engineers laid two more bridges south of the city, and by noon on 5 July, the Panzer divisions were crossing the Donets, poised to sweep along the east bank, guarding the flank of Hoth's Panzer Army as it headed for Kursk.

Whether Vatutin or his tank commanders were aware of the fate of the 2nd Tank Army's counter-attack in the north, or were simply more cautious, the 1st Tank Army did not launch itself at Hoth's Panzers. A counter-attack scheduled for 6 July was cancelled and the Soviet tanks took up defensive positions behind the infantry, the anti-tank guns, anti-tank ditches and minefields. The 1st Tank Army was on high ground overlooking the River Ps'ol, south-west of Obajan; the 2nd and 5th Tank Corps were behind the 69th Army to the south-east. In reserve 90 miles further east lay the 5th Guards Tank Army of Konev's Steppe Front. If Hoth led 4th Panzer Army directly for Kursk, he would run into 1st Tank Army and leave his right flank exposed to the rest of Vatutin's armour and the 5th Guards Tank Army. Instead, Hoth veered north-east, towards the small town of Prochorovka where the Belgorod–Voronezh road intersects the Kursk–Belgorod railroad. Advancing in this direction also avoided further bridging operations. Hoth would pass between the Ps'ol and the headwaters of the Donets. Given the German dependence on heavy tanks that were too large for standard army bridging equipment, this was no small consideration.

The 4th Panzer Army crashed through the Soviet defences with incredible skill and élan. Against the most formidable entrenchments, stubbornly defended, the 48th Panzer Corps and 2nd SS Panzer Corps advanced 19 miles in a week to reach a line running from Verhopen'e, along the high ground towards Prochorovka. At Verhopen'e, combat engineers repaired the bridge and the 'Großdeutschland' Division rolled up the defences, taking numerous prisoners from the 71st Guards Rifle Division. The 2nd SS Panzer Corps broke through to the west of Prochorovka. On its left, 'Totenkopf' established a bridgehead over the Ps'ol on 10 July. For seven days, Stalin, Zhukov and Vassilevski monitored the progress of the battle, demanding hourly reports on 10 and 11 July. They were determined to preserve as large an operational reserve as possible, ready for their own offensive. The German attack in the north had been stopped without recourse to massive reinforcements, but 4th Panzer Army was still smashing its way through one defensive line after another. The Soviet 69th Army, in danger of being cut off between Hoth's Panzers and Armeeabteilung Kempf, was compelled to withdraw.

The 5th Guards Tank Army (18th and 29th Tank Corps plus 5th Mechanized Corps) was transferred to Vatutin's operational control on 9 July and ordered, as Hoth had predicted, to Prochorovka. The 5th Guards Army was dispatched too, occupying the 28-mile front between Obajan and Prochorovka on 11 July. The 5th Guards Tank Army counter-attacked on 12 July, together with 2nd Tank Corps and 2nd Guards Tank Corps from Steppe Front's reserve. A murderous, chaotic tank battle ensued to the dramatic background of a summer storm as 2nd SS Panzer Corps continued to attack as well. SS 'Leibstandarte' inflicted severe losses on the 18th and 29th Tank Corps of the Soviet 5th Guards Tank Army. 'Totenkopf', delayed by getting its tanks across the Ps'ol, bludgeoned its way into the defensive positions of the 33rd Guards Rifle Corps.

The same day Field Marshals von Kluge and von Manstein were summoned back to Hitler's headquarters in Prussia. A tense meeting ensued on 13 July. The British and Americans had landed on Sicily and Italian forces were offering little resistance. Army Group South was ordered to dispatch 2nd SS Panzer Corps to Italy, in the expectation of an attack on the mainland. Operation *Zitadelle* was cancelled.

The battle of Kursk was hailed as a great victory in Russia, and Stalin ordered a triumphal salute to be fired in Moscow. The Red Army had received the most powerful blow the German Army could deliver, parried it, and commenced two major offensives of its own. In the chaos of a great tank battle – as in an aerial dogfight – exorbitant numbers of 'kills' tend to be claimed. At Kursk they were inflated out of all proportion: the Russians claimed to have destroyed 2,952 tanks and 195 assault guns, killed 70,000 men and shot down 1,392 aircraft at Kursk.[7]

These bogus figures have become part of the legend: the presentation of Kursk as a mortal blow to the German Army in general and the Panzer divisions in particular. Army Group Centre reported the loss of nearly half its tanks; a total of 304 written off, including 39 of the *Elefants*. Army Group South had 233 tanks destroyed during Operation *Zitadelle*, including 58 Panthers. One of the unforeseen problems with the Panther was that it took three SdKfz 18t half-tracks to tow one damaged Panther, hence the large number that had to be blown up and abandoned. By the end of July Army Group South had 500 operational tanks, roughly half as many as it began the battle with. Assuming losses among the *Sturmgeschütz* battalions were in proportion, Operation *Zitadelle* cost the Germans between 600 and 700 tanks and assault guns. Yet German tank strength on the Eastern Front was approximately 1,500 at the beginning of 1943 and remained level at about 2,000 through the whole year as replacement vehicles arrived from the factories.

The Panzer divisions were not wiped out at Kursk, and neither was the Luftwaffe. In the skies above Kursk the Luftwaffe once again shot down vast numbers of Soviet aircraft for little loss: 432 Russian aircraft were shot down on the first day to Germany's 23. For the German fighter arm, flying on the Eastern Front was regarded as operational training. Although several famous German aces served there for years, amassing enormous scores in the process, the majority of fighter pilots committed to Russia were transferred to defence of the Reich as soon as they had gained enough combat experience. They were replaced by newly trained pilots straight from training establishments. However, the Luftwaffe discovered that its bombers could no longer beat off Soviet fighter attacks unaided. Even the Heinkel He-111s, which had hitherto relied on close formations and relatively good defensive firepower, had to be shielded by Me-109s. Soviet fighter operations continued to improve; thanks to the arrival of British radar sets, the aircraft could be directed by ground control across the whole front by 1944.

The exploits of the Ilyushin Il-2 *Sturmovik* have dominated coverage of the Eastern Front air war, but in 1943 it was the success of the fighters – the La-5s, Yak-7s and Yak-9s especially – that had greatest impact, substantially reducing the number of effective German bombing missions. The *Sturmoviks* made regular attacks against German ground forces, but suffered dreadful losses both to fighters and to flak, once the latter were issued with armour-piercing ammunition. The fact that the position of rear gunner in an Il-2 was a punishment posting, which flight crew were given for disciplinary offences including cowardice, says much about the Red Army's confidence in its ground-attack aircraft. One useful contribution the Il-2 did make was to hinder Luftwaffe reconnaissance: it could overtake and shoot down the Fw 189s of the German recce flights, confident its frontal armour would protect it from the German rear gunner.

Orel, Kharkov and the retreat to the Dnepr

The Soviet drive on Orel saw roles reversed. The Western and Bryansk Fronts had to break through defences that the Germans had had plenty of time to prepare. If the Germans lacked massive tank reserves with which to restore the line, they nevertheless still had the Luftwaffe to provide an effective substitute for both artillery and anti-tank guns. The 9th Army and 2nd Panzer Army defending Orel were aided by

37,000 sorties, with many aircraft flying five or six missions per day. The 1st Air Division delivered some 20,000 tons of ordnance, claiming 1,100 Russian tanks and 1,300 other vehicles destroyed. The Russian Air Force was still inferior, losing 1,733 aircraft over the Orel Front to a total of only 64 German aircraft.[8]

Try as they might, the German forces were unable to stop the Soviet offensives. Although the Ostheer exacted a heavy and unceasing toll of casualties for every position it had to abandon, the front line was driven steadily westwards. The Soviet attacks were supported by intensive artillery barrages that demolished all but the most thoroughly constructed positions. Many of the Russian units engaged at Kursk were still full of fight and able to mount an offensive of their own. By 5 August the Soviet 3rd Guards Tank Army had captured Orel, and two weeks later the Bryansk salient had been overrun. Model withdrew to the 'Hagen' line of fortifications, built a few miles east of Bryansk roughly along the line of the highway running north–south of the city. So began what can be called the second battle of the Ukraine, the longest discrete campaign of the war and arguably more important than Kursk. The eight-month struggle in the Ukraine was as dramatic a defeat for Germany as the more famous destruction of Army Group Centre in June 1944; as five Soviet fronts defeated the Germans in a succession of battles and drove them first to the Dnepr and then all the way back to the Carpathians and the pre-war Polish border.[9]

A Russian attack south of Kursk smashed through the German defensive lines to take Belgorod on 5 August and fight another major tank action with the 2nd and 3rd SS Divisions on the outskirts of Kharkov. Von Manstein fought – and lost – the fourth and final battle for Kharkov in August 1943. He told Hitler that it was essential to retreat to a solid defensive line before winter. After a series of meetings with his senior commanders on the Eastern Front, Hitler was eventually persuaded to allow a withdrawal to the River Dnepr. Supported by the greater share of Luftwaffe resources, in the form of 750–1,000 sorties per day, half of them bomber missions, Army Group

Centre gave ground slowly against repeated Soviet offensives. The Soviet Western and Kalinin Fronts eventually recaptured Smolensk in early September, but at a terrible cost. The South–Western and Southern Fronts drove back Army Group South to prepared defensive positions running from Zaporezhe to the Black Sea, and succeeded in isolating the Crimea, occupied by the German 17th Army.

The German Army conducted an intensive 'scorched earth' policy as it fell back towards the Dnepr. In many villages every building was destroyed. This was nothing new; it had been standard operating procedure for the Ostheer, but it was carried out by soldiers who were increasingly suspicious that they would never be passing this way again. The savagery of the German Army in retreat had already been a feature of the War in the East. When the Wehrmacht had fallen back in winter 1941, it had destroyed what it could not take with it. Deportations and outright massacres of civilians had accompanied all subsequent withdrawals, a policy for which many senior army officers were brought to trial after the war.

While this does not excuse the actions of these units, the German Army had practically abandoned all judicial process by 1943. The court martial system was frequently bypassed and soldiers simply shot out of hand. Rule of law was replaced by rule of terror. More than 15,000 military executions were carried out by the German Army in the Second World War, almost all on the Russian front. With the Russians at hand, partisans itching for revenge, and their own officers increasingly ready to resort to the pistol, it is small wonder that some German soldiers employed excessive violence against those least able to defend themselves.

Even more grotesque activities began behind the front line. In August 1943 SS-Standartenführer Paul Blobel, former commander of Sonderkommando 4a, returned to Babi Yar (see Chapter Three) with his new unit Sonderkommando 1005. His task was to destroy the evidence of mass murders before the areas were overrun by the Soviets. Three hundred prisoners-of-war were used to disinter the bodies, pile them on improvised grates – the iron gates from the local cemetery – soak them in petrol and burn them. The bones were ground up with iron rollers, mixed with sand and scattered in the fields. When the job was done, the prisoners were ordered to fire up the grates once more, then the SS men shot them and disposed of their bodies the same way – except that one group of prisoners made a run for it when it became obvious what was about to happen.

The retreat was not only marked by German atrocities. The Luftwaffe methodically blew up airfield facilities, cratering runways and then sowing them with mines to prevent the Soviets using them. That practice was abandoned when it was discovered that the Russians were marching German prisoners-of-war across the runways to detonate the bombs.

Soviet mechanized forces reached the Dnepr either side of Kiev in late September. An attempt to use three airborne divisions to storm the river crossings at Kanev and Bukrin, 50 miles downstream, met with bloody defeat. One division was parachuted directly on to the positions of the 10th Panzergrenadier Division, which Soviet intelligence had not located. A bridgehead was established at Bukrin, but sealed off by the Germans. A month later, the 3rd Tank Army and 7th Artillery Breakthrough Corps abandoned the bridgehead, crossed back to the east side of the river and headed north. Some of their radio operators remained behind, still broadcasting, so their arrival in the tiny west-bank foothold at Lyutlezh, 12 miles upstream of Kiev, came as a very disagreeable surprise to the Germans. On 3 November, the German infantry divisions hemming Lyutlezh were struck by a hurricane bombardment from 2,000 guns, mortars and rocket launchers. The 3rd Tank Army overran the defences and surged towards Kiev, which the Germans evacuated three days later.

The Voronezh Front surged west another 60 miles to take Zhitomir and Korosten before Von Manstein counter-attacked with the 48th Panzer Corps in mid-November. The core of his force consisted of the 1st and 7th Panzer Divisions, SS Division 'Leibstandarte Adolf Hitler' and the 68th Infantry Division, plus the weakened 19th and 25th Panzer Divisions and a *Kampfgruppe* made up of the survivors from 2nd SS Division 'Das Reich'. The Germans recaptured both towns and re-established the direct railroad link with Army Group Centre. A more ambitious counter-stroke, aimed at attacking Kiev from the south-west and cutting off a large proportion of the Voronezh Front was abandoned in favour of an almost frontal attack, which failed. Major-General Mellenthin blamed Colonel-General Rauss, the commander of 4th Panzer Army, for excessive caution here.[10] Konev's Steppe Front stormed the German defences on the Dnepr further south and captured Cherkassy in early December. German forces still held the river line between the original Soviet bridgehead at Bukrin and the city of Kiev, but were becoming dangerously exposed to an encirclement. While vainly continuing his counter-attack towards Kiev, Von Manstein repeatedly requested permission to evacuate this dangerous salient. Hitler just wanted someone to blame for the continual advance of the Russians and sacked Colonel-General Hermann Hoth. This highly experienced Panzer general was placed on the retired list until April 1945, when he was briefly tasked with organizing the defence of the Harz mountains.

★

CHAPTER EIGHT

THE WRITING ON THE WALL

'The policy of clinging on at all costs in particular places
repeatedly changed the campaign for the worse.'

LIEUTENANT-GENERAL KURT DITTMAR

During their counter-attacks around Zhitomir in November
1943, the Germans took several thousand prisoners-of-war.
Most were either young teenagers or older men, some in their
fifties. Perhaps Russian manpower was not inexhaustible after all,
a revelation that, as General Mellenthin observed, 'strengthened
our determination to stick it out'. Indeed, the authorized strength
of a Russian rifle division had been reduced twice during 1943;
the numbers of replacements were insufficient to sustain existing
units, even when newly liberated villages and towns were combed
for young men to fill out Soviet units.[1] The Germans regarded
the Russian infantry division of late 1943 as only half as capable
as that of mid-1942. Nevertheless, the Russians had enough
infantry, even of reduced quality, and morale was high. Desertion
rates were a quarter of what they had been in the summer; and
the Red Army now included an incredible number of guns, rockets
and mortars — 80 artillery and mortar divisions, in addition to
organic heavy weapons of the infantry and tank units. There
were five tank armies, and a sixth was created in January 1944. The
correlation of forces by the end of 1943 was very unfavourable to
the Germans:

	German	Soviet
Men[2]	2.5 million	6 million
Tanks and SP guns[3]	1,500	5,600
Guns and mortars[4]	8,000	100,000
Aircraft[5]	2,000	13,000

The numbers of armoured vehicles listed here are total strengths; the number of operational German vehicles was even smaller. The same applies to the 2,000 Luftwaffe aircraft on the Russian front: no more than 1,500 were serviceable, and most of the aircraft were transport, liaison, trainer, or obsolete types. There were just 385 German fighters (301 operational) in Russia and 238 bombers. The Germans had an additional 706,000 men, the armies of their various allies; but very few of them fought effectively in 1944. By the same token, the Germans had stationed disproportionately large forces in Finland; the 20th Mountain Army had 176,000 on its ration strength. By the end of 1943 this was about the only German Army with its infantry divisions at full establishment, but the Finns refused to hazard another offensive against the Russians, or even to declare war on the USA. They were looking for a way to end their part in the war.

In February 1944, a year after the 6th Army surrendered at Stalingrad, Hitler managed to cause a similar disaster, albeit on a smaller scale. The Führer temporarily forsook his headquarters in East Prussia for his beloved Berghof. Camouflage netting blotted out the celebrated alpine views, but there was an ominous glow on the northern horizon where RAF Bomber Command was attacking Munich. From his mountain eyrie, he continued to try to micromanage operations along the Russian front, while his generals in France prepared to meet the Allied invasion.

German forces still held a section of the west bank of the Dnepr between Kanev and Cherkassy. The 52nd Corps, part of 1st Panzer Army, defended the northern sector, but it was being outflanked. The Soviet bridgehead around Kiev, 50 miles upstream, extended westwards despite the counter-attack described above. By the end of December 1943, the corps was bent back to hold an east–west front line just north of Boguslav. Vatutin's 1st Ukranian Front, formerly the Voronezh Front, continued to attack from this direction during January, and drove the Germans back to the River Rossava. The area around Cherkassy, which now formed the southern side of a salient extending back westwards to Lys'anka, was defended by the 11th Corps of the German 8th Army. The Soviet 2nd Ukranian Front under Konev steadily edged around it. All the evidence pointed to a potential encirclement, but Hitler adamantly refused to allow a timely withdrawal.

Konev launched a full-scale offensive on 24 January, with the 4th Guards Army and the 5th Guards Tank Army attacking from the south-east. German resistance was extremely determined, and the assault made little progress despite very strong artillery support. However, General Kravchenko's newly formed 6th Tank Army broke through in the north to link up with Konev's troops on 3 February. The two German corps were trapped in an oval-shaped perimeter that extended east–west 60 miles from the high ground around Medvin and Korsun'-Shevchenkovsky to Cherkassy, and north–south 25 miles from the River Rossava to Gorodishche.[6] The 11th Corps consisted of the 57th, 72nd and 389th Infantry Divisions, but they lacked anti-tank weapons and only the 72nd was strong enough for offensive operations. The 52nd Corps had the 88th and 112th Infantry Divisions, 5th SS Panzer Division 'Wiking' and the Belgian volunteer brigade 'Wallonien'.[7]

The commander of the trapped forces, General Werner Stemmermann, conducted a staunch defence. He stockpiled supplies in expectation – duly proved correct – that air supply would be inadequate. The Soviet Air Force concentrated its fighters above the pocket, and deployed large numbers of anti-aircraft guns along the path of German transport aircraft. A Russian lieutenant-colonel arrived on 9 February to offer terms, was treated to a glass of champagne and was sent on his way. One of the German commanders captured at Stalingrad, General von Seydlitz, wrote to at least one officer in the pocket suggesting he follow the example of the 19th-century Prussian hero Yorck, who went over to the Russians in the war of 1812.

Field Marshal von Manstein counter-attacked with the 3rd Panzer Corps: the 1st, 16th, 17th Panzer Divisions plus 1st SS Panzer Division. On 11 February the Germans crossed the River Gniloy

Tikich but were unable to expand their bridgehead. Ironically, it was unseasonably warm weather that was the problem. Unusually warm days alternating with the normal winter cold had turned the unmetalled roads into a glutinous mass. Soviet tanks, with their wider tracks and lower ground pressure, could cope with the conditions better. Their more homogeneous wheeled transport (mainly American) was also more able to keep moving than the bizarre collection of lorries operated by the Germans.

By 15 February it was clear that the relief force was spent. It could hold its ground, but further progress was impossible. Stemmermann would have to break out. The weather closed in, grounding the Luftwaffe but not the Soviets. Konev found volunteer pilots in U-2s to locate and bomb the village of Shanderovka, where Stemmermann's survivors were assembling for a 'do or die' assault in the morning. They ignited enough fires to guide in more bombers and provide a marker for the Soviet artillery.

The encircled German troops formed up in two columns to fight their way across the 10 miles separating Shanderovka from the River Gniloy Tikich and safety. The retreat began and ended with a grisly massacre. Setting out into a snowstorm on 17 February, the Germans blew up all immobilized vehicles and heavy guns for which there was no ammunition. They shot their own wounded in the back of the head – 'as they usually shoot Russians and Jews', one Soviet officer noted – and 'in many cases they set fire to the ambulance vans with the dead inside. One of the oddest sights were the charred skeletons in those burned-out vans, with wide bracelets of plaster-of-Paris round their arms or legs. For plaster-of-Paris doesn't burn …'[8]

Progress was deceptively easy for the first few miles. Then the Soviets attacked with tanks and mounted cavalry and the columns were split into pieces. The German units dissolved into a mass of fugitives, and they were hunted down and slaughtered without mercy. Several desperate bands broke through to the river at Lys'anka, including a couple of tanks which were lost trying to ford it – the river was a good 9 feet deep. As the Soviets realized how many Germans had reached the bank, they concentrated their artillery on the area. Hundreds drowned trying to swim across before the T–34s arrived.

The Russians discovered the body of General Stemmermann, killed when his command half-track was knocked out, among the bloody wreckage of his columns. He was identified by his Black Forest gun licence. Several SS officers shot themselves rather than surrender. The Soviets claimed to have killed 55,000 men and captured 18,000, but this would have meant Stemmermann's divisions were all at full strength. There were between 50,000 and 60,000 men trapped at Cherkassy/Korsun, and it is likely that fewer than half of them escaped. The SS 'Wiking' and 'Wallonien' formations retained their unit integrity and crossed the river, but the Belgians suffered 70 per cent losses in the process. Konev was promoted to Marshal of the Soviet Union and Rotmistrov of 5th Guards Tank Army became the first Marshal of Armoured Forces.

Konev celebrated his promotion by resuming the offensive, despite the persisting freeze/thaw weather conditions. In what Soviet veterans would remember as the 'mud offensive' – the roads consisted of liquid mud deeper than the soldiers' boots – the 2nd Ukranian Front drove back the German 8th Army (Hube) and liberated Uman. The advance continued to the River Bug, and by March 1944 Konev's men had crossed the border into Romania. While the T–34 could slither its way across the waterlogged terrain, few German vehicles could do the same, and hundreds of tanks, half-tracks and other vehicles had to be blown up and abandoned while their crews squelched westwards on foot. Neither Konev's guns nor his supply lorries could keep up with the advance, and the leading elements were supplied by Soviet aircraft.

Zhukov took personal command of the 1st Ukranian Front for another ambitious attempt to encircle the Germans. His intended victims – the 20 understrength divisions of 1st Panzer Army – were cut off by the end of March after the Soviet 1st Tank Army stormed across the River Dnestr. Once again, Hitler insisted his soldiers hold their positions regardless, but Field Marshal von Manstein won a furious argument with him and permission was granted for the army to break out. The 2nd SS Panzer Corps mounted a vigorous relief effort, wrong-footing Marshal Zhukov, who deployed his forces in expectation that the Germans would fall back into Romania. Instead, the Germans drove directly west for 180 miles to the German front in Galicia. The Luftwaffe concentrated its remaining strength in the east to support the operation, delivering 200–250 tons of supplies per day throughout the two weeks it took 1st Panzer Army to fight its way free.

After brooding for a week or so, Hitler removed Von Manstein from command of Army Group South. Von Manstein, without doubt one of the best commanders of the Second World War, was compelled to sit out the rest of the conflict. His actions behind the front line in Russia earned him an 18-year sentence at the Nuremberg war crimes trials, but he was released in 1953 to write the best-selling *Lost Victories* and play a key role in founding the post-war West German Army. Like Guderian, the urbane and charming Von Manstein persuaded many British and American officers that he was a 'simple soldier', untainted by the activities of the Nazis. Basil Liddell-Hart championed both of them, and Von Manstein is remembered today as a brilliant military commander, which he certainly was, but one of his own orders, cited at his trial, reads:

> The Jewish-Bolshevist system must be exterminated ... The German soldier comes as the bearer of a racial concept. [He] must appreciate the necessity for the harsh punishment of Jewry ... The food situation at home makes it essential that the troops should be fed off the land, and that the largest possible stocks should be placed at the disposal of the homeland. In enemy cities, a large part of the population will have to go hungry. Nothing, out of a misplaced sense of humanity, may be given to prisoners-of-war or to the population unless they are in service of the German Wehrmacht.[9]

Nor was this an isolated instance. When commanding the 11th Army in 1941 his orders also harped on about the German soldier as the 'bearer of a racial concept', and 'an avenger of all the atrocities which have been committed against him and the German people'.[10]

On the other hand, Von Manstein was aware of at least some of the plots against Hitler; several other generals hinted they were prepared to serve under him in a post-Hitler Germany, and he never passed on such contacts to the security agencies. While he refused requests to join the plotters with a trenchant statement that 'Prussian field marshals do not mutiny', how seriously he took Hitler's regime can best be gauged by the fact that he taught his pet dog to give the Nazi salute.

Von Manstein's removal was the latest in a series of sackings that began with the disastrous winter of 1941–42. The three army group commanders of 1941 (Von Leeb, Von Bock and Von Rundstedt) were all removed then, although Von Rundstedt was reinstated later – only to be sacked again in 1945. General Guderian was removed at the same time, although he became Inspector-General of armoured troops in 1943. Two other highly competent officers, Colonel-General Hoth and Field Marshal von Kleist, were sacked in 1943 and 1944 respectively. Hoth was sentenced to 15 years at Nuremberg in 1948; he served six and retired to write his memoirs, dying in 1971 at the age of 86. His criticism of Germany's wartime leadership in *Panzeroperationen* was as accurate as it was caustic. He damned Hitler and his lackeys 'for so lightly undertaking a war without written plans on basic strategy, all moves being made as a consequence of day-to-day conversations between Hitler and his staff'.[11] Kleist was handed to the Yugoslavs in 1948, who jailed him for war crimes but then sent him to Russia the next year. He died in captivity in 1954 at the age of 71.

Hitler's penchant for dismissing some of his best field commanders has often attracted comment, but if he failed to appreciate their military skills, he was acutely aware of their political potential. Might sidelining so many senior figures stimulate the German officer corps to make the sort of political intervention it had so signally avoided in the 1930s? Whereas Stalin had shot his generals to head off the – admittedly unlikely – threat of a military coup, Hitler simply bribed his potential malcontents. Field Marshal von List, commander of Army

Group A in 1942, was sacked that September but, like others of his kind, he received cash payments from the Nazi Party until 1945. In his new role, Guderian continued to clash with Hitler over many strategic issues but still found time to spend 'months travelling around eastern Europe looking for an estate which the government could steal for him – and he did not think the one he received was adequate'.[12]

Von Manstein's replacement was the acerbic Walter Model, at 53 Germany's youngest field marshal. His brusque manner terrified subordinates and irritated superiors, and even Hitler hesitated to argue with him. Despite a period in disgrace in late 1943, he had taken command of Army Group North in January 1944, restored order in a brilliant rearguard action and won his promotion. Strangely, since no part of the country remained under German control, Army Group South was renamed Army Group North Ukraine.

On 10 April 1944 General Malinovsky, commander of the 3rd Ukranian Front, liberated his home-town of Odessa. Until a few weeks before its hurried evacuation, the city had been occupied not by the Germans, but by the Romanians. Alexander Werth visited Odessa some days after it changed hands. He was immediately struck by the large numbers of young people there – in vivid contrast to his experience of liberated Russian and Ukranian towns, where only the old and very young remained. The Romanian regime regarded Odessa as a valuable prize; its people were citizens of 'Romanian Transniestria' and not to be dragged off as slaves by the Germans. Except for Jews, of course. What the journalist did not realize was that the city had been the scene of a full-scale pogrom in 1941. A week after the city's fall in October 1941, Romanian troops conducted a pitiless slaughter throughout the area, killing every Jewish person they could find. Recent estimates suggest a death toll of tens of thousands.

Liberation of the Crimea
On 11 April the Soviet 3rd Ukranian Front, commanded by General Fyodor Tolbukhin, broke into the Crimea from the north, while a diversionary offensive crashed against the heavily fortified Perekop

isthmus. Tolbukhin's divisions fanned out to overrun the northern part of the Crimea and the German–Romanian forces in the eastern Crimea stampeded back to Sebastopol to avoid being cut off. The German attempt to cling onto the Crimea was perhaps foolhardy, but it had many good airfields equipped for all-weather operations in range of the Romanian oil fields that were crucial to German fuel supplies. It was also the best place from which to fly strategic materials between Germany and Japan: in April a Junkers Ju-290 flew from Odessa to Mukden, Manchuria, with 4 tons of optical equipment, returning with a consignment of molybdenum (used for alloys and high-temperature steels required for advanced aircraft and missile parts). Planned missions from the Crimea were out of the question, as by 16 April the German 17th Army was hemmed into Sebastopol. Hitler ordered 'Fortress Sebastopol' to hold on until the last man; after all, the Red Army had defended it for 250 days in 1941–42. What he got was a German Dunkirk. The commander of the 17th Army, Colonel-General Jänicke, reported the position to be untenable – and he knew an impossible situation when he saw one. He had commanded 4th Corps in the Stalingrad pocket, but was flown out and replaced by General Pfeffer before the surrender. Hitler sacked Jänicke, the bearer of bad news. Evacuation began in the first days of May as the Soviets pounded the hastily dug entrenchments. Approximately 40,000 troops were shipped to safety, with strangely little interference by Soviet naval forces which remained unwilling to challenge German control of the Black Sea. Although the Black Sea Fleet had a battleship, six cruisers, 21 destroyers, and 30 submarines, the threat of air attack, mines and the 16 'S'-boats and six coastal U-Boats operated there by the Kriegsmarine meant that it spent most of 1942–44 inactive at Batum.[13] It did make a couple of forays in autumn 1943, only to lose three destroyers to air attack in October.

In the absence of a naval threat, the evacuation could have continued, but the perimeter collapsed on 9 May. Tolbukhin had brought forward his heavy artillery, which blasted enough gaps for his infantry divisions to break in. The Germans abandoned the city and conducted a fighting withdrawal to the Khersonese peninsula, a few miles down the coast. Some 30,000 men found themselves trapped on this tiny spit of land, no more than 1,000 yards across at its neck. A few thousand were rescued until Soviet artillery drove off the boats; once the beach itself was under fire from Katyushas, the game was up. On 12 May the survivors surrendered. Total German losses in the Crimea were 50,000 dead and 61,000 captured.

The return of Soviet rule to the Crimea involved more than the usual hunt for collaborators. Since the Crimean Tartars had cooperated with the Germans, helping to hunt down Soviet partisans and volunteering for military service, Stalin deported the entire population — 500,000 people — to central Asia/Siberia. Similar treatment had been meted out to the peoples of the North Caucasus after the German withdrawal: altogether more than a million civilians were uprooted from their villages, often with no warning. Since most of the collaborators slipped away with the Germans, Soviet vengeance fell mainly on women and children. More than 100,000 NKVD troops were devoted to organizing the deportations, which continued, especially in the Baltic States, until after the war. At the Party Congress in 1956, Khruschev joked that Stalin would have deported all 40 million Ukranians too, if only he had had the rail capacity, and somewhere to put them.

CHAPTER NINE

★

PRUSSIAN ROULETTE

'There is only one thing worse than fighting a war with allies: and that is fighting one without them.'

WINSTON CHURCHILL

By the spring of 1944 it was obvious that the western Allies were poised to land in France. It was planned to be the biggest amphibious operation in history, and if it came off, Germany would lose the war. The D-Day landings were such a triumph that their success is often regarded as inevitable, and certainly by 7 June the Germans had lost their only serious opportunity to liquidate the beachheads. However, the Allied victory in Normandy was the product of many factors, and was by no means assured when the spring thaw spread through Russia and *Stavka* began to plan its operations for the summer.

German strategy for 1944 was based on three assumptions: had they been right, history might have followed a very different course. The first was that the Allied invasion would be in the Pas de Calais. This involved the shortest sea crossing and would position the Allied armies on the most direct route to the Reich. The second assumption was that the next Soviet offensive would fall in the south, further exploiting the spectacular success of the winter offensive that had brought them to the borders of Romania and up to the Carpathians. This made political and economic sense. From here, the Soviets could strike directly into southern Poland, break into Hungary and/or push south into Romania to overrun the oil fields that sustained the German forces. The third basis for German strategy was a new-found ability to strike back at strategic targets. Hitler had seen to it that enormous resources were devoted to the development of the V1 and V2 ballistic missiles: films of them being launched were instrumental in sustaining the belief that German technology could still turn the course of the war in their favour.

The D–Day campaign is celebrated for the brilliant deception plan that played on German fears, fooling them into maintaining large forces around Calais even after the Allies were ashore in Normandy. The Soviet summer offensive of 1944 – Operation *Bagration* – was preceded by an equally successful deception scheme that drew the bulk of the Ostheer to Army Group North Ukraine. Even after the blow fell on 22 June, the anniversary of the German invasion three years earlier, German intelligence persisted in its belief that the major Soviet effort was still to come. The result was the greatest German defeat of the war: the annihilation of Army Group Centre. Meanwhile Hitler's last hope, that his secret weapons would turn the course of the war, was to prove equally false. The Allied air forces mounted an intensive campaign against the launch sites and missile factories, reducing the number of missile launches to a fraction of what they could have been.

The Ostheer had 700 tanks and 1,000 assault guns ready for operations in May 1944.[1] There were 22 Panzer and Panzergrenadier divisions on the Russian front, divided equally between north and south, with nine in Army Group North Ukraine and nine in Army Group South Ukraine. Army Group Centre, in the middle, had very little armour, and what it did have was almost all provided by batteries of StuG assault guns. The Army Group was commanded by 69–year–old Field Marshal Ernst Busch, who had won Germany's highest award for bravery, the *Pour la Mérite*, as a junior officer on the Western Front during the First World War. A committed Nazi, he led the 16th Army during the initial invasion of Russia; by the time he succeeded Von Kluge in command of Army Group Centre he had the Knight's Cross with Oak Leaves for his stubborn defence at Demyansk in the winter of 1942–43. In June 1944 he had three armies, totalling 38 infantry and two understrength Panzer divisions. His infantry divisions had six battalions each, with average ration strengths of 300 men.

The Soviet offensive was conducted by four army groups, the 2nd Baltic Front (General Andrei Yeremenko), 1st Baltic Front (General Ivan Bagramyan), 3rd White Russian Front (General Ivan Chernyakovsky) and 1st White Russian Front (General Konstantin

Rokossovsky). Between them they had 2,715 tanks, now including Guard battalions with IS-2 heavy tanks. Each of the eight tank corps had three regiments of SU-76/122/152s; a total of 1,355 assault guns took part in the attack. The assault was supported by some 24,000 guns which pulverized the thinly held German front line with a hurricane bombardment. Above the battlefields, Soviet fighters were practically unchallenged and neither Heinkel He-111s nor Junkers Ju-88s could survive in daylight. Even Junkers Ju-188s were being intercepted at 30,000 feet. The only German bombers that could get through were Heinkel He-177s, which relied on close formation flying and their heavy defensive firepower, but the Luftwaffe simply did not have enough of them.

The front collapsed within days. Vitebsk was surrounded on 24 June; Soviet forces advanced rapidly around Bobruisk and crossed the Dnepr to bypass the Germans in Mogilev, who were ordered to hold their ground to the last man – as if it mattered. Within a week, the ominous gaps between major German forces showed no signs of closing. The Soviet 5th Guards Tank Army drove a wedge between the German 3rd Panzer and 4th Armies; into the gulf between the 4th Army and 9th Army plunged the Soviet 4th Guards Cavalry Corps.

Hitler's micromanagement of the war in Russia had reached such ludicrous depths that it was said officers were afraid to move a sentry from the window to the door without permission from OKH. His reaction to the disaster was entirely consistent. On 27 June, he sacked the commander of the 9th Army, General Hans Jordan, who at least was able to fly to East Prussia to be dismissed and thus survive the war. Field Marshal Busch lasted only another day before he was removed and Field Marshal Model was placed in command of Army Group Centre. But not even the 'fireman of the Eastern Front' could rescue much from the wreckage. Although German reinforcements were rushing to stem the tide, the Soviet staff work was of a high order and their armoured forces exploited the open front with the same panache the Panzers had demonstrated in 1941. They broke through to Minsk, trapping thousands of Germans east of the city.

So many pockets were created by the disintegration of the front that there was no prospect of relief efforts – there were not enough troops in reserve to re-establish a coherent front line, so isolated units were on their own. Since the local partisans had been subjected to the most savage counter-guerrilla operations earlier in the year, they seized the opportunity to take terrible revenge against those German soldiers unlucky enough to fall into their hands. As the advancing Soviet formations discovered more than one train packed with Russian children, awaiting deportation, the Red Army was not in forgiving mood either. Nevertheless, the Russians received the first mass surrenders by German units: four German corps laid down their arms in the forests outside Minsk. Across Belorussia the Red Army took 150,000 prisoners. To mark the turn of the tide, the Russians paraded 57,000 captured Germans through Moscow on 17 July. In five weeks, the German Army had lost 300,000 men. A total of 30 divisions were removed from the German order of battle, of which 17 never re-formed.

The mass of German forces in Army Group North Ukraine were unable to help. On 13 July, Konev's 1st Ukranian Front attacked into Galicia, liberating Lwow and pressing on to the River San and the old First World War fortress at Premysl. At the end of the month, the Soviet 1st, 3rd and 4th Tank Armies reached the Vistula around Sandomierz and established several bridgeheads. These were subjected to furious counter-attacks. However, as the Germans had learned, Soviet bridgeheads were all but impossible to dislodge, and despite intensive fighting, they failed to drive the Russians into the river.

Many people, in Russia as well as the west, had dismissed talk of concentration camps as just propaganda. There had been innumerable atrocity stories in the First World War that had subsequently proved false, and the rumours about German concentration camps were generally regarded in similar light. But on 23 July 1944, the full horror of the Nazi regime was exposed by the Red Army. Not far from the Polish city of Lublin, the Germans had built the extermination camp of Majdenek. Similar establishments at Belzec, Sobibor and Treblinka had already been closed and burned down after the extermination of Polish Jews was completed; Treblinka had even been turned into a farm and pine trees planted to hide the evidence.

There had not been time to do the same at Majdenek. All the machinery was still in place – concrete gas chambers labelled *Bad und Desinfektion*; the crematorium capable of burning 2,000 bodies a day; a barn containing 850,000 pairs of shoes; and a fresh mass-grave where the remaining prisoners were shot and buried as the SS departed. *Pravda* printed a full account which confirmed the revelations of escaped prisoners-of-war who had been swept back into the Russian Army as it approached the German border. 'It was with a whiff of Majdenek in their nostrils that thousands of Russian soldiers were to fight their way into East Prussia,' noted Alexander Werth whose own report on the death camp was spiked by the BBC.[2] The War in the East had been merciless enough since 1941, and as the Soviet forces prepared to invade Germany, the opportunity to take vengeance was openly anticipated.

On 20 July Hitler survived the penultimate of the nine assassination attempts made against him between 1933 and 1945. It was the most nearly successful too – a bomb exploded under the conference table at his headquarters in East Prussia. Had the meeting taken place as originally planned, in a concrete bunker, the blast would have killed everyone in the confined space. But at the last minute it was switched to a wooden building. Hitler was shielded from the worst of the explosion by the stout oak table. The plotters failed to establish that he was dead before attempting a gallant, if amateurish, *coup d'état*. Their networks in Berlin, Vienna and Paris were soon rounded up as a vengeful Führer coordinated the machinery of state by telephone from Rastenburg.

Even the most well-adjusted individual might have come to believe that he did indeed benefit from divine intervention, having been spared from death on so many occasions. In Hitler's case, this latest manifestation of Fortuna reinforced all of his most odious beliefs and sentiments, which had an immediate impact on the War in the East.

Proclaiming he now knew why Stalin had Tukachevsky shot, Hitler appointed Nazi political officers to military headquarters. Martin Bormann and Heinrich Himmler became regular attendants at the Führer's daily military conferences. Discipline in the German Army became completely dislocated from the pre-war legal system. 'Flying military courts', a dreadful mixture of Gestapo officials, military police, SS and SD men, conducted arbitrary executions of soldiers and civilians alike. Kurt Zeitzler was replaced as chief of staff at OKH by the officer whose vigorous action against the coup attempt had restored order in Berlin – Colonel-General Heinz Guderian.

Meanwhile, the Soviet advance continued across Poland until it approached Warsaw. The Polish capital was at the heart of German road and rail communications and a key crossing of the Vistula. It was so strategically important to the Germans that they counter-attacked aggressively from 30 July. Newly arrived in the east, and with a full regiment of Panzer IVs and a battalion of JagdPanzer IVs, the 'Hermann Göring' Division attacked alongside 4th Panzer Division and SS 'Wiking' Division, both from Army Group North Ukraine. They drove the Soviet 3rd Tank Corps and 8th Guards Tank Corps 10 miles back north-east of Warsaw. The Soviet forces had fought their way across more than 400 miles in little more than a month and were reaching the culminating point of their offensive, but from 1 August political calculation combined with military necessity to slow the Russian advance. The Polish Home Army had risen in Warsaw.

The Warsaw Rising

The Soviet regime had been waging war on the Poles for longer than it had been fighting the Germans. Stalin ordered the NKVD to murder 15,000 Polish officers taken prisoner in September 1940 before the end of that year. During the 18 months of Soviet rule in eastern Poland, more than a million Poles were deported to the *gulag*. Nevertheless, such was the impact of the Nazis in Poland that by the summer of 1944 the Soviet forces included two Polish armies with a strength of some 90,000 men. The Nazi regime regarded Polish people as no more than a slave-labour force, and it is significant that Poland was about the only country in eastern Europe to provide no volunteer units for the Wehrmacht or Waffen-SS. Some six million Poles, half of them Jewish, were put to death by the Germans, giving Poland the highest proportionate casualties of any nation in the Second World War.

Warsaw had already been the scene of one uprising: the Jews in the ghetto had fought to the death rather than be deported to the extermination camps, holding off SD and SS units for several days in April 1943 with nothing but pistols and petrol bombs. In August 1944 the Polish Home Army had something like 40,000 men and women under its command, loyal to the government-in-exile in London. Although only 10 per cent had weapons, the decision was taken to seize control of Warsaw before the Red Army did so. Unfortunately for the Poles, they failed to secure any of the bridges across the Vistula and during the next few weeks, the sudden passivity of the Soviet Army enabled the Germans to assemble enough forces to counter-attack. Hitler demanded the city be destroyed altogether, and the German units that he sent there included the most infamous in his army, including the Dirlewanger Brigade[3] – and Borislav Kaminski's private army (see Chapter Six). Few barbarities known to man were absent in the slaughter that followed.

Some Soviet units – including Polish divisions under Russian command – crossed the Vistula and entered the eastern outskirts of Warsaw in mid-September, but they were unable to break through to the insurgent Home Army before German counter-attacks drove them back across the river. No doubt the front-line troops, Russians as well as Poles, were fighting as hard as they could, but the Germans had deployed major new armoured formations in the east. Stalin refused to allow US aircraft to use Soviet airfields when they tried to parachute supplies to the Polish resistance. 'Power-seeking criminals' was Stalin's description of the Home Army, and it suited the Soviets perfectly for the Germans to finish off what the NKVD had started in the killing fields of Katyn.

The Home Army surrendered on 2 October, and to medieval cruelty Hitler added his own brand of vindictiveness. Warsaw was systematically destroyed, buildings blown up block by block so that when the city was finally abandoned to the Russians in January 1945, little more than blackened rubble remained. One person lucky enough to escape was Marshal Rokossovsky's sister, Helena, whom he had not seen since 1915; finding her way to her brother's headquarters, she stayed there until the fall of Berlin, and was ultimately introduced to Stalin.

Germany's defeats in both east and west led Heinrich Himmler to drop his racial objections to the use of Russian soldiers. The Wehrmacht had quietly made official its use of the *Hilfswillige* or '*Hiwis*', Russian volunteers who worked as anything from laundry staff to ammunition carriers and drivers. Between a million and 1.5 million Soviet citizens donned some form of German uniform during 1941–45. The official establishment of a German infantry division in 1943 included 2,000 *Hiwis* and their total strength rose from 300,000 in 1943 to 500,000 in 1944. Soviet General Andrei Vlasov, an insanely ambitious officer who had championed the German cause since his capture in 1942, was wheeled out to take command of a new Russian army in 1944, just as the Germans were driven out of Russia. The ROA (Russian Liberation Army) was set up by the SS and eventually included three divisions. Poorly equipped and of doubtful motivation, they went into action in the winter of 1944–45, and were quickly destroyed. General Vlasov and other senior officers the Russians managed to capture were tried and executed for treason in 1946. He remains written out of history: even a 2001 account of the Moscow battles ignores the vital role of Vlasov and his 20th Army in the victory of December 1941.

The ROA was part of the Reichsführer's expanding state-within-a-state. The Waffen-SS eventually included a bewildering galaxy of units recruited in eastern Europe. By the end of 1943 Himmler had snatched both Cossack divisions raised by the German Army, then employed on anti-partisan operations in the Balkans. They were grandly retitled 15th SS Cavalry Corps, and continued to develop their reputation for indiscriminate slaughter.

The decisive defeat of German forces in the east, and the presence of Allied forces in France and halfway up the Italian peninsula, suggested that the end of the war was only a matter of time. Italy had already changed sides; General Franco had withdrawn the 'Azul' Spanish division and Hitler's remaining allies moved quickly to finish on the winning side too.

On 20 August, the 2nd Ukranian Front (General Radion Malinovsky) and Tolbukhin's 3rd Ukranian Front, liberators of Sebastopol, launched an operation intended to conquer Romania. For Malinovsky, this was also a matter of personal revenge: the Romanians had occupied his home-town, Odessa. Malinovsky and Tolbukhin had 92 infantry divisions between them and six tank/mechanized corps, a total of more than a million men. Malinovsky attacked north-west of Iasi and established bridgeheads over the River Prut, threatening to cut off the German 6th and 8th Armies. The 3rd Ukranian Front already had a foothold on the west bank of the Dnestr near Tiraspol, but fierce German resistance checked the assault until the Romanians followed the Italian example. On 23 August Marshal Antonescu was arrested on the orders of the Romanian king, Mihai. Romanian units surrendered en masse to the Soviets and within weeks they were fighting against the Germans. The German 6th Army was annihilated for a second time in this war, after its fighting retreat from Chisenau was blocked by the Soviets at the River Siret. In just ten days, Army Group South, re-named Army Group South Ukraine on 1 September, shrank from 500,000 Germans and 400,000 Romanians to just 200,000 Germans.

Bulgaria had been allied to Germany since 1941, and had declared war on Britain and America that December. However, Hitler failed to compel King Boris to join the war against Russia. Bulgarian military assistance was limited to the provision of troops for anti-partisan duties in Yugoslavia, a role which became more important after Italy changed sides. King Boris died of an apparent heart attack while flying back to Bulgaria in August 1943, an incident that might well have been an assassination.[4] The approach of the Red Army concentrated minds in Sofia, and on 5 September 1944 Bulgaria severed diplomatic relations with Germany. Stalin wanted more than gestures, so the Soviet Army poured across the frontier and the Bulgarian Army – including units inside Yugoslavia – changed sides. Elements of the Bulgarian Army served under Soviet command in the subsequent fighting in Hungary, while a pro-Soviet political structure was put in place. King Boris's brother, the regent Prince Cyril, was shot by the NKVD in February 1945.

Two days after Romania's defection, Finland concluded an agreement with the Soviets and the German forces there withdrew to Norway in October after the Soviet Karelian Front attacked and captured Petsamo.

Germany's last significant ally was Hungary, but the regent, Admiral Miklos Horthy, was already having secret talks with Stalin; his representatives were arriving in Moscow on 1 October 1944. An armistice was signed ten days later, but German forces in Budapest carried out a coup before it could take effect. Horthy was dispatched to a concentration camp and a fanatical pro-Nazi called Ferenc Szalasi took his place. Adolf Eichmann was able to supervise the last great round-up of Jews – 437,000 people were shipped straight to Auschwitz. The Hungarian Army was reorganized under direct German control, with new formations recruited directly by the Wehrmacht. The SS began recruitment for four Hungarian SS divisions too, but these embryonic units were caught up in the retreat that began in October as the Soviet 3rd Ukranian Front forced the Carpathian passes, with the Romanian 1st and 4th Armies now under Russian command. Only the arrival of substantial German reinforcements, including 3rd Panzer Corps, prevented the Soviets attacking Budapest itself in early November. In the teeth of repeated German counter-attacks led by 4th SS Panzer Corps, Malinovsky nevertheless succeeded in encircling the Hungarian capital at the end of December. The 8th SS Cavalry Division 'Florian Geyer', the 13th Panzer Division, the SS 'Feldherrnhalle' Division and several Hungarian divisions were trapped there. On the other side of the lines, the former commander of the Hungarian 1st Army, General Miklos, emerged as head of a pro-Soviet provisional government, ready to be installed as soon as the Red Army could complete its conquest.

Army Group North was not destroyed in the same way as Army Groups Centre and South, but its likely fate was evident at the end of July when a Soviet offensive broke through to the Gulf of Riga. Army Group North was no longer connected to Germany by land. In mid-August the German 3rd Panzer Army managed to cut through to re-establish a slim corridor, and Army Group North fell back on Riga, but on 5 October the reorganized Soviets mounted a far greater effort, using the 50 divisions of 1st and 2nd Baltic Fronts. Breaking through either side of Memel (Klaipeda), where the German 28th Corps found itself trapped, the Soviets reached the coast in overwhelming strength. Army Group North was marooned at the end of the Kurland peninsula from Libau (Liapâja) on the Baltic to the Gulf of Riga around Tukums, a front of about 100 miles.

By the end of 1944 Germany had been defeated in France, with the loss of 400,000 men, and crushed in eastern Europe, losing 900,000 men. The Allied armies were poised to dismember the 'thousand year Reich', and German military deployments were almost calculated to help. Hitler refused to evacuate Army Group North while his navy could still operate with relative impunity in the Baltic; major forces were retained in Norway for no apparent reason, and the fighting in Hungary drew off what remained of Germany's armoured reserves after the lunatic adventure known to history as the Battle of the Bulge. Hitler's quixotic attempt to repeat the victory of 1940 across the same ground in December 1944 expended his last significant reserves of men and fuel and ended in predictable defeat.

CHAPTER TEN

★

GOODBYE TO BERLIN

'The hour of revenge has struck!'

ILYA EHRENBURG

Six months after the Ostheer was so badly wrong-footed and Army Group Centre driven from Belorussia to Warsaw, Colonel-General Heinz Guderian realized Hitler was poised to repeat the error. For what he described as 'political reasons', Hitler diverted significant German forces to Hungary to attempt a counter-attack at Budapest. Guderian highlighted the obvious danger, that the Soviets would attack straight across Poland and into Germany: it was here, Guderian argued, that all available reserves should be concentrated. He cited Colonel Gehlen's prediction that the Russian assault would begin on 12 January with an 11:1 superiority in infantry, 7:1 in tanks and 20:1 in artillery. Hitler told him to fire his intelligence chief, to which Guderian retorted that he might as well fire his chief of staff too.

Hitler kept them both, for the time being, but Army Group Centre was not spared. On the very day Guderian had predicted, five Soviet fronts attacked in what subsequent Soviet accounts labelled the 'Vistula–Oder' operation. The Russians tore a 25-mile gap in the German front and their massed armoured forces pushed on at top speed, leaving isolated pockets of resistance to be wiped out by follow-on forces. Warsaw was encircled, then stormed on 17 January by the 1st Polish Army; Cracow was liberated the next day, overrun so quickly that planned demolition work in this beautiful city was not carried out. German units assembling for a counter-attack at Lodz were caught deploying and swept back to the River Oder.

Two of the Soviet fronts stormed into East Prussia, pinning the 3rd Panzer Army into Königsberg (Kaliningrad) and the Samland peninsula. The beleaguered Germans were joined by the former garrison of Memel, evacuated on 29 January under the guns of the surviving units of the German navy, including the heavy cruiser *Prinz Eugen*. The 'pocket battleships' *Lutzow* and *Scheer* bombarded the Soviet lines too, before withdrawing to Kiel and Gotenhafen. From the Baltic to Southern Poland, improvised *Kampfgruppen* fought desperately, firstly to win time for German forces to make good their escape, and then to break free themselves. In a fortnight, the Soviet Army had advanced 250 miles and was poised to invade the German heartland. Berlin was but an hour's drive along the autobahn from their bridgeheads on the River Oder.

The siege of Budapest continued as the Soviet forces raced across Poland. On 1 January the garrison struck westwards, while 4th SS Panzer Corps tried to punch through from the outside. They failed to break the iron grip of the Red Army, but got within 12 miles of linking up. Throughout the rest of the month, Soviet troops fought their way into the Hungarian capital, house by house, street by street, grinding their way to the Danube at incredible cost. With the bridges down and the river at their backs, the defenders were split into several pockets which finally surrendered on 18 January. The same horrific process then began on the opposite bank as Buda was systematically conquered with the same combination of flame-throwers, demolition charges and point-blank fire from 203mm howitzers. With the end in sight, 16,000 German and Hungarian troops tried to break out on 16 February but they were annihilated by overwhelming numbers.

The last German offensive of the Second World War began on 6 March along the shores of Lake Balaton, Hungary. A total of 31 divisions, including 11 Panzer and Panzergrenadier divisions with up to 800 tanks took part, although many formations were at much reduced strength. The 6th SS Panzer Army which spearheaded the advance was commanded by SS-Oberstgruppenführer 'Sepp' Dietrich, once an NCO in Germany's tiny tank force of 1918, and the original commander of Hitler's bodyguard.[1] To preserve security, reconnaissance of the ground had been minimal; the early thaw had left the low-lying countryside heavily waterlogged. Even Dietrich recognized the impossibility of his orders in the first hours. His 60-ton Tiger II heavy tanks sank up to their turrets when they tried to move off the road, and 15 of these precious vehicles had to be abandoned. As one SS-Obersturmbannführer signalled him when ordered to attack, ' I have tanks, not submarines. You can kiss my arse but I won't do it.'²

For a few days the old magic still worked. The Germans broke into the Soviet defences. Even the phlegmatic Tolbukhin had to request assistance from 9th Guards Army. But the German attack faced impossible odds and sputtered out in the swamp. Leaving hundreds of new tanks immobilized in the mud, the 6th Panzer Army fell back towards Vienna. Tolbukhin was left to prepare the next leg of his offensive.

The appearance of the Soviet Army on German soil prompted a mass exodus and, in some cases, mass suicide. Refugees poured westwards as the embattled German Army fought for time. For years the Nazi propaganda machine had painted the most bloodcurdling images of what the 'Jewish–Bolshevik hordes' would do if they broke into the Reich, and from the moment it crossed the frontier, the Red Army's appetite for destruction and, above all, rape was practically insatiable. H.G.Wells once observed that if you push even the most civilized man far enough, you will be confronted by the hot red eyes of the caveman. The Soviets had won a war using every tool of 20th-century industrial civilization, yet they marked their victory in the most bestial, primitive fashion. In village after village, town after town, Soviet soldiers burst into rooms of terrified civilians waving machine-guns and bellowing, '*Frau, Komm!*' Such was the scale of horror that after the fighting had ended, the Roman Catholic bishop of Berlin gave Catholic doctors permission to perform abortions. Not for the first time in the War in the East, army officers condoned their men's savagery – some even exhorted them to do their worst. For Colonel-General Pavel Rybalko, bullet-headed commander of 3rd Guards Tank Army, it was personal: the Germans had abducted his daughter.

Among the most eager for vengeance were the slave labourers and released prisoners-of-war, who were pressed into service with Soviet divisions as the front line rolled forwards. One moment they were at the mercy of the Germans, to be starved or killed at their whim; an instant later, the roles were reversed and they were back in the Red Army, rifle in hand. Some even carried out their own imitation of the selection at the concentration camps, wading into columns of refugees to pick out all the children, whom they then machine-gunned in front of their distraught parents.[3]

Between January and May 1945 some five million German civilians fled their homes. Two million were evacuated by sea from German-held ports along the Baltic, an epic amphibious rescue mission notable for the worst maritime disasters in history. Two were caused by the same Russian submarine, S13. On 30 January the 25,000-ton liner *Wilhelm Gustloff* was torpedoed and sunk within sight of the cruiser *Admiral Hipper* and the torpedo boat T36. The warships themselves already had 1,700 refugees embarked and the cruiser steamed off to avoid another torpedo. Only 650 people of the 8,000 on board survived. S13 struck again two weeks later, sinking the 14,700-ton *General Steuben* off Pilau; she was carrying 2,000 wounded soldiers. On the night of 16–17 April the submarine L3 (*Frunzovets*, ex-*Bolshevik*) sank the 5,200-ton freighter *Goya*, which was literally crammed to the gunwales. An estimated 6,000 people went down with her.

Such was the power of the SS by 1945 that German civilians were left to face the Russians while the SS commandeered shipping to empty those concentration camps near the coast. Stutthof, near Danzig, was evacuated as the Soviets approached, although half its 4,500 remaining inmates were murdered in the process, many driven into the sea and shot.

A total of 1.39 million German civilians remain officially unaccounted for in the wake of 1945. If some reached safety but never advertised it, many more people died lonely deaths not included in the cold statistics of the Second World War. Unknown numbers of Allied prisoners-of-war, slave labourers from Poland or the Balkans – and even the USSR – were all subjected to the dreadful vengeance of the Red Army.

The Soviet leadership tried to rein in its soldiers as early as February, a *Red Star* editorial proclaiming that just because the Germans 'publicly raped our women, it does not mean we must do the same'. Controversial writer Ilya Ehrenburg's rabid cries for revenge were explicitly criticized in *Pravda* which proclaimed the obvious truth that 'it is unwise and un-Marxist to think all Germans were Nazis, to be treated only as subhumans'. Stalin was more concerned that his soldiers were destroying all sorts of facilities that would be useful for rebuilding the USSR's shattered economy after the war.

The final battle

The German Army had fewer than two million troops left on the Eastern Front by spring 1945. Of these, up to three-quarters of a million soldiers were trapped in various ports like Königsberg, and in Army Group North, now re-named Army Group Kurland, on its remote and irrelevant Baltic peninsula. The Red Army was more than six million strong, and its objective was Berlin.

By March 1945 British and American armies had reached the Elbe, 75 miles from the German capital. The Russians were much closer, about 40 miles east of Berlin, and Stalin was determined that his forces would take the city. In the Kremlin it had not gone unnoticed that while the Germans surrendered readily in the west, they fought with incredible tenacity to keep the Russians at bay. Every yard of Germany the Red Army conquered, it paid for in blood. Throughout 1942–43, the British and Americans had held back from fighting in mainland Europe, while the Red Army took on the main body of the German Army. The Soviet leadership remained convinced that this was a deliberate, cynical policy.

Zhukov's 1st White Russia Front consisted of nine armies, including two tank armies, formed up directly east of the city along the River Oder. Konev's 1st Ukranian Front was to the south and comprised eight armies, two of which were tank armies. Closed up to the River Neisse, Konev's forces had the River Spree to cross before they could sweep up to Berlin.

As preparations for the final Soviet offensive began, the fighting continued without a break along the Baltic shores and in Austria. Unlike many cities declared a 'fortress' by Hitler, Königsberg did actually have some modern concrete defences, soon augmented by every defensive measure German engineers could devise. With the sea at their backs and evacuation impossible under such constant air attack, the German garrison held each position with the same cold courage as the defenders of Sebastopol had displayed three years earlier. When the casemates were blown in by heavy artillery and the defensive guns beaten into silence, the Russian storming parties swarmed into the trenches and tunnels; but there were always handfuls of survivors fighting on with sub-machine-guns and grenades. Despite the fearful odds, they continued to counter-attack, disputing every yard until 9 April when the Soviets finally broke into the middle of the city. When General Lasch and 92,000 German soldiers surrendered, 42,000 troops lay dead in the ruins, along with an estimated 25,000 civilians – a quarter of the city's population. Russian troops committed the most ghastly atrocities on German soldiers and civilians alike as the city fell.

An equally ferocious battle was under way in Vienna, where the defenders had to be prised out of every building, and a cadre of SS troops put up the most incredible resistance around the remaining Danube bridges. An attempted coup by Communist sympathizers failed, but it enabled elements of 5th Guards Tank Corps to penetrate the defences, and the city fell on 13 April.

The Soviet attack on Berlin involved more than two million men and women, 6,000 tanks and self-propelled guns and some 40,000 guns, mortars and rocket-launchers. Their route was barred by between 750,000 and a million German troops, with about 500 tanks and 1,000 assault guns. Zhukov opened his part of the offensive with an artillery barrage that would have impressed veterans of 1917–18: with up to 295 guns per 1,000 yards of front, his gunners fired 7.1 million rounds of ammunition.

The German forces were under the command of Army Group Vistula, initially commanded by the head of the SS, Heinrich Himmler, whose empire had grown in inverse proportion to that of his master. Guderian shrewdly persuaded Himmler to lay down this particular burden; the defence would be masterminded by Colonel-General Gotthard Heinrici, for two years the commander of the 4th Army on the Moscow Front. The latter's first task was an impossible counter-attack at Küstrin, demanded by the Führer, which began with great courage and ended in heavy casualties and failure: they did not break through. Possibly emboldened by a few pre-prandial brandies with Göring, Guderian rose to the bait when Hitler berated him and the soldiers committed to this futile mission. Guderian defended the honour and reputation of the army until he was literally red in the face. Hitler sent him on compulsory leave.

It may have been at this time that Heinrici and other senior commanders like Busse, commander of the 9th Army, and Wenck, 12th Army, accepted that it was over: the war was lost and Hitler was doomed. All that mattered now was to save as many of their men and German civilians from the revenge of the Russians. Hitler's previously sensitive political antennae failed to detect this hidden agenda, even when Heinrici's forces conspicuously failed to protect Berlin and fought instead to preserve escape routes either side of the city. Heinrici's troops facing the western Allies were shuttled east to prolong resistance as long as possible. The Führer's devoted Generals Keitel and Jodl scented treachery, but when Keitel visited Heinrici's headquarters to remonstrate, he was stopped by staff officers with drawn weapons.

Konev's troops stormed the River Neisse on 16 April. Bridges weighing 60 tons were in position that afternoon, and his tanks were ready to exploit all the way to the Spree. Zhukov's attack faltered, the staggering intensity of his artillery barrage notwithstanding. On the

Seelow Heights, enough German defenders emerged from their bunkers to cut down the Soviet infantry, in spite of – or possibly because of – a line of searchlights shining in their faces as the attack went in. Not for the first time, Zhukov allowed his impatience to overcome his judgement, and he ordered both his tank armies – six corps including 1,337 tanks/assault guns – to attack, without waiting for the infantry to break into the defences.

Zhukov could override both the battle plan and his furious infantry commanders, but he could not command the Germans to give in. Carefully concealed anti-tank guns and a few surviving tank destroyers commenced a frightful slaughter of the Soviet armour as the vehicles struggled across the swampy plain below. When the tanks fought their way on to the German position, they found themselves among minefields and were attacked by infantry teams with *Panzerfausts*. Smarting after an angry telephone exchange with Stalin in Moscow, Zhukov piled in extra tanks as the battle continued into the night. Still suspicious that the western Allies might drive on Berlin – Eisenhower's willingness to give the Soviets a free run at the city appeared too naïve to be true – Stalin chose this moment to stoke the notorious rivalry between Marshals Zhukov and Konev. He removed the agreed front boundaries just in front of Berlin: whoever advanced the faster would have the honour of storming the Nazi capital.

Zhukov's men stormed the Seelow Heights the next day, after 800 aircraft bombed the defences and the gunners delivered another formidable concentration of fire. However, Konev's tanks had not only reached the River Spree, but a T-34 had taken the plunge and driven straight into the river where the map marked a ford. Under fire all the way, it roared across, water surging around its hull until it clattered up the opposite bank, firing its machine-guns. Exploitation continued, with Konev's armour heading north where Rybalko's 3rd Guards Tank Army met Katukov's 1st Guards Tank Army, part of Zhukov's front, trapping the remains of the German 9th Army between them.

At the daily briefings in the Berlin bunker to which Hitler had withdrawn in mid-January, Colonel-General Hans Krebs, Guderian's replacement as chief of staff, brought a welcome professional calm to the proceedings. No defeatism here; no hysterical demands for reinforcements or complaints about attempting the impossible. Albert Speer realized it was a cunning game. The Führer ordered this or that division to fall back on Berlin, others to hold on to 'fortresses' from Czechoslovakia to Pomerania, and Krebs played along with the fantasy. Just as Speer raced around the collapsing Reich countermanding Hitler's vindictive demolition orders, so Krebs kept Hitler busy manoeuvring phantom armies across the briefing maps. It diverted Hitler from issuing more lunatic orders that the SS were still all-too-ready to insist were obeyed. Field Marshal Kesselring played along too: during his last visit to the bunker he committed his forces in the west to a massive counter-attack, with not the least intention of carrying it out.

Hitler turned 56 on 20 April. There was a brief party held in the Chancellery before a gloomy military briefing in the bunker. It was the last time he would see Göring and Himmler, his leading henchmen. Before he vanished underground again, cameras recorded Hitler's last public appearance, shambling along, distributing medals to 20 teenage boys from the *Hitlerjugend*. Below with his generals, Hitler committed himself to dying in Berlin, disagreeable news to those in his diminishing entourage eager to fly away to Bavaria.

On 21 April the Soviet 3rd Guards Tank Army stormed Zossen, just 15 miles south of Berlin. This leafy hamlet was nothing less than the brain of the Wehrmacht. Forty feet underground, its entrances hidden among the trees and scattered buildings, lay a labyrinth of tunnels, conference rooms, and the largest telephone exchange in Europe – 'Central 500', code-named *Zeppelin*. In continuous operation since 1939 and connected to every major German headquarters, it was to here that Hitler had been urged to retreat, not to the incomplete shelter beneath the Berlin Chancellery. While the Nazi leaders gathered for Hitler's last party, German officers grabbed their paperwork and piled everything moveable on to lorries bound for Berlin. The evacuation was carried out in such a hurry that when Rybalko's men broke into the complex they found telephones still ringing and teleprinters churning out signals.

On 22 April Hitler finally blurted out the obvious – the war was lost. The same day, the bunker echoed with the incongruous sound of youthful laughter as Magda Goebbels shepherded her six children inside. She carried a small case with just one spare dress; the children were allowed one toy each. By 24 April the last roads out of Berlin were cut and, just a day later, the Soviets overran Tempelhof airport. Communications between the capital and the remainder of the Reich were precarious. Hanna Reitsch flew into the city using the Unter den Linden as a runway, leaving by Arado Ar 96 from the Brandenburg Gate. In its last aerial resupply missions of the war, the Luftwaffe delivered crates of anti-tank shells from Junkers Ju-52s, putting down on the road after Speer's giant lamp-posts were removed. Hans Baur, Hitler's personal pilot, still had several long-range aircraft at Gatow, the last airfield in German hands, including a Junkers Ju-390 with enough fuel to reach Manchuria. But the perimeter was steadily shrinking and Soviet soldiers were on the edge of the Tiergarten, less than 2 miles from Hitler.

The atmosphere in the Berlin bunker was doom-laden, claustrophobic and poisonous. Treachery was in the air. Hitler eventually commanded the arrest of both Göring and Himmler, for secretly trying to negotiate their own peace deals with the Allies. Himmler's representative in Berlin, the cavalry general SS-Gruppenführer Hermann Fegelein, was shot outside the bunker on the orders of Gestapo chief Müller. Nothing, not even his marriage to Eva Braun's sister, could save him after the revelation of Himmler's faithlessness – although the exposure of his mistress as a British secret agent did not help his case.[4]

The army defending Berlin was an odd mixture of teenage conscripts, old men recruited into the *Volkssturm* and hard-bitten army veterans like the men of 9th Parachute and 18th Panzergrenadier

Divisions. There were plenty of non-Germans too, many evacuated from Kurland via Danzig to make their final stand. The 11th SS Panzergrenadier Division 'Nordland' was originally a regiment in the SS 'Wiking' Division. In 1943 it had been expanded to divisional size, with a regiment of Danes and one of Norwegians. The 23rd SS Panzergrenadier Division 'Nederland' consisted of Dutch volunteers. The 15th SS Waffengrenadier Division 'Lettische Nr.1' was recruited in Latvia and its soldiers now had no home to return to. These units were joined in Berlin by one foreign company that had to fight its way into the city from the west. Assembled from the surviving members of the French SS Division 'Charlemagne' after its disbandment, this fanatical band included a tank-killer team, each of whom had won the Iron Cross 1st Class.

Both leading Soviet commanders were in at the kill. Although the battle for the Seelow Heights cost his men excessive losses, Zhukov pushed on to assault the city from the north and east, while Konev's men attacked from the south. Zhukov's post-war attempt to claim sole credit is not just petty but irrelevant – Konev's front line was within 200 yards of the Reichstag when the fighting ceased. The German defenders included some of the most lethal professional soldiers the world has ever seen. What some of the others lacked in military skills, they made up for with the courage of despair. As the perimeter steadily shrank, each city block, each storey, each room, cost the Soviets dearly. Since ancient times the storming of a city that refuses to surrender has been accompanied by gruesome acts of brutality, and in Berlin the fearful casualties suffered by many Russian units were enough to trigger savage retaliation when opportunity presented itself. And, as the capital of the Nazi regime, Berlin was the obvious target for Soviet vengeance. The city's population was already swollen with refugees when Soviet tanks blocked the last escape routes, and carnage followed.

At 6.00am on Monday 30 April, SS-Brigadeführer Wilhelm Mohnke, the commander of the Chancellery area defences – the citadel – was woken by a telephone call from the bunker. Mohnke was just 34 years old. Despite the loss of a foot in a Yugoslav air strike in April 1941, he had commanded a Panzergrenadier regiment of the 12th SS Panzer Division 'Hitlerjugend' in Normandy and led Panzer Division 'Leibstandarte Adolf Hitler' during the Ardennes offensive.[5] Now he was summoned to keep his promise to the Führer. As the Soviet grip on the city had tightened, Hitler had asked Mohnke to report when, in his professional judgement, the enemy was within 24 hours of breaking into the bunker. Since the Russians had captured the Tiergarten and even penetrated the subway under the Friedrichstrasse, Mohnke had no choice but to tell Hitler it was finished. The SS general was treated to a Hitler monologue that could have come straight from the pages of *Mein Kampf*.

Armed with a copy of Hitler's last will and testament, Mohnke returned to his headquarters to conduct a last-ditch defence. Hitler and his new bride committed suicide that afternoon. Mohnke returned to the bunker the following evening, shortly after Magda Goebbels systematically murdered her sleeping children with cyanide capsules. Then he watched Joseph and Magda Goebbels walk upstairs to the courtyard where they committed suicide. General Krebs, who spoke fluent Russian, had already opened negotiations, coming face-to-face with none other than General Chuikov, defender of Stalingrad. Brigadeführer Mohnke found himself leading one of the breakout groups, side-lining the odious Martin Bormann who was now just another refugee. In teams, in groups, in ones and twos, the surviving Nazi leaders, SS bodyguards, soldiers, Hitler's secretaries and cook crept away under cover of darkness ... and into captivity, or history.

Organized resistance ceased on the morning of 2 May, although a die-hard group of Germans held out in the basement of the Reichstag for a few hours longer. Far above their heads, a 28-year-old Ukranian Jew working for the Tass news agency clambered on to the roof. Yevgheny Khaldei was an enterprising war photographer.[6] Fired up by Joe Rosenthal's famous picture of US Marines raising the flag on Iwo Jima, he had made several red flags from tablecloths for just this moment. As German resistance sputtered out, Khaldei persuaded a Russian soldier called Alexei Kovalyov to perch precariously over the edge, his legs held by a soldier from Dagestan (wearing watches on both wrists – one was airbrushed out of the final picture by Soviet censors). Kovalyov unfurled the flag, Khaldei pressed the shutter, and the final image of Hitler's war was created: the red banner floating in the wind above the ruins of Berlin.

NOTES

INTRODUCTION

1   The German Army suffered 6.1 million casualties on the Russian front between June 1941 and March 1945; twice the number of men who took part in the initial invasion and 80 per cent of German casualties over that period. Omer Bartov, *Hitler's Army*, Oxford (1991).

2   From the definitive study of Soviet mobilization: Walter Dunn, *Hitler's Nemesis: The Red Army, 1930–45*, Westport, CT (1994). Dunn argues that the Russians had effectively won the Second World War by autumn 1943; after that, it was just a matter of time.

3   *The Trial of the Major German War Criminals*, 1946, Vol. 26, quoted in Klaus Fischer, *Nazi Germany*, London (1995).

4   Stalin visited the front line on just one occasion. In August 1943 he left Moscow for two days to meet the commanders of the Western and Bryansk Fronts, Generals Sokolovsky and Yeremenko.

5   Niklas Zetterling and Anders Frankson, *Kursk 1943: A Statistical Analysis*, London (2000).

6   The 'Wolf's Lair' was one of several fortified command posts Hitler had constructed across Germany from which to oversee military operations.

CHAPTER ONE

1   General der Flieger Paul Deichmann, *German Air Force Operations in Support of the Army*, USAF Studies 153, USAF Historical Division (1962).

CHAPTER TWO

1   Dimitri Volgonov, *Triumph and Tragedy*, London (1994). See Evan Mawdsley, *Thunder in the East*, London (2005) for a contrary view that the effect of the purges has been much exaggerated.

2   Robert Conquest, *The Great Terror*, London (1990).

3   Norman Stone, *The Eastern Front*, London (1975).

4   Harold Shukman (Ed.), *Stalin's Generals*, London (1993).

5   Rodric Braithwaite, *Moscow 1941*, London (2006). Blokhin ended his career a highly decorated major-general but was discredited by Khruschev and reportedly hanged himself in despair shortly afterwards.

6   Russian acronym for 'Chief Administration of Corrective Labour Camps'.

7   Bryan Fulgate and Lev Dvoretsky, *Thunder on the Dnepr*, Novato, CA (1997).

CHAPTER THREE

1   General der Flieger Paul Deichmann, *German Air Force Operations in Support of the Army*, USAF Studies 153, USAF Historical Division (1962).

2 The standard load was 430 tons of fuel for a Panzer division at full establishment. An additional 400–500 tons were carried by the Panzer and mechanized divisions in 1941, enabling them to make a fighting advance of 250–300 miles.

3 Operational report from Einsatzgruppe C, 2 November 1941.

4 See Omer Bartov, *The Eastern Front 1941–45: German Troops and the Barbarisation of Warfare*, New York (1986) and *Hitler's Army*, Oxford (1991).

5 Robert H. Jackson, Chief of Counsel for the United States in his opening statement at the first Nuremberg trial, 21 November 1945.

6 One Moscow cinema repeatedly screened a George Formby film, which was an odd way to encourage people to stay in the city.

7 Walter Dunn, *Hitler's Nemesis: The Red Army, 1930–45*, Westport, CT (1994).

8 For the strange disparity between German automotive manufacturing capability and military production, see Richard Overy, *Why the Allies Won*, London (1995).

9 Martin van Creveld, *Supplying War: Logistics from Wallenstein to Patton*, Cambridge (1977).

10 If you don't have a set of stirring Red Army marches in your CD collection, you can hear the tune at http://www.barynya.com/mp3/Alesha_Misha/Katyusha.mp3

CHAPTER FOUR

1 Quoted in John Erickson, *The Road to Stalingrad*, London (1975).

2 The jail term was set at six years. Von Sponeck was later executed by the SS without further judicial process as part of the revenge for the July 1944 bomb plot. His widow was sent to a concentration camp but survived. His son, six years old when his father was shot, became a diplomat and was an Assistant Secretary to Kofi Annan at the United Nations.

3 Modern estimates vary from 3.2 to 3.9 million. A total of 16 generals were captured too with another 19 missing in action. See John Erickson's essay in Addison and Calder (Eds), *A Time to Kill*, London (1997).

4 Matthew Cooper, *The Phantom War*, London (1979).

5 Richard Overy, *Why the Allies Won*, London (1995).

6 *Fremde Heere Ost*, under the painstaking Colonel Gehlen, consistently underestimated Red Army strengths by a margin of about 500,000. However, its assessment of the Soviet order of battle compares incredibly well with post-war documentation: the Germans were out by only seven divisions over the four years of war.

7 Evan Mawdsley, *Thunder in the East*, London (2005).

8 Not 'Von Paulus' as many writers continue to call him. Like Hitler's other favourites, Rommel and Model, Paulus was a technocrat, not an aristocrat, which was more likely to endear him to the Führer, who had little time for the blue-blooded officer corps. Married into the Romanian aristocracy, he was a fastidious man who bathed twice a day and washed his hands with such frequency as to arouse comment.

CHAPTER FIVE

1 John Erickson, *The Road to Stalingrad*, London (1997), p.403.

2　Nevertheless, Lopatin went on to command other armies and ended the war a Hero of the Soviet Union, with a chestfull of other medals.

3　Tank/assault gun strengths were: 14th Panzer Division, 41; 16th Panzer Division, 31; 24th Panzer Division, 55; 3rd Infantry Division, 32; 60th Infantry Division, 21.

4　See Paul Carrell, *Stalingrad and the Defeat of the German 6th Army*, Atglen, PA (1993), for an unreconstructed view of Hitler's responsibility. He assigns further blame to Hitler, criticizing the decision to withhold 29 divisions in the west including the three SS Panzergrenadier divisions, and 6th and 7th Panzer Divisions. He makes the contentious claim that just a quarter of this force could have liquidated the Russians in Stalingrad.

5　Heim was expelled from the army on Hitler's instructions, without judicial process. He was reinstated and allowed to retire, then ordered back into uniform on 1 August 1944. Sent to command the 'fortress' of Boulogne just as it was about to be sealed off by Allied troops, he held it for six weeks until surrendering to Canadian troops.

6　These four corps commanders had very different fates. Hube and Jänicke were among the lucky few officers ordered out of Stalingrad before the end; Hube was killed in an air crash in 1944 but Jänicke commanded the 17th Army and survived ten years in Russian prison camps 1945–55. Heitz died in a Russian prison camp in 1944. Strecker was released by the Russians in 1955 and lived until 1971.

7　Generalmajor Fritz Morzik, *Airlift Operations*, USAF Studies 167, USAF Historical Division (1961).

8　Paulus's last active command had been that of an armoured reconnaissance unit in 1934. Like General Eisenhower, Paulus had never commanded a regiment, division or corps in action before he was placed at the head of an army.

9　See David Glantz's essay in Robert Cowley (Ed.), *No End Save Victory*, London (2002).

10　David Glantz and Jonathan House, *When Titans Clash*, Kansas (1995).

11　In *Stalingrad – Memories and Reassessments*, London (1990), Joachim Wieder and Heinrich Graf von Einsiedel argue that only Von Manstein could have saved the 6th Army, by demanding permission to retreat from Stalingrad on 24 November and threatening to resign if Hitler refused. Would Hitler have accepted the loss of one of his greatest generals, they speculate. Or did Von Manstein support Hitler's decision to hold the city so that he could be the saviour of the 6th Army?

12　Major-General von Mellenthin's famous account, *Panzer Battles*, London (1955), concludes his account of the Stalingrad battle with 'The tactical conduct of the battle by the Russians was on a high level'. Badanov fought his unit to destruction, but to brilliant effect. He rose to command 4th Tank Army 1943–44 and became commandant of the Soviet Army's tank training schools.

13　Alexander Werth, *Russia at War 1941–45*, London (1964).

14　Paulus entitled his account '*Here I Stand Under Orders*': the classic defence.

15　Marshal Chuikov, *The Beginning of the Road*, London (1963).

CHAPTER SIX

1　So memorably recounted in Guy Sajer's *Le Soldat Oublié*, Paris (1968), translated as *The Forgotten Soldier* and still in print both sides of the Atlantic (USA, Brassey's; UK, Orion).

2   Omer Bartov, *Hitler's Army,* Oxford (1991). See Niklas Zetterling, *German Ground Forces in Normandy,* Winnipeg (2000), for an excellent analysis of this issue.

3   These Bundesarchiv figures do not include SS casualties or losses after January 1945 when administration broke down. Another 500,000 losses were probably incurred before May. Of the nearly two million missing-in-action, at least half were dead.

4   Richard Overy, *Why the Allies Won*, London (1995), p.188.

5   Manufacturing figures vary significantly (see introductory note regarding statistics) but even expressing it roughly like this reveals just how sluggish German aircraft production was compared to that of the Allies.

6   The Me-109 received successive upgrades to keep it in front-line service until 1945, and more than 30,000 were built – more than almost any other aircraft of the war. However, its narrow undercarriage and unforgiving flight characteristics led to almost half of them being lost in training accidents.

7   In *RAF Bomber Command 1939–45: Reaping the Whirlwind*, London (1996), Richard Overy demonstrates how the bombing of Germany not only checked Speer's attempt to expand production, but diverted enormous resources away from the fronts in Russia and Italy to the defence of the Reich itself.

8   General der Flieger Paul Deichmann, *German Air Force Operations in Support of the Army*, USAF Studies No.153, USAF Historical Division (1962).

9   General der Flieger Paul Deichmann, op. cit.

10 Thomas Jentz, *Panzertruppen,* Vol. II, Atglen, PA (1996), p.43.

11 John Erickson, *The Road to Berlin*, London (1983), pp.82–84.

12 Thomas Jentz, op. cit. These are monthly inventories including all newly built and not yet delivered vehicles, but they are much higher than the orders of battle the author quotes on p.176 (forces in the west, June 1944) and p.205 (forces in the east, May–June 1944).

13 Includes production totals for Panzer III and IV, Panther, Tiger, Tiger II tanks; Marder II and III and Nashorn self-propelled anti-tank guns; StuG III and IV, Hetzer, Elefant, JagdPanzer IV, Jagdpanther and Jagdtiger assault guns; Wespe, Hummel, Brummbär and Sturmtiger self-propelled guns.

14 The best recent account is Richard Woodman's *Arctic Convoys*, London (1994).

15 Although some sources quote more than 6,000.

16 Walter Dunn, *Hitler's Nemesis: The Red Army 1930–45,* Westport, CT (1994).

17 Although an SS battlegroup committed to Finland was expanded into the 6th SS Division during 1942 and the mounted SS regiments in Poland became 8th SS Division 'Florian Geyer'. The 7th SS 'Prinz Eugen' was an anti-partisan unit recruited in the Balkans where it spent most of the war.

18 Orlando Figes, *The Russian Revolution: A People's Tragedy*, London (1996).

19 Generalleutnant Klaus Uebe, *Russian Reactions to German Airpower*, USAF Studies 176, USAF Historical Division.

CHAPTER SEVEN

1   Even then, there was not enough room. Some former Nazi concentration camps were

put back into use by the Soviets to hold not just German captives but former Soviet soldiers and workers deported by the Germans for slave labour. The Soviet regime firmly believed that it was better to hang 99 innocent men than let one guilty man go free.

2   John Erickson, *The Road to Berlin*, London (1983), p.48. They had lost 90 tanks in the previous two days, and the South-Western Front had lost half its tanks to damage or breakdown before the German counter-attack was delivered.

3   Gerhard Weinburg, *A World at Arms*, Cambridge (1994).

4   The Red Army had 27 artillery divisions by July 1943. It had about 100,000 mortars and anti-tank guns in service too.

5   David Glantz and Jonathan House, *When Titans Clashed*, Kansas (1995).

6   Dimitri Volkogonov's *Stalin* supports Rokossovsky's revelations, quoting interviews with senior survivors of Kirponos's staff. Rokossovsky's memoirs were published after his death in 1968, but the degree to which they had been censored has only recently been exposed. See Richard Woff's essay in Harold Shukman (Ed.), *Stalin's Generals*, London (1993).

7   John Erickson, op. cit., p.112.

8   General der Flieger Paul Deichmann, *German Air Force Operations in Support of the Army*, USAF Studies 153, USAF Historical Division (1962).

9   Evan Mawdsley, *Thunder in the East*, London (2005).

10 F. W. Mellenthin, *Panzer Battles*, London (1955).

CHAPTER EIGHT

1   Partisans were also swept into the Red Army as areas were liberated, but about 20 per cent had to be rejected on medical grounds. Tuberculosis was commonly cited.

2   John Erickson gives the Soviet figure for German manpower (4.9 million) which has proved to be a massive overestimate. On the other hand, the Germans underestimated Soviet manpower: they thought they faced five million Soviet troops.

3   Thomas Jentz, *Panzertruppen*, Vol. II cites German tank unit returns of 2,053 tanks (1,043 operational) in December 1943. This does not include assault guns. However, the divisional unit strengths he quotes on p.205 add up to a grand total of only 1,390 tanks and StuGs for May 1944. Since *Panzeroffizier beim Chef Generalstab des Heeres Nr. 561/44 GK*, Captured German Records, Series T-78, Roll 620 shows German operational strength fluctuating between 400 and 600 tanks and about 700 assault guns on the Russian front from the end of September 1943 to early May 1944, it is more likely that the total armoured strength of the Ostheer (including tanks, StuGs and other tank destroyers/assault guns) was no more than 1,500 at the beginning of 1944. Note also that despite prodigious production totals, Soviet front-line tank strength had fallen from 8,500 at the beginning of 1943 to 5,600 in December.

4   John Erickson states that the Germans had 54,000 guns and mortars, a figure that presumably includes 81mm and smaller weapons within divisions: Glantz and House, *When Titans Clashed*, Kansas (1995), p.184 credits the Germans with 8,037 guns and mortars. Production figures indicate that the Soviets could well have enjoyed a 5:1 superiority in heavy artillery by early 1944. The Soviet attack on Army Group Centre in 1944 involved more than 25,000 guns, mortars and rocket launchers.

5　The German total is from Generalleutnant Herman Plocher, *The German Air Force in Russia*, USAF Studies 154, USAF Historical Division (1966). John Erickson gives 8,818 aircraft for the Russians, but Generalleutnant Walter Schwabedissen, *The Russian Air Force in the Eyes of German Commanders*, USAF Studies, USAF Historical Division (1960), credits the Soviets with 13,000 aircraft in January 1944, rising to 20,000 by the end of the year despite monthly losses of 1,500 aircraft at the front and 1,200 in the rear.

6　High ground is a relative term in the Ukraine. Medvin lies at 896 feet above sea level. Heading west, it marks the start of the higher ground (all above 656 feet) of the western Ukraine that extends all the way to the foothills of the Carpathians.

7　A three-battalion brigade formed and led by Belgian Fascist leader Léon Dégrelle, the 'Wallonien' brigade fought under Wehrmacht control until 1943 when it was transferred to the SS. Of the 2,000 men trapped at Cherkassy, 632 managed to escape to form the nucleus of 28th Panzergrenadier Division 'Wallonien', which fought on until 1945.

8　Alexander Werth, *Russia at War*, London (1964).

9　*The Trial of German Major War Criminals: Proceedings of the International Military Tribunal Sitting at Nuremberg, Germany*, London (1946–51), Vol. 21, p.72.

10　Omer Bartov, *Hitler's Army*, Oxford (1991). Space precludes a fuller examination of the Nuremberg trials, but the treatment of German war criminals was lopsided. Rocket engineers went free to work for the US government. Many convicted officers were released within a few years. On the other hand, the Soviet judges were led by the man who ran the show trials in Moscow, an expert in trumped-up charges and confessions extracted under torture.

11　One wonders what 'Papa' Hoth would have made of American strategy in Iraq and Afghanistan …

12　Gerhard Weinberg, *A World at Arms*, Cambridge (1994).

13　German naval units reached the Black Sea from Hamburg; they travelled up the River Elbe to Dresden where they were partially dismantled and driven along the highway to Ingolstadt, thence to Linz and down the length of the Danube.

CHAPTER NINE

1　*Panzeroffizier beim Chef Generalstab des Heeres, Nr. 561/44 GK*, Captured German Records, Series T-78, Roll 620. Much higher figures – more than 4,000 – are sometimes quoted, but probably include new production and unserviceable vehicles; they may even be counting rebuilt vehicles twice. The Ostheer had at least another 700 tanks on its strength in May 1944 but they were not operational.

2　Alexander Werth, *Russia at War*, London (1964), p.768.

3　A one-time army colleague of the SS chief of staff Gottlob Berger, Dr Oscar Dirlewanger enjoyed Himmler's patronage and was awarded some of Germany's highest medals for gallantry. He was killed in 1945 and his unit wiped out during the battle for Berlin.

4　Stephen Constant, *Foxy Ferdinand: Tsar of Bulgaria*, London (1979), p.329.

CHAPTER TEN

1　Ridiculously overpromoted, the former NCO knew how the army generals laughed at him behind his back, but his combat record was by no means as disastrous as it might have been. He was shrewd enough to surround himself with competent staff officers. Convicted of numerous war crimes, including the Malmédy massacre, he was jailed from 1946 to 1957, when he was released on health grounds. He died in 1966, his funeral marked by the attendence of more than 6,000 of his old soldiers: the acid test of a general's reputation.

2   Quoted in John Toland, *The Last 100 Days*, London (1965), p.188.

3   John Toland, op. cit. See also John Erickson, *The Road to Berlin*, London (1983), p.508 and Alexander Werth, *Russia at War*, London (1964), pp.963–66 and 986.

4   James O'Donnell, *The Berlin Bunker*, London (1979).

5   In 1940 the battalion under his command conducted a cold-blooded massacre of 80 British prisoners-of-war on 28 May 1940 at Wormhoudt. In 1944 the regiment under his command murdered 35 Canadian prisoners at Fountenay le Pesnel, Normandy. Attempts to bring him to justice in the 1990s never succeeded and he died, unpunished, in 2001.

6   His mother was shot by a Ukranian mob while he was just 12 months old, the bullet passing through his side to kill her. His father was beaten to death in a subsequent pogrom. The Germans killed his sisters. It is pleasant to record that in his final years he received recognition in the west, and met the famous Associated Press photographer whose work had so inspired him. Khaldei died in October 1997.

★
SELECT BIBLIOGRAPHY

Addison, Paul and Calder, Angus (Eds), *Time to Kill*, London (1997)

Adelman, Jonathan and Gibson, Cristann (Eds), *Soviet Military Affairs: The Legacy of World War II*, Boston (1989)

Andrew, Christopher and Gordievsky, Oleg, *KGB: The Inside Story*, London (1990)

Bartov, Omer, *The Eastern Front 1941–45, German Troops and the Barbarization of Warfare*, New York (1986)

Bartov, Omer, *Hitler's Army*, Oxford (1991)

Bekker, Cajus, *The Luftwaffe War Diaries*, London (1967)

Bekker, Cajus, *Hitler's Naval War*, London (1976)

Berenbaum, Michael, *Witness to the Holocaust*, New York (1997)

Bishop, Christopher and Drury, Ian (Eds), *War Machine*, London (1983–85)

Bishop, Christopher and Drury, Ian (Eds), *Combat Guns*, London (1987)

Boldt, Gerhard, *Hitler's Last Days*, London (1973)

Brown, Eric, *Wings of the Luftwaffe*, London (1977)

Bruce, Robert, *German Automatic Weapons of World War II*, London (1996)

Bullock, Alan, *Hitler and Stalin*, London (1993)

Butler, Rupert, *Gestapo*, London (1992)

Carrell, Paul, *Stalingrad and the Defeat of the German 6th Army*, Atglen, PA (1993)

Chuikov, Vasili, *The Beginning of the Road*, London (1963)

Conquest, Robert, *The Great Terror*, London (1990).

Cooper, Matthew, *The Phantom War*, London (1979)

Creveld, Martin van, *Supplying War: Logistics from Wallenstein to Patton*, Cambridge (1977)

Creveld, Martin van, *Fighting Power: German and US Army Battlefield Performance 1939–45*, London (1983)

Deichman, Paul, 'German Air Force Operations in Support of the Army', USAF Studies, USAF Historical Division (1962)

Dunn, Walter, *Hitler's Nemesis: The Red Army 1930–45*, Westport, CT (1994)

Einsiedel, Heinrich Graf von, *The Onslaught: The German Drive on Stalingrad*, London (1984)

Elkins, Michael, *Forged in Fury*, Loughton (1981)

English, John, *On Infantry*, New York (1981)

Erickson, John, *The Road to Stalingrad*, London (1975)

Erickson, John, *The Road to Berlin*, London (1983)

Fest, Joachim, *The Face of the Third Reich*, London (1970)

Figes, Orlando, *The Russian Revolution: A People's Tragedy*, London (1996)

Fischer, Klaus, *Nazi Germany*, London (1995)

Fulgate, Brian and Dvoretsky, Lev, *Thunder on the Dnepr*, Novato, CA (1997)

Gallagher, Hugh Gregory, *By Trust Betrayed: Patients, Physicians and the Licence to Kill in the Third Reich*, Arlington, VA (1995)

Glantz, David, *Soviet Military Deception in the Second World War*, London (1989)

Glantz, David and House, Jonathan, *When Titans Clashed*, Kansas (1995)

Griess, Thomas *Atlas of the Second World War: Europe and the Mediterranean*, West Point Military History Series, New Jersey (1985)

Guderian, Heinz, *Panzer Leader*, London (1952)

Gudmundsson, Bruce, *On Artillery*, Westport, CT (1993)

Hooton, E. R., *Eagle in Flames*, London (1997)

Jentz, Thomas, *Panzertruppen*, Atglen, PA (1996)

Jukes, Geoffrey, *Kursk*, London (1969)

Keegan, John, *Waffen SS: The Asphalt Soldiers*, London (1970)

Lang, Jochen von, *Bormann: The Man who Manipulated Hitler*, London (1979)

Lewin, Ronald, *Ultra*, London (1980)

Liddell Hart, Basil, *The Other Side of the Hill*, London (1950)

Lord Russell of Liverpool, *The Scourge of the Swastika*, London (1954)

Manstein, Erich von, *Lost Victories*, London (1959)

Mawdsley, Evan, *Thunder in the East*, London (2005)

Mellenthin, F. W. von, *Panzer Battles*, London (1955)

Morzik, Fritz, 'Airlift Operations', USAF Studies 167, USAF Historical Division (1961)

O'Donnell, James, *The Berlin Bunker*, London (1979)

Overy, Richard, *The Air War 1939–45*, London (1980)

Overy, Richard, *Why the Allies Won*, London (1995)

Overy, Richard, *RAF Bomber Command 1939–45*, London (1996)

Padfield, Peter, *Himmler*, London (1990)

Pipes, Richard, *The Russian Revolution 1899–1919*, London (1990)

Plocher, Herman, 'The German Air Force in Russia', USAF Studies 154, USAF Historical Division (1966)

Sajer, Guy, *The Forgotten Soldier*, New York (1971)

Schwabedissen, Walter, 'The Russian Air Force in the Eyes of German Commanders', USAF Studies, USAF Historical Division (1960)

Sereny, Gitta, *Albert Speer: His Battle with Truth*, London (1995)

Shukman, Harold (Ed.), *Stalin's Generals*, London (1993)

Simkin, Richard, *Tank Warfare*, London (1979)

Snyder, Louis, *Encyclopedia of the Third Reich*, London (1976)

Stone, Norman, *The Eastern Front*, London (1975)

Toland, John, *The Last 100 Days*, New York (1965)

Toland, John, *Hitler*, New York (1976)

The Trial of German Major War Criminals: Proceedings of the International Military Tribunal Sitting at Nuremberg, Germany, London (1946–51)

Tsouras, Peter (Ed.), *The Anvil of War*, London (1994)

Tsouras, Peter (Ed.), *Fighting in Hell*, London (1995)

Uebe, Klaus, 'Russian Reactions to German Airpower', USAF Studies 176, USAF Historical Division (nd)

US Government Printing Office, *Handbook on German Military Forces*, Washington (1945), reprinted by Louisiana University Press (1990)

Volgonov, Dimitri, *Triumph and Tragedy*, London (1994)

Weinburg, Gerhard, *A World at Arms*, Cambridge (1994)

Werth, Alexander, *The Year of Stalingrad*, London (1946)

Werth, Alexander, *Russia at War*, London (1964)

Whiting, Charles, *Gehlen: Germany's Master Spy*, New York (1972)

Wieder, Joachim and Graf von Einsiedel, Heinrich, *Stalingrad – Memories and Reassessments*, London (1990)

Woodman, Richard, *Arctic Convoys*, London (1994)

Zaloga, Steven and Grandsen, James, *The Eastern Front: Armor Camouflage and Markings 1941–45*, London (1983)

Zank, Horst, *Stalingrad, Kessel und Gefangenschaft*, Herford (1993)

★
INDEX